Strangers in a
Not-So-Strange Land

Indian American Immigrants
in the Global Age

Arthur W. Helweg
Western Michigan University

 Case Studies in Cultural Anthropology: George Spindler, Series Editor

THOMSON

———✳———™

WADSWORTH

Australia • Canada • Mexico • Singapore • Spain
United Kingdom • United States

THOMSON
✳
™
WADSWORTH

Anthropology Editor: *Lin Marshall*
Assistant Editor: *Nicole Root*
Editorial Assistant: *Kelly McMahon*
Marketing Manager: *Diane Wenckebach*
Marketing Assistant: *Tara Pierson*
Advertising Project Manager: *Linda Yip*
Project Manager, Editorial Production: *Jennifer Klos*
Print Buyer: *Rebecca Cross*

Permissions Editor: *Kiely Sexton*
Production Service: *Buuji, Inc.*
Copy Editor: *Cheryl Hauser*
Cover Designer: *Rob Hugel*
Cover Image: *Arthur W. Helweg*
Cover Printer: *Webcom*
Compositor: *Buuji, Inc.*
Printer: *Webcom Limited*

The logo for the Cultural Anthropology series is based on an ancient symbol representing the family: man, woman, and children.

Printed in Canada
1 2 3 4 5 6 7 07 06 05 04 03

For more information about our products, contact us at:
Thomson Learning Academic Resource Center
1-800-423-0563

For permission to use material from this text, contact us by:
Phone: 1-800-730-2214 **Fax:** 1-800-730-2215
Web: http://www.thomsonrights.com

Library of Congress Control Number: 2003112645

ISBN 0-534-61312-8

Wadsworth/Thomson Learning
10 Davis Drive
Belmont, CA 94002-3098
USA

Asia
Thomson Learning
5 Shenton Way #01-01
UIC Building
Singapore 068808

Australia/New Zealand
Thomson Learning
102 Dodds Street
Southbank, Victoria 3006
Australia

Canada
Nelson
1120 Birchmount Road
Toronto, Ontario M1K 5G4
Canada

Europe/Middle East/Africa
Thomson Learning
High Holborn House
50/51 Bedford Row
London WC1R 4LR
United Kingdom

Latin America
Thomson Learning
Seneca, 53
Colonia Polanco
11560 Mexico D.F.
Mexico

Spain/Portugal
Paraninfo
Calle/Magallanes, 25
28015 Madrid, Spain

To Monica
with my whole heart

Contents

Foreword

ABOUT THE SERIES

These case studies in cultural anthropology are designed for students in beginning and intermediate courses in the social sciences, to bring them insights into the richness and complexity of human life as it is lived in different ways, in different places. The authors are men and women who have lived in the societies they write about and who are professionally trained as observers and interpreters of human behavior. Also, the authors are teachers; in their writing, the needs of the student reader remain foremost. It is our belief that when an understanding of ways of life very different from one's own is gained, abstractions and generalizations about the human condition become meaningful.

The scope and character of the series has changed constantly since we published the first case studies in 1960, in keeping with our intention to represent anthropology as it is. We are concerned with the ways in which human groups and communities are coping with the massive changes wrought in their physical and sociopolitical environments in recent decades. We are also concerned with the ways in which established cultures have solved life's problems. And we want to include representation of the various modes of communication and emphasis that are being formed and reformed as anthropology itself changes.

We think of this series as an instructional series, intended for use in the classroom. We, the editors, have always used case studies in our teaching, whether for beginning students or advanced graduate students. We start with case studies, whether from our own series or from elsewhere, and weave our way into theory, and then turn again to cases. For us, they are the grounding of our discipline.

ABOUT THE AUTHOR

Arthur W. Helweg is a professor of anthropology at Western Michigan University. He has done anthropological research regarding economic development and migration in India, Pakistan, the United Kingdom, Canada, Romania, and the United States. He has also researched extensively the South Asian diaspora. Professor Helweg has written over 120 publications. The *London Times Literary Supplement* lauded *Sikhs in England. An Immigrant Success Story*, coauthored with Usha Helweg was awarded the Theodor Soloutos Award by the Immigration History Society for being the best work on immigration history in 1990. *Ethnicity in Michigan: Issues and People*, which he wrote with Jack Glazier, was selected by the governor of Michigan and his advisors for Read Michigan Week. The selection was made by the Great Lakes Book Dealers Association and the Michigan Heritage Society and announced by Michigan governor, John Engler.

Professor Helweg has also consulted for the United States Agency for International Development and the United States Office of Education. He has been awarded research grants from the Fulbright-Hays Program of the U.S. Office of Education, U.S. State Department, Smithsonian Institution, and Institute for Indian Studies. He has also received considerable local funding.

Professor Helweg is currently an editor of the Discovering the People of Michigan project—a series of books focusing on the various ethnic communities in Michigan—while actively teaching and researching anthropology.

ABOUT THIS CASE STUDY

Everyone knows that Asian Indians have come to America in large numbers and that they have been extraordinarily successful. One can hardly cross the country without staying at least one night in an Indian-owned motel formerly owned and run by a white American couple. The whole Indian family will take part in the management and the actual work involved—cleaning, changing sheets, collecting used towels and substituting new ones, registering clients for the night, assigning rooms, answering calls, keeping the peace, and so on and on. They will make a profit where it had become impossible for the white owners to do so because it is the Indian family labor that keeps the enterprise running and running well. And in the cases that we (my wife and I) encountered, the senior man in the family was a member of the Chamber of Commerce and of business organizations such as Kiwanis in the town with which the motel is associated.

One can hardly have contact with the electronic industry without realizing that many responsible management positions are held by Indians, as well as other positions involved with manufacture, servicing, and promotion of electronic equipment. "Silicon Valley," wherever it may be, is always a stronghold of Indians, many of whom migrate from Silicon Valleys in India. A substantial number had migrated to the U.S. by 1900 but various anti-migration laws had been enacted that kept the immigration to a minimum until the Immigration law of 1965 eliminated most of the more blatantly racist provisions of exclusion.

Most of these people have immigrated from India rather recently, however. In 1975 there were an estimated 175,000 Asian Indians in the United States. In 1997 there were 1,215,000 and they were spread throughout New York, New Hampshire, Pennsylvania, Ohio, West Virginia, New Jersey, Mississippi, California and Washington, in substantial numbers, with fewer in nearly all of the states excepting Montana and Wyoming. The Indian population of the state of Michigan became 0.6 percent of the total by 1998.

The more recent immigrants have been most successful. Eighty percent come with college degrees and 65 percent are employed at the managerial-technical level earning 25 percent more per household than the average for mainstream households of comparable background. This influx of highly qualified immigrants has occurred throughout the world, particularly in Canada, England, and Australia, all Commonwealth countries. They are not welcome in much of South America (though the Caribbean is a stronghold), Fiji, and in several African countries (though they are numerous in South Africa).

There is no doubt that Asian Indian immigrants are numerous and successful. This case study treats the reader with the details of their success story. Arthur Helweg has had extensive experience with this immigrant population, both in the U.S.A. and in India. Anyone interested in immigration dynamics should find his treatment compelling and useful.

George Spindler
Editor
Stanford University

Preface

The saga of the Indian American[1] community in the United States is one small, recent, yet extremely significant, phase in the process of globalizing human capital. Their story is one of hope and despair, tears and joy, bondage and freedom, and poverty and wealth. They are part of a process that started when Christopher Columbus, and subsequent explorers and colonizers, tried to force indigenous people into slavery. The people already inhabiting America were not considered good laborers, especially on plantations—they were perceived as poor workers who tended to run away. The people of Africa were later judged to be harder working and easier to control. As a result, the African slave trade started and opened[2] a new period in the process of globalizing human cargo.

When the British Parliament yielded to abolitionist pressure and passed legislation prohibiting slavery, plantation owners around the globe began clamoring for cheap labor. The answer was found in indenturing people[3] of India. Thus, a new system of slavery (1830–1920) was instituted, along with a third change in the globalization process of human capital. People of India followed the British flag to the remotest parts of the British Empire to fulfill a dream of acquiring wealth—a dream generally dashed by abuses. Nevertheless, it was the foundation of what is now termed the "Indian Diaspora"[4] and the more inclusive term, the "South Asian Diaspora."[5]

---

[1]The people residing in the United States who claim India as their land of ethnic origin have been identified by various terms—"Indian," "East Indian," "Asian Indian," and "Indian American" to name a few. Asian Indian was the most prominent identifier in the 1990s and is the official designation still. However, as the labels "South Asian American," and "Pakistani American," "Italian American," and so on, are coming into use, "Indian American" is becoming more popular. In this book, I will use "Indian," "East Indian," "Asian Indian," and "Indian American" interchangeably to identify people who claim India as their ethnic land of origin, but are living in the United States.

[2]For this study, a migrant is an individual not living in his or her country of birth.

[3]The indenture system is when an individual contracts him or herself into servitude. It was a prominent way many people, including Scottish, Irish, and others, financed their way to America.

[4]I realize that the term "diaspora" is most commonly used to refer to the dispersed Jewish community residing outside its homeland. In the last decade, however, usage of the term has been expanded to include other groups residing outside their place of ethnic origin, such as the Chinese diaspora and so on.

[5]The South Asian Diaspora consists of India, Pakistan, Bangladesh, Sri Lanka, and the mountain countries of Nepal, Bhutan, and Sikkim. The consolidation of all South Asians into one community by scholars is not necessarily agreed to by the people who originate from South Asia.

Shukla (2001) puts it well when he concludes:

If the category "South Asia" makes the most sense in constructed political alliances in the subcontinent in the solidarities of new identities in diasporas, it also comes into direct conflict with the hyperproduction of more nationalist groupings that evacuate the term of its meaning for a range of communities. New forms of technology have not been established as a position in this debate, they have aided and abetted both kinds of subjectivity. A broader analytical question that emerges from this social impasse is whether the ethnographic field is able to accommodate subject matter (as well as communities) that only provisionally hold together when "South Asian" defines a field of inquiry, does it create a new knowledge or does it simply do the work of description? These are questions implicit in a variety of historical renderings of, not least of all, material in the present.

My knowledge is primarily that of the people of Indian origin and that is my focus here.

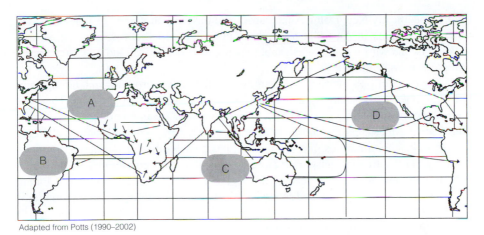

Adapted from Potts (1990–2002)

A - Migratory labour within colonial Africa, 1880–1920
B - Forced importation of African workers, 1780–1850
C - Export of Indian coolies, 1830–1920
D - Export of Chinese workers, 1845–1880

Overview of Colonial Globalization of Human Resources. The movement of human capital from and to India, which comprises about 15 million people, is part of a larger process that currently comprises 150 million people.[6] The process has its origins back to the voyages of Christopher Columbus; and Spanish attempts to use Native Americans in America for cheap or free labor. The above map shows the development and current movement of human capital on the global scale. Sources: Khadria, Binod. 1999. The Migration of Knowledge Workers: Second-Generation Effects of India's Brain Drain. *New Delhi: Sage. Potts, Lydia. 1990.* The World Labour Market: A History of Migration. *London: Zed.*

The current phase in the globalization of labor is a result of, among other things, the 1965 U.S. immigration legislation, increased efficiency of travel, instantaneous communications systems, and the type of migrant. These changes cause the reevaluation of institutions like economic development processes and strategies, immigration, citizenship, national responsibility, and many other concepts and institutions.

This study differs from the traditional approaches to immigrants in that it considers the globalizing and transnational[6] processes taking place as well as the holistic nature of the Indian Diaspora networks. This study is not limited to the Indian American community or the immigrant community and their home village, but ideally includes all relevant units impinging on the community of focus. Also, it will become apparent that a social unit can exist and be cohesive while at the same time being residentially dispersed. Such a view is very important in this day of rapid travel, instant communication, and the changing nature of national boundaries.

Officially, my research methodology was qualitative with participant observation. In actuality, it was much more than that. I devoured all the literature on India and its emigrants I could get my hands on. I lived within the Indian community in the United States, specifically New York City and Kalamazoo, Michigan. I lived in

---

[6]The slave trade was one leg of the famous Triangular Trade—New England traders and manufacturers were one group, among others, who capitalized on the situation by exchanging cheap manufactured goods in Africa for human cargo to enslave.

[7]"Transnational" is a term that refers to the realization that cultural images and objects flow across national boundaries and have a global impact. Put another way, national and territorial boundaries are becoming less and less significant.

India, specifically New Delhi, Ahmedabad, and the Punjabi village of Jandiali. I also spent six months in Australia researching in Sydney, Melbourne, and Canberra. I asked anyone who was knowledgeable open-ended questions, and I learned something from every interview.

The order of presentation in this study is holistic, not chronological. Going from general to particular enables the reader to observe the contextual situation. Thus, the Introduction sets forth an explanation of concepts and a framework for understanding Indian Americans and other immigrant communities. Part I deals with three Asian Indian communities that strongly influence each other in an ongoing process, namely (1) the Indian Diaspora, (2) the Indian Returned community in India and (3) Indian Americans. The rest of the text focuses on topics concerning Indian Americans. I have also included several appendixes that quantify Asian Indian immigration trends, accomplishments, and history. It is my hope that you, the reader, will enjoy this work as much as I have enjoyed researching it and writing about the Asian Indian community in America as well as in other locations around the world.

ACKNOWLEDGMENTS

In doing the research for this book, help came from so many people that listing them would fill many pages. Some are unsung heroes who helped a great deal with little recognition. In my particular case, N. Gerald Barrier, Paul Wallace, Pashaura Singh, and other scholars provided superb comments, support, and "second chances" on many conference papers.

Funding from the U.S. Office of Education Fulbright-Hays Program, with able and helpful administrators, like John Paul and the late Robert Dennis, have helped me and other scholars maximize the benefits of being a Fulbright scholar. If not for John Paul's interest in me and timely advice, I would not have been able to accomplish the research in the field that I did.

George Spindler and the Wadsworth team composed of Brad Rogers, Lin Marshall, and Analie Barnett far exceeded their editorial parameters in encouragement and help. Brad Rogers introduced the proposal, and Lin Marshall and George Spindler were most encouraging while Analie Barnett kept track of things in a marvelous way. Thank you to Cheryl Hauser and the team at Buuji, Inc. for their production work on this manuscript.

I have been fortunate to be employed at Western Michigan University, where, under the presidency of Diether Haenicke, my research was supported financially as well as with leave time.

In the field, J. S. Grewal, J. S. Sandhu and family, O. P Mehta and family, B. S. Randhawa and family as well as John Lowe, have been a great help, and they were not always aware of the benefits they were bestowing on me.

To my wife and children, I will always be grateful for their involvement in my research and willingness to relinquish the comforts of home so our family could remain together while doing field work.

In general, I owe a great debt to the Indian people who took me in and opened their lives so I could better understand their trials and victories. It must be remembered that in spite of their generous help, any errors or misrepresentations are solely my responsibility.

Introduction
New Land, New Laws, New People, New Theories

ONE MAN'S STORY

I first met Jasbir Singh in the Punjabi village of Jandiali, where I was living in 1970. He was a charming Sikh who took his faith seriously. He, his wife, and children lived in his father's house, along with his brothers, his brothers' families, and unmarried sisters. Soon after I arrived in the village, Jasbir and I became good friends, and we spent a lot of time together as he explained to me about village life in India's Punjab.

As we talked, I never dreamed that he would immigrate to the United States 12 years later. During the interim, Jasbir obtained a degree in mechanical engineering and studied computers. He learned from his sister, who had married an American resident and was living in the United States, that these were marketable skills in the States. Thus, on a hot June morning in 1982, my friend and his sister, who was a resident in the States but visiting her home in India, took the train to New Delhi, where he was going to have his final interview at the American Embassy—the last hurdle before obtaining the coveted "green card," signifying permanent residence status.

Jasbir was very different from the stereotypical immigrant that had graced America's shores during the past 200 years. He came from a democratic Asian country and was part of an upper middle class family. True, he was born and raised in a Punjabi village, but he was well-educated and due to the Western orientation of his curriculum, which was based on the British system,[1] and the interaction he had with American professors,[2] he was familiar with American ways and a fluent writer and speaker of English. Jasbir's family consisted of his wife, Goodi, and their three children: Nimi (age 16), Raju (age 12), and Shobi (age 8).

---

[1]In colonizing India, the British set up an educational system, the basics of which still characterize India's schools, colleges, and universities.

[2]After India obtained independence in 1947, many American professors taught in Indian institutions of higher learning under the Fulbright-Hays and Ford Foundation education and economic development programs. Indian and American universities formed joint ventures such as Punjab Agricultural College in Ludhiana and Michigan State University and Ohio State University. Later on, the Peace Corps also made its impact.

Jasbir was a Punjabi,[3] a people noted for their hard work, innovative behavior, and tradition of emigration. Land was and is a scarce commodity in Punjab, and Jasbir knew that when his father died, the family land would be divided among him and his brothers. Thus, the plots would be too small to support him and his family. He also had to plan for the education of his children and the marriages of his two daughters. He was making enough to meet current expenses, but he was not saving and the future was not promising.

Jasbir's younger brother, who lived in the United States, was prosperous and the favorite of his parents. His younger sister had reversed a desolate future by crossing the seas to marry an American citizen. His parents constantly glorified the emigrants of the family because they had plenty of money.

Emigrants sometimes tend to look down on those who remain behind. One evening, Jasbir heard his father asking the younger son, who was home for a visit, to sponsor Jasbir. Roshen, the younger brother, replied, "Dad, I don't think Jasbir has the ability or the intelligence to survive in the United States."

Not only did Jasbir suffer this humiliation, he also heard the adulation of those who had emigrated and concluded that he too would have to take advantage of that option if he were to provide adequately for his family, as well as regain the respect that an elder son should have in the family.

His loyal wife, Goodi, did not share his views. She had heard stories about the decadent lifestyle of Americans. She heard that every girl in the United States loses her virginity by the age of 11. She did not want her daughters subjected to those temptations. She saw white people in India hooked on drugs and feared that her children would be exposed and pressured to participate in America's drug culture.

After many long hours of conversation, which included assurances from Jasbir's sister that their Indian morals could be maintained in the United States, Jasbir and Goodi decided to emigrate. Thus, with sponsorship from his sister, he joined the thousands of Indians leaving their homeland for America.

When Jasbir arrived in the United States, friends provided lodging and contacts so that within a month he had a job with a reputable engineering firm in New Jersey. It was a difficult job under hard conditions. The worst hurdle was that the job required a great deal of time away from his beloved family. He detested the separations but took the job to gain the necessary "American experience"[4] that would make him marketable in the future. In the meantime, his eldest daughter obtained a job at the local Burger King while his wife clerked at a nearby fabrics store.

It was difficult, but by the third year, they had enough money to place a substantial down payment to buy a house. They now have a four-bedroom $200,000 home and three cars (one is a new Chrysler). Jasbir has put his children through Rutgers University. His oldest daughter majored in computer science, the second in engineering, and his son in business.

---

[3]Punjabis are people who claim the geographical region of Punjab as their ancestral homeland. They have a distinct language and culture. Subsequently, there are Punjabis who are Pakistanis or Indian. They can also be Hindu, Sikh, or Muslim.

[4]Asian Indians, like other groups, are humiliated when their experience or education in their land of origin is not accepted. American employers, by not recognizing foreign qualifications or experience, get highly trained labor at a lower cost. Jasbir was a good example, he had to spend time overseas to get his American experience. His company saved money because they paid him a much lower salary than they paid those who had "American experience."

Jasbir arranged the marriage of his eldest daughter to a fine Indian boy Nimi met while doing her studies at Rutgers University. Nimi and her husband now live in an affluent suburb near New York City. They have a live-in Indian servant[5] to look after their children during the weekdays, and she and her husband each pull in six-figure salaries. Her husband put things well when he said in a joking manner, "We are making so much money that we are having difficulty spending it."

Jasbir arranged the marriage of Shobi to a fine lad from India. The initial meeting took place when the boy was visiting relatives in the States with the hopes of finding an Indian girl to marry who had permanent U.S. residency or U.S. citizenship. It has turned out to be a good marriage. The couple has two children, good incomes, and a fine apartment in Manhattan near the site of the former World Trade Center. Fortunately, they narrowly escaped injury when terrorists flew planes into the building on September 11, 2001.

Jasbir also arranged Raju's marriage to a girl from India and the marriage ceremony was held there as well. It was a time of pride, for friends and relatives alike saw the success of Jasbir and his offspring.[6] Raju works with his maternal uncle in his uncle's import/export business, which is doing very well.

Jasbir looks with pride on his family and constantly blesses his sister for his good fortune. His offspring are all doing well, and he is proud of them. Jasbir now enjoys his retirement. His American Express gold card eliminates the necessity to carry much cash and his retirement plus his wife's fabulous success in the real estate business make for a very comfortable life for a proud man in New Jersey.

THE NEW IMMIGRATION

Of course all post-1968 immigrants to the United States are not like Jasbir. There are Vietnamese, Chinese, Malaysians, and others. Every continent is represented. Some are rich, some are poor, some are educated, some are not. Some coming from India are less educated and less affluent than Jasbir. People like Jasbir, however, are more numerous and more highly represented than ever before, and they are relatively unstudied.

Jasbir and his family are typical of what Charles Keely (1971, 1980) calls the "New Immigrant" or the "New Immigration"—terms coined to signify the distinctive attributes of the post-1968 influx. Although the new immigrants may not be the majority of those entering the United States now, they have increased and become very prominent over the past 35 years. The vast majority originate from East Asia and South Asia. They are well-educated professionals in medicine, engineering, and science. They are fluent in English and have attended a university modeled after British or North American systems. As a result, they are strangers in a not-so-strange

---

[5]Having live-in servants is a common practice among middle and upper class Asian Indians in India. They desire to continue the practice in the States. As a result, a number have sponsored their servants from India. Servants, after being in the States, have sued their employer for not paying them the minimum wage and providing the required Social Security benefits. In the case of Jasbir's daughter, they hired a lady originally from Kerala who is bonded and licensed as a professional ayah or specialist in child care. There are many professional ayahs in the metropolitan New York area.

It was common to hear young Asian Indian women say, "You cannot survive in America with a career and family unless you have a servant." They, however, have survived with families and careers.

[6]Emigrants consider it prestigious to have their offspring's wedding in India. It is also an auspicious occasion as kinfolk come from all over the world to be united with family again.

land. In other words, they are newly arrived in the United States and are familiar with the country and people through their studies.

In the case of those from India, like Jasbir, they did their studies in a British-oriented college or university where English was the medium of instruction. Some were guided by American professors who taught in India under the Fulbright-Hays, Ford Foundation, American Institute of Indian Studies, or other research or exchange programs. Consequently, their language and educational experiences provide them with the skills that enable them to excel in the United States.

A significant number of immigrants from India, like Jasbir, who arrived between 1968 and 1980 came from urban-oriented, middle or upper class social positions. Those of rural origins generally had a university education and sufficient contact with city life to be comfortable in cosmopolitan America. They often came from families belonging to a high social or economic bracket in India, where their prospects for a good career and lifestyle were eminent.

The family reunification clauses in 1965 and subsequent immigration legislation made possible sponsored relatives, which became prominent in the post-1980 immigration stream. Thus, the post-1980 immigrants are on the average not as highly educated as their predecessors. Their education and qualifications, on the average, are still among the highest, if not the highest, of any ethnic community in the United States.

The type of entrants on which this study focuses have the technical, educational, and social skills to immediately and successfully enter middle class American society. In the United States, they work in air-conditioned offices and have secretarial assistance. Many wear well-tailored suits, have neatly trimmed hair, and can sit in a posh restaurant and carry on a sophisticated conversation with their U.S.-born peers. Any feelings of insecurity they may have are not noticeable to others.

These new immigrants provide a sharp contrast to those who entered the United States at the turn of the century during America's industrialization. Those immigrants were generally a non–English-speaking people, many of peasant origin, who provided unskilled labor for America's industrial machine, clothing industry, and other business enterprises. Their plight provided material for novels of social concern such as Upton Sinclair's *The Jungle*, that countered the myth of America as the land of opportunity where the oppressed could breathe free (Daniels 1990; Dinnerstein & Reimers, 1988).

Only since the 1965 revisions of American immigration legislation have non-Europeans, like Jasbir, been able to enter the United States. Immigrants became prosperous and powerful before, but not to the degree taking place now. Prosperity is greater now among legal immigrants. These people with a professional and business orientation comprise an important segment of the community in numbers, wealth, and political influence for both the United States and India. Although this study focuses on educated and trained individuals originating from India, the general conclusions concerning their situation may well be applicable to immigrants from countries such as China, Japan, Korea, Taiwan, and the Philippines.

Not only are such immigrants and their situations in the United States different from those of the past, but also the communications revolution has enabled many of them to continue to participate in Indian society while living in the United States. Unlike the migrants who left Europe at the turn of the century, realizing that they might not return, the sojourners of today are not forced to make the decision of permanently staying or leaving. They can fly home within days and give instructions over the telephone to workers, friends, and relatives in their land of origin—in essence, they can participate in one society while residing in another.

NEW LAWS

It was the Immigration Act of 1965 (PL 89-236) that strongly contributed to the radical change to the composition of America's immigration stream. Even those supporting the legislation could not have guessed that Europeans would no longer dominate the immigration flow, as had been the case since Europeans began settling in North America. With the implementation of the 1965 legislation in 1968, the gates of immigration opened to a highly educated and professionally oriented people. A vast number were Asians who were highly educated professionals, technically trained, and astute in business.

This is the story of one group of people who are a prominent component of the post-1968 influx—immigrants whose origins are from India. Officially they are termed "Asian Indians" but recently also called "Indian Americans," and they now occupy a prominent place in the American multicultural mosaic. Their story is one of trial, heartache, success, and contribution.

UNDERSTANDING THE NEW IMMIGRATION

Models, frameworks, and assumptions concerning immigrant studies have changed significantly over the past four decades. In a way, they have followed the situation and opinion of the social and cultural context of the period.

Traditionally, migration studies concentrated on four broad topics: (1) causes of population shifts, (2) social-psychological concerns of immigrant adaptation, (3) social problems caused by immigration, and (4) the nature and dynamics of migrant groups and individual social networks. The vast majority of these studies used a model that only considered the relationships between host and immigrant societies (Bryce-Laporte, 1980; Jackson, 1968; Jansen, 1970; Kasdan, 1970; and Shaw, 1975). This is especially true when examining questions concerning identity (Glazer & Moynihan, 1970, and Barth, 1963).

Until the implementation and later improvement of steamships, coming to the United States was a hazardous and trying experience for the poor. Loss of life was high, and the conditions so bad that the vast majority of those people who made the voyage swore they would never do it again for any reason. As a result, immigrants quickly developed the ideology of leaving the homeland behind and America becoming the "Promised Land."[7] Public schools were established to indoctrinate immigrants, especially their children, to be American.

Between 1880 and 1930, one-fourth to one-third of the U.S. immigrant population returned to their country of origin (Wyman, 1993), but the ideology of assimilation continued. It is not surprising those studying immigrants and immigration fell in line behind Robert Park (1928, 1950) and the Chicago School and interpreted immigrant behavior along assimilation lines.

---

[7]Concepts like the "promised land," "Manifest Destiny," or hymns with themes like "Crossing the River Jordan," all have the implication that this land is given to people by God.

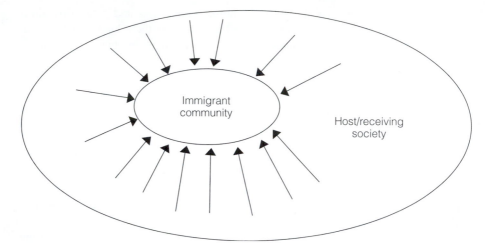

Figure I.1 Assimilation Theory. Up to 1950, it was assumed that all immigrant and minority communities would be molded by their social environment and eventually be indistinguishable from the host society. Immigration theory supported that popular perception. Figure I.1 graphically represents the process of the host society molding immigrant and minority communities to be like the host community.

Figure I.1 illustrates the assimilationist perspective. In this framework, minority and immigrant communities accommodate to the wider or host society—the flow of influence is primarily one way, although the smaller or weaker community has its impact on the majority or wider community, usually in a subtle or less conspicuous way. In cases where there was some influence between host and receiving societies, it was usually indirect and outside the immigrant's sphere of interaction.

After World War II, a communications revolution developed. Within two decades people traveled around the globe in a matter of hours and talked with family and friends in remote Asian villages in a matter of minutes.[8] Migration researchers recognized this change and it is reflected in Figure I.2. The conceptual framework here is a continual three-way interactional process between the sending, receiving, and migrant communities.

Scholars argued that three social arenas must be considered to comprehend the behavior of expatriates: (1) the sending community, (2) the migrant group, and (3) the receiving society—for a three-way diachronic process is taking place:

> [The] adaptive responses displayed by each of these three groups affects the problems confronting the others and the options open for their solutions. Thus the more holistic our view of the adaptive process, the more realistically we can understand and assess what is happening within each (Graves & Graves, 1974:118).

When analyzing my material on the Sikh community in England (Helweg, 1979), I found the three-way model to be ideal. When I went to the sending villages, I saw

---

[8]Of course, this is not always the case. The point is, however, that communication has much improved over the last five decades.

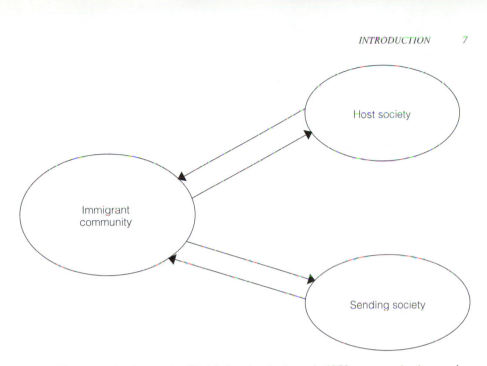

Figure I.2 Three-Way Interaction Model. Starting in the early 1970s, communications and travel was so efficient and fast that an immigrant could be an active participant in his or her place of origin as well as the new abode. Thus, a three-way interactional relationship developed between the migrant, host, and home communities. Figure I.2 illustrates that process.

how emigrants in England influenced the life of their home village, ranging from monetary remittances and social ranking to technological transfer and political participation.

In the 1980s and 1990s concepts like "globalization," transnationalism, and "world system" reflected the realization of the increasing influence various and distant places had on each other. I also saw that the interaction of the Sikh community I had studied in England was not limited to the host and sending societies but included people in Malaysia, Kenya, Canada, and elsewhere.

For me, the most helpful model to understand this complex, changing, and varied situation is field theory (Lewin, 1952). As shown in Figure I.3, the investigator determines his or her field of inquiry and then identifies the forces or force fields involved. Note that force fields can influence each other. Their relationships can be interactional or in rare cases, one way. A force field can be anything from a community to history to physical surroundings.

Of course, an ethnologist's theoretical approach depends on the goals he or she has in doing the research, but the field theory approach was in the back of my mind as I organized my research and research material, all of which necessitated that I research in India as well as Canada, England, Australia, and various communities in the United States.

In the material that follows, I will show the influence of India's Diaspora on the residents of various countries or localities. Although the chapter outline of Part I may look like there is a three-way division, there really is not.

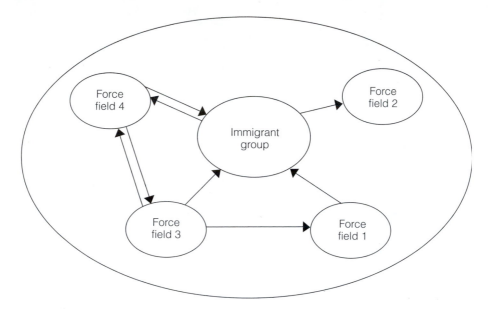

Figure I.3 Field Theory Model. Figure I.3 illustrates the current situation where people can contact whomever they chose. The nature and influence of natural and national boundaries is changing and field theory is used to aid in understanding migrant behavior.

Part I/Strangers in a Not-So-Strange Land

INTRODUCTION

When Jasbir Singh and his family decided to emigrate, they were doing more than just changing residence from India to the United States. They were joining the Indian Diaspora, which is a transnational community. They were also becoming members of the Asian Indian community in the United States. At the same time, Jasbir and his family continued to participate, invest, and leave their assets in India.

EMIGRANT COMMUNITIES

As Jasbir Singh's situation illustrates, the emigrant from India becomes a member of two or more distinct communities. The communities they join are the (1) Indian or South Asian Diaspora, also termed overseas Indians, non-resident Indians (NRIs), or people of Indian origin (PIOs); (2) the Indian returned—a community of people who returned to India or have never given up their residence and participation in their land of origin; and (3) the Asian Indian immigrant community in the United States.

Although the vast majority of the Asian Indians in the United States arrived directly from India, a notable number of twice migrants[1] came from Africa, Malaysia, the Middle East, the Caribbean, and many other areas of the globe. They brought diversity, leading to greater innovative and entrepreneurial behavior.[2]

As the diaspora returned, and immigrant communities are described in the next three chapters, it is imperative that to keep in mind that these groups exist in an ongoing, interactional relationship with each other, with India, and other sending communities as well as receiving communities like the United States and Great Britain.

---

[1]The term "twice-migrants" was initially coined by Parminder Bhachcu (1985) in reference to people of Indian origin who first went to Africa and then on to Britain. Later usage has included people that have done two or more migrations.
[2]The research of Barth (1961, 1963), Helweg (2002), Benedict (1968), and Greenfield and Strickon (1986) supports the conclusions that diversity in cultural contacts leads to greater innovative and entrepreneurial behavior.

COMMONALITIES OF PRESENT DAY
ASIAN INDIAN MIGRANT COMMUNITIES

Part-Societies

Except for the Asian Indian Diaspora in its totality, Asian Indian immigrant communities are "part-societies." This classification means that the immigrant communities are a part of a larger whole. In this age of globalization, all societies are part-societies, but in the case of the immigrant communities, they operate within the political, economic, and cultural frameworks of the hosting society. As a result, they generally occupy a niche in the host society.

The anthropologist Robert Redfield (1960) first developed the concept of part-societies in analyzing peasant communities in Mexico. The classification was not perfect and fell into disuse because of its limitations. However, like many other attempts to described and analyze human behavior, while it was not perfect, it had its degree of truth. The point he made was that peasant communities are not independent entities. They are subsystems of a larger system.

Redfield was not naive; there was some good insight into the point he was making. He rightly argued that peasant communities are not self-sufficient entities. They depend on cities for markets, off-season employment, government regulation, and so on. They exist in a symbiotic relationship with urban areas. They need the urban areas to survive, and cities need peasants for temporary labor, food, and so on.

With some similarities akin to Redfield's concept of peasants, the immigrant develops a symbiotic relationship with the host society and culture. Sometimes the sojourner creates his or her own niche, sometimes he or she fills an existing position. Either way, the immigrant is working and existing within a situation created by the social or cultural situation in which he or she finds him or herself.

Education

Another commonality of the post-1968 immigration is that immigrants were not only well educated, they were educated in a Western-oriented educational system using the English language as the medium of instruction. The British had established an educational system that the Indian government built on after independence in 1947. The Indian government capitalized on exchange and cooperative programs the United States offered. The result was and still is that the immigrants from India speak fluent English and are familiar with American culture and concepts, and thus were strangers but in a not-so-strange-land. Put another way, they do not have to adapt to and learn American ways, they were *preadapted*[3] to life in the United States, which gives them a tremendous advantage over other groups.

Transnational and Global Behavior

With the current level of development in global communications, transportation, and economic interdependence, social, ethnic, and political boundaries are taking a new meaning or no meaning at all. People talk, transmit money, write contracts, and

---

[3]I coined the term "preadapted" to signify the situation where the immigrant, if he or she has the proper education and training, can immediately step into a new community and immediately be productive. Of course, there are levels of preadaptation.

exchange ideas while being separated geographically, politically, or socially. A people may be dispersed, and yet be a cohesive community. They may be dispersed across urban areas or national boundaries. The telephone and computer enable them to communicate instantaneously. They also have local, national, and international associations to deal with common issues and concerns. Families may be dispersed throughout the globe while maintaining the overall structure and relationships they would have if they were living on their ancestral land in India.

The migrant can now operate from a transnational perspective,[4] which means national boundaries inhibit action less and in some cases are not even a consideration. As I will show, the members of the Indian Diaspora have global networks and are part of the globalization process of setting up and participating in the global networks.

I must add that participants in the globalization process think and see the world in different parameters. They think and act from a global or transnational perspective. To illustrate, Mohan Mehra is an up-and-coming entrepreneur. He has been a rising success with his computer software enterprise. Mohan immigrated to the United States, attended the University of California, and after obtaining his MBA, went on to start his company, which has prospered.

What is unique about Mohan, and a factor in his success, is that he thinks globally. When he looks for people to hire, he contacts people in India, China, South America, and elsewhere; he does not limit his inquiry to the United States. When he looks for markets, again he does not limit his search to the United States, but gets information from friends and relatives in Hong Kong, France, China, Japan, and elsewhere. He thinks in terms of the world marketplace, not just finding a niche in the American economy.

Raju Saegal, an employee of Mohan's, has a career plan for himself. As he sets and modifies his goals, he also thinks about experience in British, French, German, and other firms. He has not limited his aspirations and goals to the United States; he is thinking globally.

Migration and its ramifications are much more complicated than just analyzing the host, home, and immigrant societies. To be clear with the terminology, immigration is to enter, migration is to change, and emigration is to move out. Knowing the changes brought about by emigration or immigration on a locality are important, but often the ramifications are more widespread. Emigration and immigration can influence foreign policy, education, economic policy, social tensions, and many other things taking place around the globe.

Thus, in this era of globalization and transnationalism, migrant and other social groups interact and influence each other and have overlapping memberships. Some have developed an international social system that ignores political boundaries and territoriality.

What follows in this part's three chapters concerns communities that emigrants from India join on leaving their homeland, namely the Indian Diaspora, the Asian Indian community in the United States, and the NRIs or overseas Indians of India. Except for the possibility of the Indian Diaspora, all are part-societies, that is, subsystems within a larger social field. Thus, the three chapters of this part will describe the diaspora—sending and receiving situations with a focus on the ongoing and

---

[4]Also see Lessinger (1995) for a good explanation and illustration of transnational behavior.

interactional impact they have had on each other due to migration. Many other force fields impact the communities, but these issues are the most prominent right now.

The major question that will become apparent is what holds it all together. The answer is not simple, but I propose that along with globalization and transnationalism, sufficient agreement on cultural principles, unifying kin groups, associations, ethnic identification, or any combination of these forces working either independently or together contribute to the unity of the Indian Diaspora.

CONCLUSION

People are just scratching the surface concerning the ramifications globalization and transnationalism will have on the flow of human capital. What I see, however, is that you cannot understand an immigrant community apart from the interaction it has with the sending, receiving, and other communities. Being part-societies, the various communities cannot be understood in isolation, but must be dealt within the interactional relationships they have with others as they behave within their context. As will be shown, understanding the Indian Diaspora means knowing about the interactional relationship with India, just as understanding aspects of modern India means considering the interactional relationships with its diaspora and overseas communities.

1/The Indian Diaspora
A Global Tribe[1]

As communications in travel and word have increased in speed and efficiency, the Indian Diaspora is developing a heightened sense of identity and unity. The government of India has aided this growth as it begins to see the economic advantages of having a closer relationship with the overseas community. The overseas Indian community may be geographically dispersed, but events that impact one part of the community have influence elsewhere on the self-perception of Asian Indians.

As shown below, the coup against the duly elected government in Fiji influenced the self-perceptions of all people of Indian origin, even those in the remotest areas of the globe. One factor was NRI's increased awareness of not being backed by the Indian government and a realization of their weakness politically. The violence focused against the Asian Indian community in New Jersey raised a sense of inferiority and weakness in their self-concept, especially since the government of India and the authorities in the United States did not take adequate steps to deal with the situation.

The edited speech that follows was given by Thomas Abraham at the second Global Convention of People of Indian Origin and sets forth a partial view of how they see their situation and some of the issues as they see them.

NRI/PIO[2] COMMUNITY—A PERSPECTIVE

Whether they come from Africa, Asia, the Americas, Australia, the Caribbean, or Europe, they are Indians in body and spirit. Almost all of them maintain their Indian cultural traditions and values. They seem to have meaningfully integrated in their new countries without losing their ethnic identity.[3] A new global community of Indian origin has

---

[1]The term "tribe" is not being used here in the strict anthropological sense, but to denote a community that has some of the cohesive characteristics of a tribe.

[2]NRI stands for non-resident Indian and PIO stand for people of Indian origin.

[3]Being perceived as maintaining or keeping one's culture is a very subjective evaluation. What is important here is that the Asian Indians perceive themselves as having kept and maintained their culture abroad. Whether this is actually the case is not so important; it is the perception that they have of themselves that is important.

developed; the members are highly successful in business and the professions. They have the potential for not only helping in the homeland in a time of crisis, but they play a new role in helping their members in all places of the world.

The decision for the disapora to take a more active political and economic role in their affairs as well as those of India was triggered by such incidents as the Indian-dominated government in Fiji being overthrown by a military dictator in 1987. Also, there were human rights violations, in Fiji, Guiana, Trinidad, South Africa, Sri Lanka, United Kingdom, and the United States—the "dot buster" issue in New Jersey.[4] It resulted in the formation of the Global Organization of People of Indian Origin (GOPIO). One purpose for the formation of the GOPIO was to take up issues such as human rights violations.

In the last 10 years, human rights violations have been relegated behind economic concerns. More and more people are seeing that the creation of economic platforms as being more popular and a potentially successful route to pursue. This correlates with the fact that Asian Indians of the diaspora are becoming enormously rich, thanks to the computer/Internet revolution. There are a dozen billionaires, hundreds of PIOs with assets over a $100 million, and several thousand millionaires.

It was not until the 1970s that the government of India under Rajiv Gandhi, began to realize the potential assets and expertise in non-resident Indians (NRIs). He invited a few NRIs to develop core sectors including telecommunications while also making it easier for NRIs to invest in India.

There are enormous opportunities for NRIs/PIOs to get actively involved in India's development as well as support various social service activities. Many NRIs and organizations have taken major initiatives in supporting their former schools and colleges, while others have supported social and environmental causes. Many have worked behind the scenes to create interest among companies to take interest in India. As can be seen, India and its diaspora are growing closer and closer together.

OVERVIEW

I had studied India and its people for almost two decades. I had read Hugh Tinker's classic works *A New System of Slavery, The Banyan Tree, and Separate and Unequal.* Hugh Tinker was a mentor, scholar, and friend, whose scholarship was honest, accurate, and beyond reproach. He embodied to me what an academic should be. Thus, I studied his writings meticulously. From his works and those of other scholars, I had a detailed knowledge of the overseas Indian community. Yet, with all my knowledge, I was not prepared for what was to suddenly happen starting in the 1990s—the significant entrepreneurial activity of the overseas Indians not only exploded, it was suddenly being recognized. Business magazines started reporting on the business acumen of the Indians in the diaspora.[5] Columns and articles on management by writers of Indian origin became respected and popular.[6] Joel Kotkin

---

[4]This refers to the gangs in New Jersey who physically and violently attacked Asian Indians. The gangs called themselves "dot busters" in reference to the "bindi" or dot that many Indian women wear on their forehead.

[5]One only need to look in *Business Week, The Wall Street Journal,* and other business publications; they are not hard to find.

[6]One of my favorites is C. K. Prahaled of the University of Michigan Business School. He draws on both his experience in India and the West to develop ideas concerning business management and leadership.

(1993), in his book, *Tribes,* presented the Indian Diaspora as one of the four most prosperous overseas communities in the world today. People of South Asian origin were becoming visible in American universities and business schools, and non-resident Indians (NRIs) were being credited with the development of India's "Silicon Valley." When PBS reported on India as a world economic power, it was no accident it started by focusing on a couple who had returned from the United States to set up a business in India.

One must look at diaspora studies and the formation of the overseas Indian community to understand what seemed to be a sudden burst of entrepreneurial activity. In actuality, it was a combination of events spanning centuries and the sudden globalization process bursting in on the world order that lead to the high achievements and presence of the overseas Indians.

DIASPORA FORMATION

Using the word "diaspora" to identify the people of Indian ethnic origins residing outside of India may seem inappropriate. Many people, when they hear the word, think of the Jewish people living outside of Israel. It has also referred to the processes by which Jews were exiled from their homeland. However, current usage has followed the lead of Barrier and Dusenbery (1989), who expanded the term's definition to include the "the voluntary or forcible movement of peoples from their homelands into new regions."

Under colonialism, diasporas were multifarious movements involving the following:

1. The "temporary or permanent" movement of Europeans all over the world, leading to colonial settlements. Consequently, the ensuing exploitation of the settled areas necessitating large amounts of labor that could not be fulfilled by the local populace. . . .
2. The diaspora resulting from the enslavement of Africans and their relocation to places like British colonies. After slavery was outlawed, the continued demand for workers created indentured labor. . . .
3. Large bodies of people from poor areas of India and China (and others) to the West Indies, Malaysia, Fiji, Eastern and Southern Africa, and Southeast Asia. (Ashcroft, Griffiths, & Tiffin, 1968:68–70)

In addition, the people of the Indian Diaspora are not a homogenous community. If one travels from England to North America and on to Fiji, Australia, and other places where people of South Asian origin live, one sees diversity and variation within the communities of people of Indian origin. Yet there is a unity in the diversity. Diaspora decedents or members of the diasporas "have come to produce highly unique cultures that both maintains and builds on the perceptions of their original cultures" (Ashcroft, Griffiths, & Tiffin, 1968:68–70).

The Indian or South Asian Diasporas (Figure 1.1) are concentrated in North America, Southeast Asia (mainly Malaysia, Burma, and Singapore), Europe (mainly the United Kingdom), Eastern and Southern Africa (mostly Mauritius and South Africa), the Caribbean, the Pacific (mostly Fiji), and now as migrant workers to West Asia. Their family histories and backgrounds range: the exploited indentured laborers, innovative entrepreneurs who went out to make fortunes, the uneducated worker

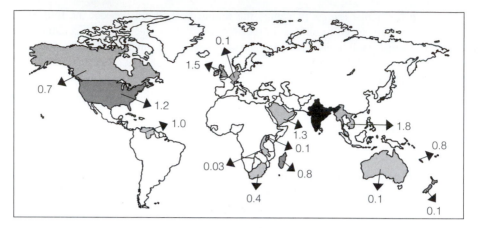

Figure 1.1 Map of South Asian Diaspora. This map of the South Asian Diaspora is not limited to only people of Indian origin. Pakistan, Bangladesh, and Sri Lanka are becoming prominent contributors to the new immigration stream also. Numbers in this map are by millions. Source: Patel, 2001.

in the industrial heartland, and the highly educated, well-trained professional. Some descend from people who emigrated more than a hundred years ago who no longer know from where in India they originate, and others are individuals who recently left India for a better life. But they all have in common their Indian heritage, in varying degrees, and a quest for a better future.

Over 2000 years ago people from India were settling in Southeast Asia, Central Asia, Japan, and the coast of East Africa. In fact, emigration from South Asia has been a dominant behavioral pattern on the subcontinent for centuries. It has its origins in the Indus Valley civilization (2500 B.C.–1000 B.C.) whose merchants frequented far-off lands. With the Aryan[7] invasions, merchants became incorporated into the caste system in the south. Prominent movements began after the death of Buddha (563 B.C.–483 B.C.) when his disciples traveled to Eastern and Central Asia to propagate his teachings—an effect that expanded under Emperor Asoka (265 B.C.–237 B.C.).

When the Mughals came to power around 1526, Hindu elites clung tenaciously to the caste system to exclude the rulers from their dominant social institutions. The elite and Brahmans, often one and the same, maintained Hindu institutions, especially the caste system and concepts of superiority, by mediating between the rulers and ruled—a structure that lasted through British colonial rule. The caste system informally trained people in patron/client relationships. As a result, the people of India became very skilled in knowing their place in a social system and how to act properly within that system. They quickly surmised who was superior and who was inferior and how they should behave towards each. They perceived society as a hierarchical system, not an egalitarian community. Also, during this time, the greater part of the population subsisted on agriculture with the village being the main unit. Villages were relatively self-sufficient units with their own craftsmen. Thus, Romila

[7]Although the term "Aryan" is often used in a political manner, it is and had been the term for the Central European tribes that spread out and entered ancient India.

Thaper could rightly say, "Although the Muslims ruled the infidels, the infidels called them 'Barbarians'" (Thaper, 1966). The social structure remained in tact and reliance on family unity became a basis for the social organization of the people to the present day.

After the fall of Rome, the Indian traders established strong commercial ties with the Byzantine, Persian, and Arab neighbors, as well as trading partners as far away as Europe and the Middle East. By the 13th century India had mastered a world-class spinning wheel and weaving technology[8] with products, such as Kashmiri shawls prized by civilizations like the Chinese.

Trade and the influence of Indian culture came from both Hinduism and Buddhism. Buddhism was the dominant religion, but the epics of the Ramayana and Mahabharata became a prominent part of the mythology of East and Southeast Asia to this day. However, virtually no lasting colonies comprising people of Indian origin were established (Tinker, 1974:8, 11, 13, 26, 3, 33, 43, 53).

WESTERN ENCROACHMENT

Theoretically, the entry of the West began with the Aryan invasions. However, the invasions of Alexander the Great (325 B.C.) brought a sustained relationship with the West. In fact, the great Indian ruler Asoka may have had a Greek mother.[9] In either case, the Hellenistic kingdoms on the northwestern border of South Asia lasted several centuries and were a meeting ground for Buddhist, Greek, and later Christian ideas.[10] In fact, contacts between East and West remained plentiful through the Roman rule of Antonine (131–168 A.D.). It was during this time that St. Thomas the Apostle took the message of Jesus Christ to South India and Alfred, King of Wessex, sent emissaries to find the Thomasite Christians, who became the Malabar church.

The sixth to eleventh (A.D.) centuries saw Indians from the eastern seaboard developing trade networks and sending commercial expeditions into Southeast Asia. The impact of these forays is still evident in Central and East Asia, where Indian mythology, dance, and theater continue to be prominent.

Movement from Western India to Africa dates to the second century A.D. with the development of trade (which continued through British rule) between the continents. Indians then maintained a "commuter existence," leaving wives and families and returning home periodically. Those who remained in Africa were called "passenger Indians" because they were considered sojourners, not permanent settlers (Manget, 1969:1–26; and Tinker, 1977:1–3).

With the rise of Islam militancy in the Arab world, communications between Europe and Asia ceased. So great was the social chasm that accounts of people like Marco Polo and Friar Odule were dismissed by their skeptical countrymen.

Several factors drove Western Europeans to expand their control over much of the world. First, the increased militancy of the Arab middlemen made the trade much more precarious. Second, Europeans wanted spices. They were crucial for the preservation of food as well as improving the taste. As a result, spices from Asia were in

---

[8]A technology the British would attempt to destroy.

[9]There are suggestions that Asoka's father married a daughter of Seleucus.

[10]Even the Buddha was assimilated into the saint worship of medieval Europe. Josaphat, an Indian prince, underwent all the experiences of Buddha. Josaphat and his disciple Balaam were accepted as saints by the Greek Orthodox Church and later by Rome.

high demand in Europe. Third, Europeans embraced the philosophy of capitalism, which emphasized the quest to always maximize profit and to never be satisfied. Consequently, no matter what the gains, the countries, merchants, and people of Western Europe always sought more. Fourth, to maximize profit, Europeans needed to bypass the Arab middlemen, which led to the exploration for alternative trade routes. Although it came later, the influence of Calvinists that equated wealth with godliness (Weber, 1958) was a driving force that not only led to expanding trade and the elimination of the middlemen, but also to colonize much of the world.

When the Portuguese made contact, they quickly realized the superiority of their guns and ships over the local inhabitants. In 1509, the Portuguese survived an attack at Diu by Egypt and Turkey, when the Sultan of Egypt teamed with Sulaman the Magnificent of Turkey. The various Portuguese then seized Goa in 1511 and were in control of the gold, spices, and other commodities of the East-West trade.

The encroachment of Portugal into Asia came at a time when that the internal conditions in South Asia were in disarray as king and potentate fought each other continually. Thus, opposition to Portuguese inroads was comparatively light. As a result, Portugal was able to control the maritime trade with Asia while interisland and intercontinental trade remained in the hands of the Arabs, Malaysians, Indians, and Chinese.

With the formation of the East India Company in 1600, trade from Britain started expanding. Although it was a private company, it had its own military force and in essence ruled much of South Asia until the Indian Mutiny of 1857 set forth abuses and the weakness of the East India Company control. In 1857 the soldiers and administration were under the control of the East India Company. They staged a mutiny and almost expelled British presence in India. Government inquiry revealed many abuses and as a result, the British government took control of the holdings and ruled until India obtained its independence in 1947.

The British set up an educational system that not only indoctrinated the Indians in British culture but also trained them in management and being part of an administrative service. Those who did well in their studies were incorporated into the prestigious Indian Administrative Service (IAS). The prestige of being a member of the IAS lasted for decades after independence. The value of education became a very prominent trait in Indian culture. After the Indian government obtained independence, it invested heavily in education. The government supplemented existing universities with the elite Indian Institutes of Management (IIMs) and Indian Institutes of Technology (IITs) throughout the country. They were modeled after prestigious American schools like the Massachusetts Institute of Technology (MIT) and Harvard Business School. Many of the faculties were trained in the States and many American professors taught in India under the Fulbright-Hays and other exchange programs. This has all resulted in a large well-educated, but unemployed, contingent in India.

Under British rule, administration of rural India continued through local intermediaries so rural villages could still claim independence. As a result, people relied more on the family as an economic unit, a pattern that has continued to the present day.

As the government built railroads and a communications infrastructure, the barriers between villages and markets decreased. As a result, the world market demanded more South Asian products. Peasants saw the high prices on the world market and realized they were not getting their fair share. For crops with a world market demand, the British instituted a plantation system that made the rural villagers lose self-determination and become dependent on the world markets—in the case of Indian cotton, to feed the cloth mills in Manchester. Jute and cotton were major export crops of Bengal while the building of a canal system increased big business concerns and helped to establish colleges in Calcutta and Bombay. These cities developed a cosmopolitan and commercial character quite different from the administrative urban areas like New Delhi.

A NEW SYSTEM OF SLAVERY

The British, like the Dutch, had been involved in the lucrative slave trade. The abolitionists had their way when legislation prohibited British ships to clear a port with a cargo of slaves after May 1, 1807, and after March 1, 1808, no slave could be landed in any British colony. The British Parliament tried to include safeguards but the European plantation owners needed cheap labor, especially in Fiji, Mauritius, Trinidad, and Guiana. It was also a time of rural poverty and starvation in British India. The solution was what Hugh Tinker has termed "A New System of Slavery" (Tinker, 1974)—more specifically, an indenture system.

Indenture was a system of labor recruitment where, according to the contract, the subject worked abroad and then returned to India once the terms of the contract were honored. Abuses were rampant because the workers had no recourse to justice—they were, in essence, enslaved. Laborers initially came from the urban centers of Calcutta, Bombay, and Madras. As this source of labor was exhausted, the British turned toward tribal recruitment, and later to the states of Bihar and the United Provinces (now Uttar Pradesh). Emigration was highest during times of economic difficulty, as men resorted to leaving their families behind. Some were single when they emigrated. Others never returned to their wives and children, either by choice or by contractors not living up to their obligations. Thus, this movement resulted in the formation of Indian communities in areas of plantation economies such as Fiji, Malaysia, Mauritius, and British Guiana. The indenture system lasted from 1830 until 1920. Between 1834 and 1934 about 30 million Indians were sent out as indentured laborers. Mauritius was the first to receive indentured labors in 1834, followed by British Guiana in 1838. Trinidad, Reunion, Guadeloupe, and Martinique in 1845; Jamaica in 1854; Natal South Africa in 1860; Fiji in 1879; East Africa in 1895; and smaller numbers in other areas.

Much of the Indian culture was lost or modified among the indentured community.[11] However, these people became the foundation of the overseas Asian Indian community, or what is commonly referred to as the Indian Diaspora.

Most of those indentured originated from the south, east, or hilly areas of India. Those on the west coast remained merchants while those in the northwest were declared martial races and were enlisted in the British Indian Army. They were stationed throughout Britain's colonial empire, especially in Hong Kong and Singapore. It was from one of these contingents that a representation of Sikh soldiers visited

[11]One interesting modification is found in Fiji where the people of Indian origin believe that one of the rivers is a tributary of the Ganges. They believe it flows from India via an underground and under ocean passage and surfaces in Fiji.

British Columbia on their way to march in Queen Victoria's Jubilee celebrations. Being pleased with the reception they received, some returned to Vancouver to settle there. It was the beginning of South Asian immigration to North America (Buchignani & Indra, 1985:5, 6).

In essence, people of South Asia had followed the British flag to the far reaches of the Empire so that like the British Empire, the sun never set on the Indian Diaspora. Thus, the merchant networks for the people of South Asia became extensive and diverse.

The 19th century brought a radical change to the character of India's diaspora: small-scale emigration became a mass movement to provide cheap labor for Britain's colonies (Figure 1.2). Conditions of abject poverty in certain sections of India or the prospect of gaining wealth overseas motivated people to sell themselves into servitude. As slavery became uneconomical, the colonial governments used Indians and other South Asians as plantation workers and clerks under an indenture system (Tinker, 1977:118–150).

Under the indenture system, about one-third of the indentured returned home. Of those, about 76 percent returned with nothing and 10 percent had between 100 and 180 rupees. Most, however, returned with their health shattered. Although they were virtually cut off from India, the laborers still maintained some of their cultural heritage, which included elements of language, religion, food, and music.[12]

The movement of Indians to East Africa was not the indentured form; it consisted primarily of artisans and clerks who worked on public projects (such as the Ugandan Railway), manned the bureaucracy, developed agriculture, and built business and industry. Emigrants came from the northwestern sector of India, primarily Punjab and Gujarat. Unlike their counterparts in the Caribbean, the Punjabis and Gujaratis maintained their culture abroad and promoted ties with their homeland. However, some professionals from Bengal adopted foreign behavioral patterns that emphasized higher education, English food, and British literature. They remained apart from their less educated rural counterparts.

During the three decades following the end of the indenture system (1920–1950), the Indian Diaspora began to shift from positions of servitude to active roles in the urban societies of their adopted lands. Certain emigrant groups, like the Sikhs,[13] Patels, and Ismailis,[14] consciously adhered to their culture, often drawing their strength from "Mother India." The vast majority who had been laborers under the indenture system were "creolized, bastardized in some respects, and almost everywhere fragmented and weak in leadership" (Tinker, 1976:8).

It was a time when going to the West was not prestigious. Indians considered emigrants polluted because they associated with what Hindus considered the defiling

---

[12]Initially, the overseas Indians lost much of their culture, but as contacts with the homeland increased, Indian culture began to reestablish itself.

[13]Sikhs are a small religious community. Founded by Guru Nanak (1469–1538), their original goals were to synthesize Muslim and Hindu tenets in a coherent whole. In response to severe persecution, they gradually evolved into a martial group. Under their tenth and last leader, Guru Gobind Singh, the *khalsa* or soldier-saint brotherhood was formed. Devout Sikhs now maintain their distinctive symbols of *kes* (uncut hair) to represent manliness or prowess, *kara* (bracelet on the right wrist) to protect the sword arm, *katcha* (specially designed shorts) to promote freedom of movement and remind them to use their life-giving fluids properly, *kanga* (comb to keep the hair orderly to symbolize saintliness, not madness), and *kirpan* (dagger) for defense.

[14]"Patel" is a common given name for many Gujaratis; the Ismailis are a sect of the Shiah, one of the major branches of Islam. The latter are also found in South Asia.

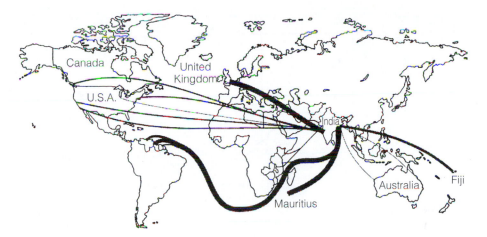

Figure 1.2 The Indian emigration streams lead to the development of the current Indian Diaspora. Source: Tinker, 1989.

behavior of Westerners. Hence, the saying, "half a loaf of bread at home is better than a whole loaf abroad" exemplified the feelings of many. Nevertheless, non-resident Indians were able to influence the foreign policies of both India and their host societies. On the one hand, exploitation of Indians on plantations and discrimination against them were continual issues to the governing body in India. On the other hand, the Indian emigrant communities in the United States, Great Britain, and Canada worked hard to promote India's freedom movement by supplying money, manpower and influence to the government under which they were residing. The Indian expatriate community played a definite role in the decline of colonialism.

Around 1945, changes began in the Caribbean Indian communities. The Indians became more affluent and travel became faster and more comfortable. With the advent of better steamships and air travel, contacts with India intensified. Travel back and forth to India rapidly increased, entrepreneurs arranged for artists and entertainers to visit diaspora communities while the government of India sent parliamentarians—all helped to reestablish relationships with the homeland, which included kinsmen. Indians in East Africa were not so isolated from India. For example, where a steamship voyage took 3 weeks between East Africa and India, it took 26 weeks between India and the Caribbean. From East Africa, the Indian culture resurgence spread to Mauritius. Due to the severe oppression experienced in South Africa, Indian culture was slow to reestablish itself. The search for marriage partners also aided in communications with India.[15]

THE NEW IMMIGRATION

Since India gained its independence in 1947, emigration has continued; it has not been limited to Great Britain and the New Commonwealth,[16] but has spread to the United States, Australia, and the Middle East (Figure 1.4). Until the last decade,

---

[15]Patel's (2001) article was a big help in organizing this section.

[16]The "New Commonwealth" is a consortium of countries that were part of the British Commonwealth. Not all Old Commonwealth countries belong. For a long time, Pakistan was not a member, but recently joined the New Commonwealth.

Figure 1.3 This map shows the South Asian emigration to the Caribbean. The tentacle-like migration streams stretched out from India to the other side of the world. Today the people of Indian origin are a significant political and social force in the countries they traversed to—their populations are sizable and influential. Source: Potts, 1990.

1 - Cuba
2 - Jamaica
3 - Dominica
4 - Haiti
5 - Puerto Rico
6 - St. Croix
7 - Nevis
8 - Guadeloupe
9 - Dominique
10 - Marinique

11 - St. Lucia
12 - St. Vincent
13 - Barbados
14 - Grenada
15 - Tobago
16 - Trinidad
17 - Venezuela
18 - Br. Guiana
19 - Dutch Guiana
20 - French Guiana

Great Britain undoubtedly was the destination of preference because Indians, like many other colonials, had developed an admiration for the believed superiority of their former rulers. Sikh Jats from Punjab and later Patels from Gujarat dominated the population flow from India to England, which was curtailed by the passage of legislation beginning in 1962 (Gordon & Newland, 1986).

Large scale movement to the United States began in the mid-1950s, especially among students. Financial aid was available, and those who did not have it could obtain jobs to pay for their studies. The United States was perceived as superior in technology, business, and general sciences. Wider scale migration to the United States, Canada, and Australia began in the mid-1960s, when revised immigration regulations removed racial barriers and began to emphasize skills that would guarantee economic self-sufficiency. Educated Indians, primarily from Punjab, Gujarat, and Kerala, took advantage of these policy changes. As a result, the West gained a cadre of educated immigrants who contributed to both their homeland and their country of residence.

Since the mid-1970s, the oil-rich Middle East has become a focus for South Asian immigration. Initially artisans dominated the group, but Indians increasingly occupy prominent administrative and management positions, replacing the more expensive Western professionals (Kondapi, 1951, and Singh, 1979). India sees the Gulf region as important from both a security viewpoint and for the 2.5 million people of Indian origin in the region who remit 200 crores ($44 million) annually. Economically the region accounts for 15 percent of India's total foreign trade and two-thirds of India's energy requirements. Of course there has been the centuries-old interaction, and the Gulf's centrality to the Islamic world makes it politically significant.

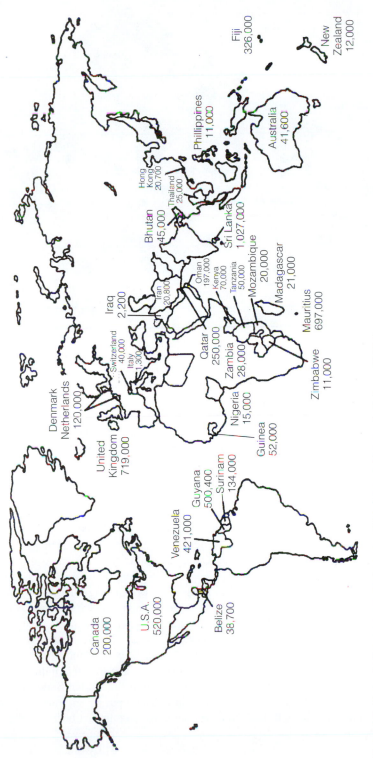

Figure 1.4 Major Indian overseas settlements, 1984. Source: Helweg & Helweg, 1990:6.

Hugh Tinker

To paraphrase Hugh Tinker, indentured laborers from India were bastardized, creolized and dehumanized, but they managed to maintain their cultural and religious ties to their homeland and keep their culture alive while residing outside their homeland, even for generations.

In Bahrain, exchange and interaction occurs in the private sector. In 1966, India's Minister of State for Commerce, while participating in the 13th International Congress of Non-Resident Indians, signed a Memorandum of Understanding with the Bahrain Chambers of Commerce and Industry. India has also strengthened relations with Iraq and has gifted Iraq with baby food, wheat, and rice to alleviate the hardships caused by UN sanctions on the Iraqi people. In Kuwait, the Indian government monitored compensation claims of Indian nationals. Now the Asian Indian population exceeds 240,000, which is more than before August 1990. Exchanges, trade, and visits continue with Oman, Qatar, Saudi Arabia, United Arab Emirates, Yemen, and Iran.

Migration has not been limited to emigration originating on the subcontinent. When virtually the entire Indian population of Uganda was expelled on August 4, 1972, a few Indian refugees returned to India and Pakistan, but the vast majority went to Great Britain, the United States, Canada, Sweden, the Netherlands, Switzerland, Austria, Norway, Belgium, Denmark, New Zealand, and the Persian Gulf states. The Ugandan experience sent a shock wave through India's overseas community; Indians began to fear that Great Britain or the United States might also expel them by a legislative act. As one Sikh in England put it, "all Parliament has to do is pass a law and we will have to leave." Indians have in fact been expelled from Burma and Sri Lanka.

Indians, primarily Tamils, were recruited as laborers to work on estates in Sri Lanka during British rule. They continued to live under adverse conditions and experience the brunt of resentment, especially during times of economic hardship (Tinker, 1977:118–150). In the 1970s, the Tamils in India felt akin to the Tamils in Sri Lanka, but as the government in Sri Lanka increased their oppression of the Tamils there, the Indian Tamils started fighting back. The Indian government has had a peace-keeping force in the region for several years, but at present about five groups (two of which are Tamil rebels) are fighting each other. These groups have generally returned to India, but the influence of their plight has not been as dramatic as for those from Uganda.

Travel and communications between India and its diaspora is high, but according to Hugh Tinker (1977), the status of the people of Indian origin outside India (see Appendix A and Figure 1.4) can be classed by country into six categories: (1) countries where the rights of Indians have been reduced or frozen to holding second-class citizenship (South Africa, Sri Lanka, and Zimbabwe); (2) countries where Indians remain downtrodden (Trinidad, Guiana, Mauritius, and Fiji);[17] (3) places where Indians are a separate community but are forced to conform (Malaysia and East Africa); (4) places from where Indian communities are likely to be deported (Burma and Uganda); (5) societies where Indians hope to integrate (United Kingdom, United States, Canada, and Australia); and (6) regions where Indians are temporary workers (Middle East). Although this study focuses on the Indian community in the United States, it represents only one contingent of a much wider social system.

ENTREPRENEURS AND ENTREPRENEURIAL NETWORKS

The history of the Indian Disapora shows that by the late 1960s the basis had been laid for the creation of what of Joel Kotkin (1993) could call a tribe of entrepreneurs. Traditionally, the concept of the entrepreneur was significant in the neoclassical equilibrium-oriented view of economics.

> To the theoretical economist in the neoclassical tradition, the entrepreneur was an abstract figure assumed to be unaffected by external influences to the rational operation of the firm he directed (Greenfield & Strickon, 1986:5).

Put another way, the entrepreneur was considered the manager, trader, or merchant par excellence. This concept of the entrepreneur as the rational manager was changed after the World War II to that of an innovator, trendsetter, or challenger to the established order. Thus, the entrepreneur can be a force for change or stability. Also, the concept broadened to include participation in non-economic institutions (Barth, 1961, 1963). Thus, the focus of entrepreneurial studies has shifted from decision making to that of analysis of structural and institutional factors influencing entrepreneurial activity.

Emigrating exposes people to new ideas, which result in new combinations while old restrictive norms are left aside. Whereas a Muslim and Hindu would not work together in South Asia, they will abroad.

One man who illustrates the South Asian entrepreneur is Rajiv Mahotra. When Rajiv Mahotra arrived at Michigan State University in 1969 to commence graduate studies in business, it was a time when many American students were looking to India for enlightenment. The Beatles, probably the most popular music group ever,

---

[17]In most cases, the Indians in these countries had been used for plantation labor. Trinidad is now a major oil exporter with less emphasis on agriculture, and Fiji is placing an increased emphasis on tourism.

claimed to be devotees of a guru in India, as did many other celebrities. Interest in India and things Indian was a prominent part of student culture in particular and youth culture in general.

Rajiv was born into a Marwari family, a caste group known for their acumen in business. He felt, as many believed, that he had "business in his blood," for he was born into a family that had been in a business going back to ancient times. In fact, he had plans to obtain a graduate degree in business administration.

Although he came to the States on a student visa, Rajiv had an idea that he felt would make him rich. He noticed how Americans not only were fascinated with Indian religion but also how they bought things in "packages," which contained items used together to obtain a desired goal. Thinking how he could use these ideas, Rajiv came up with idea of selling "guru kits" to students. That is, he would have an attractive package consisting of wood sandals, wood beads, incense, saffron, and an instruction book on how to meditate, with names and addresses of gurus and *ashrams,* both in the States and in India. Immediately, Rajiv wrote to his parents in India explaining his idea and asking them to supervise the assembling of the guru kits in India and send them to him, so he could market them in the States.

Everything went according to plan. Rajiv's family members in India supervised the creation and assembly of guru kits—family members were used because they were better known concerning their reliability and they were likely to be more trustworthy than a person who was not a relative. The guru kits were sent to Rajiv who marketed them in the States while still doing his studies at Michigan State University.

Rajiv Mahotra represents the ideal entrepreneur. The issue is not whether he was successful or not or whether he was a businessman, middleman, trader, or inventor. An entrepreneur may or may not be any or all of these things. What made Rajiv an entrepreneur was that he was an innovator. What he did was put together a new combination of existing factors. He did not invent anything; all the ideas were already in place, whether in India or the United States. What Rajiv did was put existing units together in a unique way and that is what made him an entrepreneur.

It follows that people who have bicultural or multicultural experience are more likely to be entrepreneurial. Thus, migrants and people with extensive contacts outside their realm of influence are most likely to be entrepreneurial. Add in the fact that being away from home means they have fewer strictures and they can try new things without facing censure from society. And some people, like Rajiv, have the financial backing and benefit of years of family experience to draw on.

The role of the entrepreneur on social behavior is of recent interest and realization in the social sciences. Until 1949 and the publication of Joseph Schumpeter's *The Theory of Economic Development,* the entrepreneur was, especially in neoclassical economic thought, a rational figure unaffected by external influences in the rational operation of his or her firm or business. The entrepreneur was perceived as a force for resisting change.

Two works brought about the sudden rethinking concerning entrepreneurs and their place in social dynamics. Joseph Schumpeter saw the entrepreneur as the focal point and key to economic development and growth. Fredrik Barth showed the crucial role the entrepreneur can play in non-economic institutions as well as being a key element in determining the direction of social change or inhibiting the direction or social dynamics of a community. Barth demonstrated that entrepreneurial behavior was not limited to the economic realm but could include fishermen or people of any other social institution.

As has been illustrated, the entrepreneur can be a force for change or stability. The entrepreneur can be crucial in setting the direction of a particular social group or society. In the case of Rajiv Mahotra, he is the ideal entrepreneur. He took ideas from the West (i.e., kits and quest for knowledge of the East) and items from the East (i.e., wood sandals, beads, instructions in eastern Hindu religion) and came up with the idea of something new—the guru kit. He did not invent anything; he just created something new out of existing items. However, what he did was novel and innovative.

In creating and marketing the guru kit, Rajiv, like other entrepreneurs, was a force for change and stability. In India, people saw that Westerners wanted to learn from them. Thus, they felt superior and as a result, many did not want to change their living habits. However Rajiv did initiate change in that a new product was being produced in India, and they were taking a more favorable attitude towards themselves and their religion.

In the West people like Rajiv were also a force for maintaining Indian culture as they saw it. By borrowing and buying Western techniques and technology, it reinforced the feeling of superiority Westerners felt. Thus, they worked from a position of confidence. However, a large enough group of people oriented toward Indian religion and culture in the West wanted change, so forces pulled or pushed for change.

The entrepreneurial network Rajiv used was kinsmen, in this case his parents. In the case of many societies, business and economic networks are formed from kinsmen because (1) people believe they are more likely to be loyal and (2) people have had a closer relationship with family so they know what they are getting.

These general observations of entrepreneurial behavior may vary when put into practice. As the entrepreneurial and trading routes and networks are discussed below, rest assured that entrepreneurs are responsible for social and cultural change whether the entrepreneurs are specifically mentioned or not.

The export of labor gave the people of India influence in diverse places, which resulted in the development of a large entrepreneurial community for emigrants and immigrants. Indian migrants generally aid or dramatically lead in the development of an area because they quickly exhibit entrepreneurial behavior; they see ways to develop new combinations out of old units or ideas.

There was one more problem to overcome before Indians, overseas and domestic, could be galvanized into a viable economic force. They had maintained their culture since the Indus Valley civilization, which helped maintain a purpose in life and provide a rationale for unified experiences. The family and village as social units had maintained an organized lifestyle, while mediators insulated the rural people from their rulers. The caste system, along with the British and Americans, instilled ways in which the Indian learned to work in a bureaucracy or an administration. But something else was needed to weld all of these residentially dispersed individuals into a producing community. The problem of territoriality, national boundaries, and nationalism had to be dealt with as well as making communications fast, efficient, and inexpensive—without these innovations the flow of materials, products, and capital were inhibited.

Globalization is the process of economic development by which all aspects of production, distribution, and consumption are done on a global scale. Keep in mind that globalization is a direct counter to regionalism. Globalization assumes (1) all human beings are similar and political leaders will embrace this assumption by promoting democracy; (2) there is a worldwide technological interdependence; (3) the planet earth is a single place—there is only one world; (4) pollutants, drugs, ideology, and other things freely flow across boundaries; and (5) humans are heading towards a global civilization of shared values, processes, and structures. All global theories would not agree on the above processes and assumptions. What is happening is that (1) economic transactions are faster and denser in relevant localities, (2) international migration emphasizes contractual and temporary settlement over establishing a permanent abode, and (3) there are countercurrents to globalization, such as the nation-state (Cohen, 1997:155–76).

What globalization did for the Indian Diaspora, and other diaspora, was nothing short of revolutionary. Kaushak Patel is an example. He runs his real estate business in Chicago. On the last week of every month, he flies to his home village in Gujarat to perform his duties as village headman. Another example are the Mehta brothers. One lives in Chicago, one in Hong Kong, and another in London. They have relatives scattered in major cities around the globe. The family is on the phone to each other almost every night talking over strategy, investment, and family matters. The way they operate is just as efficient (or more) as being at a desk with the same offices as one's brothers.

What has developed from the Indian Diaspora is what Joel Kotkin terms the "Global Tribes." By this he means:

> [a people that] combine a strong sense of a common origin and shared values correlating with essential tribal characteristics with two critical factors for success in the modern world: geographic dispersion and a belief in scientific progress. . . . Such cosmopolitan groups . . . do not surrender their sense of a peculiar ethnic identity at the altar of technology or science but utilize their historically conditioned values and beliefs to cope successfully with change. (Kotkin, 1993:4)

In the global economy, ethnicity is becoming a defining factor in the post–Cold War era, and global tribes are well-suited to functioning in the "progressively more integrated worldwide economic system." Thus, three characteristics are critical for a group's success in the new globally integrated economy:

1. A strong ethnic identity and sense of mutual dependence that helps the group adjust to changes in the global economic and political rules without losing its essential unity.
2. A global network based on mutual trust that allows the tribe to function collectively beyond the confines of national and regional borders.
3. A passion for technical and other knowledge from all possible sources, combined with an essential open-mindedness that fosters rapid cultural and scientific development critical for success in the late-twentieth-century world economy. (Kotkin, 1993:4, 5)

The Indian Diaspora of 18 million is spread over 53 countries with 10 countries having over a half million people of Indian origin. In spite of the rapid growth, Indians maintain the characteristics of a cohesive "tribe." In 1960, only 5 million were scattered with a few thousand unskilled laborers. The vast majority were Punjabi Sikhs living in California, demoralized, as was the case in Mauritius, Fiji,

Trinidad, and elsewhere. This society of diverse countries, castes, and religions has a unity in their diversity. They descended from a rich tradition stemming back to the Indus Valley at the dawn of human history. The vast majority adhered to some form of the caste system. Hindu mythology pervaded their culture. Being so dispersed worldwide broke the idea of travel overseas being polluting. The merchants, craftsmen, and entrepreneurs could now come as far as they desired. Even places in the diaspora regions took on a sacred significance. For example, in Fiji, there is a sacred river believed to be a tributary of the Ganges that flowers from the Ganges underground and resurfaces in Fiji. It is a place of pilgrimages.

India had instituted an exceptional education system that trained a ready core of highly skilled and highly educated professionals, businesspeople, and entrepreneurs to stimulate trade. In some ways, the emigration of Indians was unique to the annals of education. They made quick and successful adjustments to the industrial societies in which they entered and consistently led in obtaining high levels of technical, management, and business education. The Indian Institutes of Technology and Indian Institutes of Management, along with other notable higher educational institutions, developed people who were qualified and highly motivated to step into upper level professions, such as doctors and engineers, as well as capitalize on business opportunities abroad, especially in North America and Western Europe and to share their economic gain with India in the forms of remittances, public works, investment, and consulting. Not only were those in India well trained, they were familiar with the English language and Western ways. Thus, they were capable of stepping into middle and upper level jobs. Put another way, they were *preadapted* to life in the West.

Their influence is not limited to work abroad. A drive through Punjab, Gujarat, or Kerala, shows the results of emigrant remittances in the form of hospitals, libraries, computer centers, new grain varieties, irrigation pumps, large houses, and tractors.

One of the notable achievements spearheaded by emigrant capital and technical knowledge is Hyderabad. Hyderabad became cyber-center for the world, replacing the Silicon Valley of California as computer programs could be developed there for a tenth of the cost. Those who spearheaded the endeavor were primarily emigrants who were well educated in technology and, unlike American managers, saw an opportunity to maximize profit—a task they have been doing for generations. All they had to do was combine what they had learned from their American experience with what they knew of their homeland and the profit was theirs. Also, members of the Diaspora invested in their homeland. About one-third of the total foreign investment in India since the country's economic reforms began came from members of the diaspora. Also, Indians working in U.S. companies are encouraging those companies to invest in India.

Around the world, Indians have used their international networks to be successful in business, trade, agriculture, convenience stores, clothes manufacturing, science, research, motels, education, medicine, research, and so on. They are a community that has a unity in their diversity.

They are not only one cohesive tribe, but are also made up of subtribes according to region, caste, and religion. Comprised of Punjabis, Gujaratis, Tamils, Keralites, and so forth, they work as separate units but when needed, they come together under the Indian or South Asian umbrella.

Families, castes, and tribes are dispersed, but in this age of electronic communications, a brother in Hong Kong invests for his brother in San Francisco. Mountains, rivers, forests, plains, and distance are no longer barriers to rapid travel and communication. Nor does emigration necessitate cutting ties with the homeland. Overseas Indians invest and participate and administer in their village of origin as if they were residing there.

Rajiv is a good example of how family networks are used. However, if family members do not have the needed skills or knowledge, they hire and supervise outsiders. If deemed worthy, they will be treated very well so their loyalty to the firm is cultivated and assured. Thus, in the United States, Asian Indians who own businesses have a good reputation for treating their personnel very well and gaining the loyalty one would expect from a family member. Therefore, the firm is still like a family, for whether not there is a biological link, the values, behavior, and attitudes of the members, especially in positions of authority and leadership are the same.

A family firm has other advantages over other types of organizations. In a family firm, things are decided informally, often outside the firm in informal conversation, thus eliminating the need and waste of having meetings on company time, for business issues often dominate the family conversations. Also, family members have an emotional and vested interest in the firm so they work harder and longer hours without extra pay (Benedict, 1968). And, as stated earlier, outsiders are made part of the family to ensure their loyalty and devotion as a surrogate family member.

The result is a vibrant diaspora, which benefits both India and the host communities. For example, the global real estate investment of overseas Indians is $100 billion while individuals like Shashi Jogani turned a $4,000 profit in one business and converted it into a $400 million enterprise. Investment in India has been high while the economies of the host societies have benefited. When one considers that the Indian Diaspora generates US$300 billion annually, which is comparable to India's gross domestic product, one can understand why the Indian government is trying to attract Indian Diaspora investment.

A few migrants support legends among the Asian Indian Diaspora—billionaires like the Hinduja family with its multibillion dollar steel-fertilizer-finance conglomerate out of London, Geneva, and Bombay. Members of the Indian Diaspora have been successful in the corporate and managerial sectors. Thus, the median family income for Indians in the United States according to the 1990 census is $53,000, higher than for white families.[18] Indians working for U.S. companies in particular are directly responsible for obtaining foreign investment for India. In fact, members of the Indian Diaspora are responsible for about one-third of India's total foreign investment.

Overseas influence also comes in the form of what the Indians call social work. Social work can take the form of individual effort, organized processes, or working or advising an aid agency of a government or non-government organization (NGO).

Neil and Pram Shah illustrate full-time individual efforts. They both were public health specialists in the United States. After making what they considered sufficient money, they sold their assets and returned to their home region in Karanataka. In Karanataka, they use their money and share their knowledge to eradicate disease and misery in a 15-village area. They have been at it for 10 years now, with considerable success. Many returnees like the Shahs are scattered all over India.

---

[18]Some feel that this figure does not leave an accurate impression for the Indian families tend to be larger and have more earning members than white families.

G. S. Grewal

Here Gurmale Singh Grewal is being honored by Sahouli, his ancestral village. He has set up a computer center in the village that is tied to the Internet. He has brought new and better technology, seeds, farming techniques and medical facilities. He has aided members of his family and has greatly contributed to giving his homeland a far better quality of life.

Other more organized efforts include the India Development Service (IDS), which has a very good record of advising, proposing, evaluating, and sponsoring aid programs for India. The staff and advisors of Winrock International, people of Indian origin residing overseas, dominate the staff and act as consultants for these organizations.

CONCLUSION

The contemporary Indian Diaspora is a story just beginning to be researched and told. It is a global institution that wields a tremendous amount of economic and political power. The story includes more than successful individuals like Rajat Gupta who was elected managing partner of McKinsey & Co,, a prestigious consulting firm or my friend Jegdev Sandhu who went to England in the 1960s and by investing in land in Punjab is worth more than a million pounds sterling today.

Many notable personalities receive recognition, but they are where they are today because of the sacrifices of indentured laborers who preceded them. Others got their start from friends who emigrated. The story is not just of successful entrepreneurs who suddenly are wealthy and successful. They would not be where they are today if it wasn't for the people and institutions that preceded them.

2/Mother India
The Source and the Recipient

INTRODUCTION

The emigrants' communities and the community of returnees in India are part-societies. Whether in India or outside India, they see themselves as part of India. Whether they have emigrated or returned, people of Indian origin (PIO) look to their homeland for help and sustenance, whether spiritual or material, and a place where they belong—a home or homeland. It ranges from South Indian stonecutters imported to build a Hindu temple in the United States to Tamils in Sri Lanka requesting help to counter discrimination and oppression in their place of residence. This chapter will show that for those who have returned, government policies have resulted in their becoming a distinct ethnic community, which is not always appreciated by the wider Indian society.

MOTHER INDIA

India (Figure 2.1) is currently the seventh largest supplier of immigrants to the United States. With its population of over a billion people, India is the world's most populous democracy and second most populous country in the world. It has a land area of 1.6 million square miles. Put another way, India is one-third the size of the United States with three times the population. India's government is a federal republic with a duly elected parliament and prime minister. Since gaining independence, India has made considerable advances in food production, industrialization, and general economic development. It contains a large cadre of intellectually trained people and is one of the largest suppliers of engineers and other highly educated talent in the world.

When India obtained independence in 1947, many Westerners greeted the event with skepticism.[1] The departing British were certain that "they will be begging us to come back and rule their country within a year."[2] But, India is one of the few coun-

---

[1]See Collins and LaPierre (1975) for a popularized description of the independence struggle in India. Khushwant Singh (1956) and Chaman Nahal (1975) treat this topic in novel form.
[2]Dr. A. R. Mehta, personal communication (1972).

Figure 2.1 India's emigration hubs: There are four emigration hubs in India.

Not to scale

tries that, having achieved independence from colonial rule, has maintained a stable government. Although India's unity has been challenged, the country has remained in tact. It is a country with diverse cultures: three major racial groups, four prominent religious communities, and sixteen language categories (including English).[3] Hinduism, however, with its caste ideology, provides an overriding unity that sets forth common structural and ideological principles for India in particular and South Asia in general.[4]

Important to the country's development is the fact that, beginning with Jawaharlal Nehru and continuing under Indira Gandhi, India embarked on an ambitious program of industrialization. As the country developed industrially and technologically, it acquired the largest middle class of Asia; its strong emphasis on education has made it the third largest supplier of scientists in the world, behind only the United States and the former Soviet Union. India, however, cannot employ these highly educated and technically qualified people; thus, many have emigrated and now provide their expertise not only to Western countries, but also to Africa, Asia, and the Middle East.

[3]From the *Time Almanac* 2003, the racial groups are Indo-Aryan (72%), Dravidian (25%), and Mongolians (3%). The prominent religious communities are Hindu (453,292,086, 82.72%), Muslim (61,417,934, 11.21%), Christian (14,223,382, 2.6%), Sikh (10,378,797, 1.89%), Buddhist (3,812,315, 0.73%), Jain (2,604,646, 0.47%), and Zoroastrian (91,366). Hundreds of linguistic dialects are spoken.
[4]Much ink has been spilt concerning Indian culture and society, especially concerning the caste system. Some of the more noted works are Bailey (1963), Dumont (1966), Dumont and Pocock (1957, 1958a and b), Hutton (1946), and Marriott (1968). Schwartz (1967) has surveyed castes in overseas Indian communities.

Like their European counterparts, India's emigrants represent diverse cultures. Emigrants to the United States primarily originate from Punjab, Gujarat, Kerala, Tamil Nadu, Bengal, and twice migrants.

Punjab

About 35 percent of the Indians in the United States claim Punjab as their ethnic homeland. Punjab is a 50,000-square-kilometer region with a population of 16 million, of which 40.74 percent are literate. As an agricultural state, 70 percent of the people farm and 85 percent of the land is under cultivation. The green revolution has taken hold, and farmers are known for their innovative technology. Punjab has concentrated on small-scale rather than heavy industry; in 1986, over 100,000 industrial plants—valued at Rs 1,625 crore ($1,083,333)—employed almost 500,000 people. Chief products include textiles, sewing machines, sporting goods, sugar, starch, fertilizers, bicycles, scientific instruments, electrical goods, machine tools, and pine oil.

Emigrant investment has played a significant part in Punjab's economic growth: the investments have been primarily in agriculture and ideas, money, and technology have come from abroad.

Punjab's history is ancient, but unlike Gujarat it has constantly faced invasions and rebellions. Located in the northwest part of South Asia, it is on the path traditionally followed by invaders into South Asia: the early Vedic invaders, Darius of Persia in 522 B.C., and Alexander the Great of Greece in 322 B.C. Later Macedonian governors controlled the region until Chandra Gupta Maurya annexed it in 305 B.C. As the Mauryan Empire declined, Scythians, Parthians, and Casinos occupied the region, in that order. After them, indigenous rulers came into power. From the 10th century began numerous Muslim invasions that culminated with Babar, the founder of the Mughal Empire, which ruled India until the British Raj. When Mughal control declined, Punjab suffered from minor Muslim invasions until 1849, when the British annexed it. In 1947, India and Pakistan divided Punjab, and in 1956 Indian Punjab was further fragmented into the two states of Haryana and Punjab. The present-day political region thus represents a small fraction of its original area.

Sikhism[5] was born in this region of turmoil in the mid-15th century. Although Guru Nanak, its founder, preached peace and conciliation, numerous persecutions transformed the sect into a soldier-saint community. The British categorized the "Lions of the Punjab" (Sikhs) as a martial race and relied on them throughout their empire as soldiers, workers, and administrators. Sikhs have a reputation for prowess, innovation, and aggressive behavior. The religion was close enough to certain Hindu sects that many Hindu families raised their eldest son a Sikh. Since 1982, however, an element of the religion has advocated a Sikh homeland. Revolutionary actions and government insensitivity to the situation has led to violence; desecration of the Sikh Golden Temple by the Indian Army in 1984 precipitated the assassination of Indira Gandhi. Since that time, the rift deepened between the Hindus and Sikhs and vio-

---

[5]The Sikhs are a small religious community. Founded by Guru Nanak (1469–1538), their original goals were to synthesize Muslim and Hindu tenets in a coherent whole. In response to severe persecution, they gradually evolved into a martial group. Under their 10th and last leader, Guru Gobind Singh, the *khalsa* or soldier-saint brotherhood was formed. Devout Sikhs now maintain their distinctive symbols of *kes* (uncut hair) to represent manliness or prowess, *kara* (bracelet on the right wrist) to protect the sword arm, *katcha* (specially designed shorts) to promote freedom of movement and remind them to use their life-giving fluids properly, and *kirpan* (dagger) for defense.

lence escalated.[6] Kuldip Nayar, Indian political journalist and columnist, laments that there is no longer a Punjabi identity, but only "Hindu" or "Sikh" allegiance. The Sikh emigrant community has contributed both financially and politically to the fight in India.[7]

Prior to 1950, the Sikhs were the primary Indian and Punjabi immigrants to the United States, where they settled in California and took up agricultural pursuits. After the World War II, Punjabi immigration[8] into the United States continued to dominate until the 1970s when the Gujarati became the dominant group. This early Punjabi emigration was the result of Sikh service under the British. They had learned about opportunities overseas, and because the region's partition had already forced many to leave their homes in West Punjab to live in East Punjab, they were quite open to the idea of going abroad. Not surprisingly, many emigrants who claim Punjab as their ethnic homeland actually resided in Delhi before they left India.

Punjabis behave differently from their Gujarati counterparts in the United States. They are less strict in religious orientation and are not so frugal. Punjabis work hard and save money, but they also enjoy life. Punjabis may become self-employed, but they are not so apt to own a side business as Gujarati. Their expertise lies in the fields of science and engineering. Punjab, like Gujarat, has returnee enclaves and encourages emigrant investment.

Gujarat

Gujarat, the home state of Mahatma Gandhi, is a prosperous region with an area of 196,024 square kilometers and a population of 34,086,000 with a literacy rate of 43.7 percent.[9] Gujarat has both an agricultural and an industrial economy; its prominent products are cotton, ground nuts, textiles, soap, and oil. It produces 63 percent of India's infant formula and 60 percent of its salt; other industries include the largest petrochemical complex in the world; fertilizers, inorganic chemicals, drugs, and dyestuffs; and many engineering plants. Petroleum is a rising industry.

Gujarat has a cultural tradition that goes back to antiquity. The area was part of India's Mauryan and Gupta Empires, but the foundation for its present-day identity lies with the rule of Mulraj Solanki, a ruler of the Chalukyan Dynasty. By the end of the 13th century, the state had passed under Muslim rule; the resulting synthesis of Muslim and Hindu cultures has held until recent times when ethnic conflict caused bloodshed between the two groups. Unlike the situation in Punjab, Gujarat's social structure and value system have not been destroyed by invasion or domination. Even during British rule, Gujaratis were able to insulate themselves sufficiently that British culture did not significantly challenge traditional concepts.

---

[6]It is hard to gauge the degree of this rift. For example, there are many undocumented accounts of a Sikh or a Hindu risking his or her life for the other.

[7]But it may not be backed by a majority of the Sikh community in 1986. It is important to keep in mind that the revolutionary movement contains many points of view.

[8]The Sikhs are from the Indian state of Punjab and are considered Punjabis. After World War II, Punjabis dominated Indian migration to the United States, but it was the educated Hindus of urban origins that increased in prominence, not the Sikh farmer who comprised the immigration stream in the era before World War II.

[9]Based on conversations and sample census material, I estimated these statistics. Such is the case for the estimation of Punjabis and Keralites also.

Gujarat, with the longest coast line of any Indian state, has supported a trading and business tradition since ancient times. The port of Surat was at one time a world trading center, and Gujarati merchants plied their trade throughout the Far East, Middle East, and Africa. The British colonial administrators employed them in a number of ways, especially in East Africa to work on the Ugandan Railway. In fact, in Kheda district villages, it is common to meet Indians who still draw a pension from the British government because of their service to the Raj in Africa.

Gujarati emigration to the United States expanded rapidly after the 1965 legislation changes. The central district of Kheda was densely populated, but highly educated because of American influence and involvement in the universities. So when American immigration laws began to favor skills over race, a large cadre of Gujaratis took advantage of the new rules and emigrated to the United States (along with Indians expelled from Uganda under the Idi Amin regime). They quickly went into business for themselves in the motel, real estate, and retail trades. Their ranks included some who were trained in medicine or engineering: it is common for Indian professionals to own a business and have their spouse or sibling manage it while they continue to practice their profession, be it engineering, medicine, or teaching. This business mentality has manifested itself in the way Gujaratis have adapted to life in the United States. They generally start a business to control their own destiny and to gain wealth. Gujaratis are frugal because they are well aware of business cycles. During times of plenty they save rather than spend, realizing that lean times will eventually come.

Gujaratis by tradition are religious people who maintain a prominent worship center in their homes and support Hindu and Jain temples. Their social and cultural concepts have remained strong, and they have a strong orientation toward their homeland even while residing abroad. (Returned emigrants from Africa are widespread in the Kheda district, especially in Vallabh Vidya Nagar, Ahmedabad, and Surat.) This orientation is visible also in investment, for non-resident Indians have invested more than Rs 127.96 crore ($85,306,666) in about 275 industrial plants in Gujarat (Lane, 1986:625–7).

Kerala

Kerala is a small state located on the southwest coast of India, with an area of 38,863 square kilometers and a population of 25,453,680. It is the most densely populated state in India;[10] with 1.18 percent of the country's land area it supports 3.71 percent of the population. It is an economically poor area because of chronic food shortages,[11] yet it boasts a 69.17 percent literacy rate, the highest in India. The lack of food, high level of education, and high population density are all factors encouraging emigration from the region; hence, 10 percent of the Indians in the United States come from Kerala.

Keralite emigrants can be found in numbers both in the Persian Gulf region and in the United States. Keralite women are more noticeable in the medical profession (as well as domestic work and childcare) than are women from other Indian states.

---

[10]This excludes the Union Territories.

[11]For historical and climatic reasons, Kerala has emphasized commercial agriculture over food crops. Thus food grains, especially the staple food rice, are in short supply.

Medicine and nursing are a result of the high levels of education and the influence of the Christian church in Kerala. The Christian church has a long tradition in Kerala— its roots go back to St. Thomas, its founder; about one-fourth of the population are Christian (Andrews, 1983; Pais, Bhaskar, & Kurian, 1989).

Tamil Nadu

Tamil Nadu, the home of 55 million Tamils is located on the extreme southeastern portion of the Indian Peninsula and also the fourth state to become a hub in the United States–India immigration stream. Like most of India, Tamil history goes back to ancient times. It starts with the establishment of three powers: the Chera, the Chola, and the Pandya kingdoms. Aryan influence increased after 200 A.D., a time when the region was engaged in general foreign trade. Various wars and kingdoms mark the region until the British established a trading post in a small fishing village in 1649, which is now Madras.

Tamil Nadu is a beautiful state nestled in the southern Indian peninsula, on the shores of the Bay of Bengal and the deep blue Indian Ocean. It is a heady combination of tropical climate, cooler hill resorts, ancient culture, and friendly people making it an ideal holiday destination.

The pride of many Tamils is their language, Tamil itself. Scholars recognize Tamil to be one of India's two languages of antiquity. One of the distinguishing features of Tamil is that it has three different forms of the sound "l." In fact, the correct pronunciation of "Tamil" sounds like "Tamizh," for which there is no phonetic equivalent in most other languages. Today, there are sizable Tamil-speaking populations in Sri Lanka, Malaysia, Singapore, Mauritius, and other countries.

Tamilians are avid readers, and the area has a vibrant magazine publishing industry. Tamil literature is among the oldest in India, and some of it is now accessible on the World Wide Web!

The web is a forum where people can meet from many cities in Tamil Nadu. It also is a way to visit one's home area and catch up with old friends. Much of the ancient culture of Tamil Nadu is still alive. There is Carnatic music, an Indian classical tradition. Bharatha Natyam is its twin dance form, always accompanied by this music. The rich tradition of folk music continues to inspire the more popular film music.

Popular culture in Tamil Nadu is an altogether different pot of sambar. The creative force of the people has led to one of the largest film industries in the world, producing movies and film songs for several decades. Three major religions coexist in modern Tamil Nadu. The grandeur of the Hindu temple architecture in Tamil Nadu must be seen to be believed.

Twice Migrants or Multiple Migrants

The last category of Indian emigrants can be called "twice migrants" (Bhachu, 1985). These are people who had emigrated from India and after residing in their adopted land, perhaps for generations, emigrated again to yet another place. In the case of the East Indian community in the United States, the twice migrants came from primarily Uganda and Kenya in East Africa and from the Caribbean.

As noted earlier, the British recruited Punjabis and Gujaratis in 1897 to work on constructing and later running the Ugandan Railway and to occupy clerical positions in Kenya and Uganda. As a community, the Indians prospered and became prominent in the public, industrial, and professional sectors of society—very few were unskilled. Both men and women were highly educated in a British-oriented system (Bhachu, 1985:1, 26–8). Since many of them (their numbers reached about 372,000 by 1970) had opted for British citizenship at the time of independence, some entered the United States under that quota. Because the Indians held clerical positions during British rule, the native Africans saw them as enforcing distasteful imperial policies and resented them. The Indians had also maintained social distance from the black Africans by not associating with them and not condoning intermarriage between the two communities. Thus, as Africanization developed in Kenya, and Idi Amin expelled people of South Asian origins from Uganda in 1972, many arrived in Britain, Canada, India, Australia, and the United States. The numbers in North America were sufficient that the African-Asian[12] community began to take form in the United States.

Indians were deceived, kidnapped, drugged, or just persuaded to sign on, and to be transported, primarily by British but also Dutch to Guinea, French Guinea, Guinea-Bissau, and elsewhere in the Caribbean. They began coming to the United States in 1970 and settled along with other West Indians in the Jackson Heights area of New York City. Unlike the African-Asians, many of the Indians from the Caribbean have "lost their culture." They had entered the West Indies under an indentured labor system. The Indian laborers signed contracts and then were transported to work on plantations. They were usually separated from their families, lived under slave-like conditions with authorities and owners who did not live up to their contracts. The result was a loss of much of their Indian culture. They do not speak any Indian language and know little about their caste and the Hindu religion. However, they are developing their cultural identity and see themselves as different from Indians who previously resided in India or Africa.

NRI: A CREATED ETHNICITY

The preferential treatment for investments and reestablishment afforded to returnees has caused growing resentment against the NRIs. In the September 30, 1983, issue of *India Today* the editors wrote an opinion piece titled, "The Non-resident Gods": "We are seeing the birth of a new privileged class and nobody is questioning the wisdom of it." They stated that India has become a divided society and that programs favoring NRIs foster the growth of a privileged class:

> Is there justification in the heavy discrimination obvious in reserving for non-residents 599 of the 859 fully furnished Asian apartments that will be sold later this year? Or in such trusted schemes as priority for scooters and cars paid for in foreign exchange, and the allotment of coveted admissions to medical colleges for those who can pay their fees in foreign currencies? Or higher interest rates on bank deposits in foreign exchange? Or priority for telephones?

---

[12]Depending on their place of residence, these people refer to themselves as Kenyan Asians or Ugandan Asians.

They argued that these policies have created an artificial division in Indian society. This division has encouraged people to break the law (those with black market money use their foreign currency to take advantage of programs designed for NRIs) and have created a new category of foreigner (an Indian who is not just an Indian, but one with foreign currency who invests in India to obtain preferred treatment). These favored Indians, according to the editorial, will always be socially indebted to India:

> Last, among those who are favored by such schemes are people who owe this country a social debt they are unlikely ever to pay. Studies indicate that some 30,000 Indian scientists are working abroad and though statistics are hard to come by, it is estimated that in the 1960s, a quarter of all engineers and nearly one-third of all doctors trained in India left the country. It costs the Indian government about a lakh of rupees to train a doctor and Rs 50,000 for an engineer to do a graduate course at one of the IITs (Indian Institute of Technology). One estimate made by the International Development Research Centers is that India lost $144 million (Rs 144 crore) for physicians who left India between 1961 and 1972. This is a heavy debt to society, and one that a developing country cannot afford.

With the establishment after independence in 1947 of the IITs and IIMs system of higher education, the purpose was to train engineers and scientists to build an infrastructure in the country for economic development. The IITs and IIMs attract the best brains of the country. Admission is by competitive examination with around 2,000 out of 100,000 gaining entrance—a much lower percentage admission rate than the best schools in the States, including Harvard and Stanford. Businesses and educational institutions in the States heavily recruit graduates from the IITs and IIMs. Generally, the top 200 scores opt for computer science (Hattori, 2000).

The editors of *Indian Today* conclude:

> There can be no defense for pandering to those who have shown little regard for their native land, who have used its facilities to better themselves and left it poorer in the bargain. Perhaps if they were to pay the country what it cost to educate and train them, they would be entitled to a certain privilege. But as things are, there is every case for encouraging the overseas Indian to bring his skills home or to send money home to relatives, or bring it home to invest, or to buy property to settle or earn income on the same terms as the rest of us. But there is no case for extending concessions, privileged terms, or for creating a new class. Democratic India does not need to create enclaves of privilege. The relationship between resident and overseas Indians must be based on equality; it is not a commodity with a privileged price tag (Helweg & Helweg, 1990:214–16).

The returnees form social groups where prestige, social ranking, expectations, and other elements may be very different from traditional Indian society. They see themselves and are perceived of as part of and yet apart from fellow Indians who have not had the overseas experience. Those who have been abroad form their own social networks; their group and position may be defined differently from those who have not had the same experiences. They may feel they should have special privileges. The PIOs (people of Indian origin), whether abroad or returned, have had an ongoing symbiotic relationship with India and its people, although the degree and nature of that relationship has fluctuated over time according to the needs and abilities of each community.

VISIBLE EMIGRANT INFLUENCE

As I rode through the high emigrant areas of the Doab region of Punjab and the Kheda district of Gujarat, I could see the impact of emigration. I immediately noticed the presence of tractors, many being foreign brands like Massey Ferguson, and also auxiliary machinery, a Gober gas plant, and bountiful fields of grains and rice, as well as an absence of abject poverty.

In a rural Gujarat village, a dialysis machine was used to give life—a gift from the villagers residing abroad. In Punjab's Jullundur district, a village has a computer center with Internet access—a gift from one of the village's emigrants. In Gujarat, a U.S. trained doctor has built a clinic from his earnings in the United States. The clinic is now a family operation; his father manages it so the doctor can concentrate on healing patients. Many villages have a few large grandiose houses built with emigrant money. Some are in the village proper and others are apart, seeming to be self-contained units. Some houses are empty and locked and others are occupied. Emigrant money has paved roads, financed wells, and bought tractors and farm machinery. Emigrant money has built houses, medical centers, libraries, temples, and Gurdwaras.

I talked with Katar Singh in his lavish rural home. He had just returned from California. His son had just left for California. Katar Singh and his three sons are on a rotation system to return to Punjab to look after their land. He is a sharp contrast to Roshen Singh who is from England. He invested heavily in land in Punjab for the future of his sons. Tears rolled down his face as he told me that his sons wanted to stay in England; they did not want to return to Punjab to be landlords. They did not care how rich they would be, living in Punjab was not an option. Their father could not comprehend their attitude. He relayed his tale in disbelief.

In cities like New Delhi, Ahmedabad, Bombay, or Hyderabad, the emigrant presence is also visible and felt, but in a different way. Because of their wealth, returnees can join the best clubs like the Gymkhana Club of New Delhi, much to the consternation of the older IAS people. But they need wealthy emigrants to maintain economic viability. Some live in individual homes while architects have built enclaves designed just for returnees. Some live in big houses while others live in apartments.

Not visible but a major issue is that the government has set up schemes to encourage overseas Indians to return. In so doing they have created a new privileged community and a new ethnic group—the "Indian Returned" or the "Returnee." They may be able to jump the queue on such things as telephones and gas cylinders, motor scooters or automobiles. Bringing in or investing dollars warrants access to special programs that bring greater yield. Benefits and programs are changing periodically on the national level and individual states have their own programs and institutions to entice the overseas Indians to return to their homeland—with their money and needed expertise.

Outside of the policies and visible indicators, returnees from abroad have another characteristic. Whether from high caste or low caste, rich or not so rich, from the country or the city, a good family or a marginal one, the returnee has a sense of accomplishment and superiority. In some places the returnees collect together in their own group. Others take on symbols, such as implementing English words in their conversation or having "forgotten" Hindi. Some wear English clothing or something made and bought abroad.

They are not easily intimidated by bureaucrats, merchants, or other Indians. Some women become "liberated" and do not show deference to their husbands. They talk about the modern conveniences—cars and gadgets they have or had across the seas. Whether the wider Indian society agrees with them is not relevant to the overseas Indians. In their minds, they are superior because they are overseas Indians.

The myth in India since independence in 1947 has been that the overseas community always looked to India as their source of spiritual strength, guidance, and inspiration. The assumption is that the overseas Indians are successful, and they are successful because of the spiritual, educational, and cultural base they received and continue to receive from Mother India.

The place of the overseas Indian in their homeland and the policies of the Indian government toward their overseas contingent are still a matter of debate and continually changing.

LOYALTIES AND RESPONSIBILITIES

Who should be responsible for the people of Indian origin (PIO) residing overseas? What is the role of the government of India? What does citizenship have to do with it? During British rule, Indians under indenture brought abuses and exploitation to the attention of the British rulers who were considered responsible. When Asian Indians suffered under discriminatory practices in the United States and Canada, they turned to the British rulers for justice, only to be disappointed.

During the struggle for independence, Jawaharlal Nehru made it very clear that the fate of the overseas Indians was tied to the freedom struggle:

> Our countrymen abroad must realize that the key to their problems lies in India. They rise or they fall with the rise and fall of India. (Tinker, 1974)

Outside of rhetoric, the Indian government had virtually no concern for the overseas Indians during the independence movement. In fact, Nehru referred to the overseas Indians as "hirelings of the exploiters." Nehru was very clear: he saw the diaspora as not part of India, and emigrants were to live and remain in the country where they resided, not expecting any support from India.

India's policy has been more expedient than idealistic. Three things have guided the government of India's policy towards its expatriates: (1) India's international standing, (2) domestic opinion, and (3) economic gain or loss. The case of the Indians in South Africa is a case in point. When they turned to India for support, Jawaharlal Nehru made it very clear that they were citizens of South Africa and they were to find their support there. He urged them to be good citizens and maintain their place where they were residing. When the duly elected Indian leadership of Fiji was ousted in a coup, the Indian government did not lift a finger. Yet in Sri Lanka, where Tamils of India wanted the Indian government to intervene for the benefit of Tamils in Sri Lanka, military action was taken.

What obligations and expectations should the Indian government have towards its overseas community and what does the overseas community owe their homeland? Overseas Indians desire dual citizenship—the best of both worlds. India does have a special status that grants special privileges to people of Indian origin residing abroad—a kind of halfway citizenship, even if they have become citizens of another country. It is in part a way of encouraging investment into India by its overseas community as well as enticing knowledgeable and skilled expatriates to return.

BRAIN DRAIN

The term "brain drain" refers to the loss of talent and educational costs of a country as citizens and residents move to another place. It initially referred to the loss of talent from Britain to the United States. Now, however, it is used to refer to the loss of educated and trained from poor countries to developed or rich countries. In actuality, it is also a problem for developed countries such as Britain, Canada, and Germany that lose highly educated and well-trained talent to the United States.[13] Although this discussion focuses on India, India is not the only country with a major loss of educated and skilled people. For example, between 1960 and 1987, the United Nations Conference on Trade and Development (UNCLAD) states that as many as 825,000 skilled immigrants entered North America with the proportion from developing countries increasing each year. Twelve percent of the 12 million people working with science or engineering degrees are foreign born. Supporting statistics could go on for pages, but the point is that the United States is the major recipient of people trained in science and engineering.

Imagine the consternation the people in India feel each year when the entire graduating classes of India's elite IIMs and IITs take their Indian-paid[14] education and leave for the United States to attend graduate school or start a job. By 2002, India's loss of resources due to the emigration of computer professionals to the United States alone was about $2 billion annually. About 100,000 Indians are expected to emigrate annually. The cost to India for educating each one of them averages out from $15,000 to $20,000.

The alarm over brain drain stems back as far as the 1960s. UNCLAD raised an alarm over this issue, and estimated that between 1961 and 1972 the value of trained manpower leaving developing countries for the west was at $46 billion, which included an annual loss of $3.8 billion. At that time, developing countries lost 550,000 highly qualified engineers, scientists, and doctors to the West. Jagdish Bhagwati and other writers blamed the United States and they cite current statistics to support their conclusions (Bhagwati, 1976a, 1976b; Caroli, 1983; Oommen, 1989; Rockett & Putnam, 1989).

About 40 percent of the U.S. foreign-born adult population have a tertiary level education. Also, since the early 1990s, some 900,000 highly skilled professionals, mainly IT workers from India, China, Russia, and a few Organization of Economic Cooperation and Development (OECD) countries, which include Canada, the United Kingdom, and Germany have migrated to the States under the H1B temporary visa program. Also, the United States keeps about 32 percent of all foreign students studying in OECD countries. Canada, Germany, and France are net importers of skilled workers even though their skilled workers also emigrate to the United States. However, increased globalization has fueled temporary flows and accounts for a 5 to 10 percent increase in the total flow of skilled professionals, mainly IT workers from

---

[13]I was surprised to learn that even in a comparatively small city like Kalamazoo, Michigan, immigration lawyers are hired to recruit educated technical and professional talent for local industry.

[14]Entry into these elite institutions is competitive. Once admitted, all fees are paid for by the Indian government.

India, China, Russia, Canada, Germany, and the United Kingdom (Cervantes & Grellec, 2002).

In the case of India, in a 1970 UNCLAD study (Domrese, 2002) estimated that a qualified doctor who leaves India represents a $40,000 loss; for every scientist the loss was $20,000. The United States, however, gained $648,000 for each foreign-trained doctor and $236,000 for each scientist. Even back in 1975, 56,000 scientists and technicians trained in India worked in other countries. Of these, 26,000 Indian doctors were in the United States and about 10,000 in the United Kingdom. Over the 25 years since India gained independence, only 16,000 scientists, engineers, and doctors who worked abroad registered with India's Council of Scientific and Industrial Research (CSIR). Before 1981, 11,000 were offered jobs in India; of those selected, 4,770 came from the United States, 4,000 from Britain, 1,300 from European countries, and 755 from Canada. Presently, India loses 30 to 40 percent of its graduate doctors and engineers to emigration (Unsigned, 1979, Newland, 1979).

Related questions should accompany the brain drain issue. What contributions can the Western-trained returnee make to the home community? Do remunerations offset talent loss? The literature on return migration is sparse and focuses on European peasant experience, an example not applicable to the migration process being discussed here (Glaser, 1978, 1980; Khadria, 1999; Kubat, 1980; Nayer, 1991; Rogers, 1984 1988; Singh, 1989; Wyman, 1993).

Many African countries advise their diaspora members to not return. As a government minister from Ethiopia put it:

> Don't return, we don't have the jobs available. Send us money instead. Money we need and can use; educated professionals are a liability and a potential source of social tension and conflict. (National Public Radio, n.d.)

Contributions[15] have increased fourfold from $3.605 billion in 1990 to $14.396 billion in 1999–2000. In fact, NRI contributions have kept doubling every two and a half years as more and more Indians find lucrative jobs in the West, primarily in the United States. Also, traditional Indian hubs, that started with Punjab and in the early 1980 shifted to Gujarat and then Kerala and they are now being replaced by information technology driven states Karnataka and Andhra Pradesh, which results in increased foreign remittances. The new NRI is earning 10 times the traditional Gulf counterpart.[16]

Remittances have increased sixfold from $2.069 billion in the beginning of the 1990s to $12.356 billion by the end of the decade. The NRI is now an interactive participant in fueling India's economy. It did not happen suddenly. As Tables 2.1, 2.2, and 2.3 show, in the mid-1970s, remittances from industrialized countries, primarily from North America, Western Europe, Britain, and Australia rapidly increased. The increase continued through the second half of the 1980s to reach $2.021 million in 1990–1991. Remittances have become very significant in that they have played and play a large role in India's balance of payments. In the 1970s they were 5 percent of India's exports. By the early 1980s, they equaled 25 percent of India's export earnings

---

[15]Remittances are the total monies returned to the country of origin as a result of emigration; they can include wages, investments, and any other assets resulting from emigration. Direct contributions are monies sent back by the emigrant directly to family and friends.

[16]See Appendix G for a breakdown of remittances to India by region of origin and U.S. dollar equivalents.

TABLE 2.1   FOREIGN-BORN POPULATION:
TOP COUNTRIES OF ORIGIN, 1920, 1960, 1999
(IN THOUSANDS)

Country	1920 Number	Percent
Germany	1,686	12.1
Italy	1,510	11.6
Soviet Union	1,400	10.1
Poland	1,139	8.2
Canada	1,138	8.2
Great Britain	1,135	8.2
Ireland	1,027	7.5
Sweden	625	4.5
Austria	575	4.1
Mexico	456	3.1

Country	1960 Number	Percent
Italy	1,256	12.8
Germany	989	10.2
Canada	953	9.8
Great Britain	754	7.3
Poland	747	7.7
Soviet Union	690	7.1
Mexico	575	5.9
Ireland	338	3.5
Austria	304	3.1
Hungary	245	2.5

Country	1999 Number	Percent
Mexico	7,197	27.2
Philippines	1,455	5.5
China & Hong Kong	985	3.7
Vietnam	966	3.7
Cuba	943	3.6
India	839	3.2
El Salvador	761	2.9
Dominican Republic	679	2.9
Great Britain	655	2.5
Korea	611	2.3

Source: Bureau of the Census, U.S. Department of Commerce.

and enough to finance one-sixth, that is, 16 to 17 percent of India's import bill. Also, during the 1980s, remittances were large enough to finance 40 percent of the country's massive trade deficit. Also, starting in 1976–77 until 1984–85 remittances covered more than the entire debt-servicing payments, and by the end of the 1980s, they still covered about one-third of the trade deficit and half of the debt servicing, but it was a time when remittances were in a decline. This change was due to the family reunification clause in U.S. immigration policy—no one was back in India to receive the money, the entire family was in the States (Khadria, 1999:140–43).

TABLE 2.2   U.S. FOREIGN BORN POPULATION BY
REGION OF ORIGIN, 1995–2000 (IN THOUSANDS)

Region	2000	1995
Europe	4,355	3,937
Under 18	250	232
Asia	7,246	6,121
Under 18	657	767
Latin America	14,477	11,777
Under 18	1,684	1,481
Other	2,301	2,658
Under 18	245	275
All Regions	28,379	24,493
Under 18	2,837	2,726

Source: Bureau of the Census, U.S. Department of Commerce.

TABLE 2.3   OVERSEAS INDIANS SHARE OF DIRECT INVESTMENT IN INDIA

	1991	1992	1993	1994	1995	1996	1997	1998	Total
Rupees	1,602.5	1,496.6	2,604.5	11,185.4	19,705.6	20,620.4	10,396.2	3,594.8	75,354.8
Dollars	35.61	33.26	124.54	28.56	437.9	458.23	231.02	1,197.2	6674.5

As the deficit between imports and exports widened during the 1990s, NRI resources helped stabilize India's precarious balance of payments (Unsigned, 2002b).

Statistics do not tell the whole story. Emigration is a selective process where the most innovative and daring leave. India, then, is not only losing the educated population, but the best of its educated population. The United States gains highly motivated and capable individuals. There is concern, however, that India does not seem to be gaining much benefit for the amount of educational investment it makes. The November 1983 issue of *India Today* had an editorial titled "The Talent Trap" that dealt with the emigrant factor and emphasized how government policy and private industry stifle innovation among India's technically skilled and professionally trained workers.

To further understand what this loss of brain power means for India, look at the employment picture. The World Health Organization (WHO) estimates that 80,000 doctors in India are underemployed; that is, they are overly qualified for the work they are doing. Yet the doctor-to-population ratio is 2.2 physicians per 100,000. As in the West, many medical practitioners in India prefer to practice in urban areas. At the end of 1984, there were 23.547 million job seekers in India, an increase of 7.3 percent from the beginning of the year. In 1985, the educated unemployed numbered 12 million, which in August 1985 included 215,000 medical and 27,000 engineering graduates and postgraduates (Mathew, 1986:593–6). In the late 1970s, 250,000 scientific and technical personnel in India were jobless. That figure included 190,000 graduates in engineering technology; 36,000 engineering graduates; and 3,500 graduates in medicine.

*Asian Indian students in the U.S. and India have an insatiable desire to know about and
operate computers. Here, some students from Michigan State University are applying their
knowledge for Singh Development Co. of Detroit.*

These findings support the observation of one Indian:

In 1967, one-half of the engineering class of IIT-Kanpur went to the United States. In 1968
and thereafter, it was the same story; for many of them would get admissions into MIT
and from there the world was at their fingertips. India is different than the States in that
our best prefer engineering over medicine. Thus, it was a shock and disappointment to
have engineering as my field and come to the States to learn that it is ranked below doctors, who in India are second to us.

The "brain gain" for the States is much greater than the figures indicate. Asian
Indians are quickly dominating the field of computers. As people see these skilled
workers of India operating in the new Silicon Valley, it brings prestige to India as
well as United States.

Although Hyderabad is developing into the new Silicon Valley of Asia,
Bangalore is developing into a world-class technological hub, which is now challenging the actual Silicon Valley and other centers in Europe and Japan.

What should be done about the brain drain issue for India and other countries in
similar situations? Some feel India should impose an exit tax of $10,000 to everyone
who has a visa to go abroad. In this way, India could recoup billions of dollars in lost
revenue. Some argue that receiving countries, especially the United States, should
pay reparations to those countries supporting them with the talent. Taiwan and Korea
focus on return in that they are developing their resources, encouraging an invest-

ment strategy, and working on upgrading the research facilities to entice talented people to return. Taiwan uses a commissioned clearinghouse for scholars to return home as potential players right out of houses into legislation positions. Yet, the United States wants to keep the high-tech industry in the United States.

The Indians believe that their culture, language, and educational system allow students to excel in math and computer code writing. Their ability in math and knowledge of the English language make them desirable for employment in Western companies. India's "IITians," as they are called, have been significant contributors to commonly used popular software, such as Netscape and Microsoft's Hotmail. India has its share of notables in the silicon world, Kanwal Rekhi, a Silicon Valley entrepreneur; the president and CEO of U.S. Airways; and the co-founder of Sun Microsystems. Rekhi excitedly claims that those who have made big money in the States are looking homeward to India and developing businesses back in India.

With the advent of globalization, people no longer have to emigrate to tap into the world market. IIT-Bombay is changing their curriculum to reflect the changing global situation. Changes also include giving students more freedom to develop computer software. India has been successful in developing special bonds for NRI investment, which resulted in initially yielding $4 billion a month. By January 2002 the Indian government realized the need to create or maintain links with the overseas Indians who generate $300 billion annually. Thus, they began to recognize dual citizenship. To make things easier still, in June 2002 the Indian government created the "PIO Card" for NRI travelers to return to their place of origin hassle-free. The government created the category so that the overseas Indians could return to India without the normal hassles experienced by a person who was not a citizen (Unsigned, 2002b)

One of the major issues concerning brain drain is the future of the brain that remains behind. Manoranjan Dutta (1982), a professor of economics at Rutgers University made a crucial point when he said, "the brain that cannot be used is a dead brain. Therefore, what good does it do to have an emigrant return if his brain will be killed." Apa Pant, former ambassador to several Western countries, including the United States, put the issue in a similar fashion when he said, "It is better to utilize a brain abroad than put it in the drain here" (Pant, 1979). Of course the issue they are raising is whether India has the infrastructure to use or employ all the talent they create. Unemployed and underemployed doctors, engineers, and other professional/technical people are a major problem. Although the success and positive changes in the computer industry are impressive, the evidence in the other sectors of the economy are not (Helweg & Helweg, 1990:215–19). One solution being proposed is developing a Scientific Diasporas (Meyer, 1999). With the current level of globalization in the world today, it is not necessary for an individual to return to his or her homeland—for example, an overseas Indian can share his or her knowledge with those in India without ever changing residence—not even a visit to India is required. Can such important information be shared without political and economic consequences? The formation of Scientific Diasporas is still in its infancy. As the networks develop, we can only hope for the best.

THE DYNAMICS OF MIGRANT UNIVERSALIZATION

Very often, the field of migration focuses on the broad statistical implication as it relates to foreign policy or national issues. The ramifications of population movements generally make their impact on the micro-level and than spread out (a modification of the concept of universalization). For example, remittances were initially sent to family and friends. Only as they increased in quantity did they become a national issue. The prestige and power of being an NRI, overseas Indian, or returnee probably originated from family dynamics like those experienced by Jasbir Singh as his younger brother became the respected head of the family because of the money he had at his disposal. The concept spread to becoming part of the national ideology. Mark Wyman relates the fact that many Eastern European peasants did not know what country they belonged to or even the concept of nationalism until the people returned from the United States with these ideas and behaved accordingly (Wyman, 1993). It was then that nationalism started becoming a social and political force in Eastern Europe. Borrowing from McKim Marriott (1955:211–214), I call this process of spreading of migrant ideas and institutions resulting from population movements "univeralization from migration." Marriott coined the term "parochialization" to indicate the counterflow. With increased globalization, the counterflow in the migration process is increasing, whereas before, it was almost nonexistent.

The universalization process is largely ignored and yet crucial in understanding the changes population movements cause or influence. The NRI prestige and favoritism may have started from the changed position in the family or village of the emigrant. The use of new hybrid seeds, fertilizers, and water may have resulted from emigrants sending back new technology and resources. The increased use of mechanization may have come from machinery and ideas emigrants sent back. It is possible that the green revolution is more a result of overseas Punjabis sending back ideas, seeds, machinery, and associated technology than the famed development programs of USAID, UNESCO, or programs by U.S. universities. It is an area that needs more research.

In the beginning of the chapter I indicated some of the visible ramifications of emigration. The effects are not always so simple however. For example, inflation can and generally does become rampant in an emigrant area. For example, in Jandiali in Punjab, a high emigration area, the price of land and houses rose dramatically. Those abroad planned to return and were willing to pay exorbitant prices for land. The result was that some areas developed an external economy, that is, an area where the people live and can survive only because of the remittances. If the remittances stopped, the people could not survive. I argue that in the state of Punjab, the costs of production are higher than the profits from the sale of the products. The difference is made up due to remittances. Also, in the case of Jandiali, the emigrant faction challenged the traditional headman's position. The emigrants invested in Sadhu Singh, who used their money as they saw fit but also to his way of thinking, which was advantageous to him in a grab for power.

People in Jandiali tried new varieties of hybrid seeds, new farming techniques, and the latest cattle management techniques. Of course, not all fulfilled the high expectations, but enough was gained to make the efforts worthwhile (Helweg, 1989).

CONCLUSION

In spite of all the statistics and case studies, it is very difficult to know what policies should be employed. Should the migration of brains be halted? Should the United States pay reparations for attracting the brightest and best brains of the world?

Should an exit tax be placed on emigrating brains? Does a brain in India have to go in the drain?

The business consultant guru Bob Waterman makes a point in one of his lectures that it was the best thing for Japan that it did not have any natural resources except people. This forced the country to invest in people, and it is the people that have made the country the economic power it is today

India wisely employed the same strategy. Right or wrong, many left for more lucrative rewards and opportunities, but PIO remittances and technical assistance have played a major role in the progress of India's economy, society, and political development. NRIs have sent money, invested capital, and for some their lives to bring about a better life for those left behind. Should India develop different policies? Should India try to force the United States to pay reparations, or employ some other program? My view is that India is doing the right things; the government is just not doing them fast enough, or the lower level bureaucracy is inhibiting the outcomes of some programs designed to bring about economic, social, or political development.

3/Life in the Land of Milk and Honey

TRAIL OF TEARS

The British greatly exploited the people of India. India was the jewel in the British crown in many different ways. Not only was India a place of resources and talent, it also supplied manpower to work plantations in the Pacific and Caribbean, to have an army and police force governing British colonies from Hong Kong to British Guiana, and bureaucrats to administer East Africa. For the most part, however, the overseas Indians under British rule were exploited and unnoticed, that is, until Mahatma Gandhi brought their plight to public attention. The British Empire was built on the backs of Indian labor whether it be "coolie," administrative, or military. Yet, they were the pariahs of the empire. Thus, it is not surprising that their British rulers not only did not support them in North America—British agents actively supported their persecution. Thus, the Asian Indians coming to North America had three categories of concern: (1) establishing a community for themselves in the States, (2) supporting India's freedom struggle, and (3) gaining their rights as a people, which included fighting discrimination. The combination of tasks was a formidable undertaking, to say the least.

ESTABLISHING A COMMUNITY

The East Coast: The Incubator of Ideas

It is not known for sure when the first people of Indian origin entered North America. In the 1640s, Portuguese Indians were selling cloth in Mexico City. After that, the East and West coasts followed different trajectories. On the East Coast, the colonial diary of William Bently predates the meeting of a Madrasi in the company of a ship's captain. Also, a Captain Philips and his family appears to have had a Sikh in their employment who drove them to church on Sundays. It was the Parsees[1] who held a unique position as mediators for the British and Dutch traders during and after the

---

[1] A small ethnic community who live in and around Bombay. They originate from Persia and practice the Zoroastrian faith.

American Revolution. The Parsees befriended the American Consulate in Bombay starting with George Washington's administration (Buchignani & Indura, 1985).

The Parsees, especially of Bombay and Baroda, considered themselves more westernized than other groups and they carried on an export-import trade with the United States. In fact, a group of Parsees considered immigrating to the United States in the late 1800s although they never established a substantial settlement. Like other Indian merchants throughout the world at that time, establishing colonies was not uppermost in their minds. Trade was, however. Parsee and Gujarati traders followed the British flag. They had no firsthand information about the United States. The period from 1776 to 1842 was a period of unrestricted entry into the United States. Although Indians saw the United States as a place of exceptional opportunity for all, to them it was far off. Recruiters did not readily engage people from India like they did China. Also, it took three months for ships to reach New York or San Francisco from Bombay, Madras, or Calcutta and since the Indian traders needed current and reliable information, trade and immigration from India were not forthcoming. Consequently as Europeans and even Chinese flocked to America's shores, only about 200 people of Indian origin emigrated to the United States in the pre-1870 period when entering the United States was unrestricted.

There was interaction and interest in India from colonial times however. Interestingly enough, Yale University got its name as a result of a large grant made by Allah Yale who, after amassing wealth in India made a large donation to the new college in New Haven, Connecticut. His generosity made possible a new building, and Yale University got its name. In the 1760s and 1770s, before the American Revolution, reports about the wealth in India, as well as critical reports of abuse, exploitation, and kidnapping of Indian labor by the East India Company, reached the colonies. Also, tales of the 1771 famine in India, and how the East India Company officials profited from the shortage of grain, disenchanted American merchants with the British East India Company.

After the Americans under George Washington defeated Lord Cornwallis, he went to India. There he was more successful in his typically British "divide and rule" policies, defeating, among others, the great Tippu Sultan.

In the three decades after the Civil War, India ideas had a strong influence on Americans. American society began to challenge Puritanism. The role of church leaders in the Salem witchcraft trials had damaged the church leaders' prestige and people's belief in the Puritan ideology, and Americans were looking for a new value system. This search culminated in the transcendentalist movement with notable members such as Ralph Waldo Emerson, Henry David Thoreau, Margaret Fuller, and others.

No country offered the United States an alternative religious experience such as India had. Raja Ram Mohan Roy (1772–1833) was the first prominent figure to have an impact on the New England thinkers. He was a pioneer in comparative religion, and in his studies was coming to the same conclusions as the Unitarians, a liberal form of Protestantism that developed from elements of the Episcopalians, Congregationalists, and others. William Adam, a Baptist missionary in India, brought Roy to the attention of the Unitarians in America. The American intelligentsia discussed Roy's articles and ideas. His ideas were similar to his American counterparts', for his doctrine differed little from the liberal Christian view of the nature and attributes of the deity.

Charles Dall, an American Unitarian who influenced Bengalis, took Jesus out of Western context and defined him as an Eastern prophet. Dall also exhorted Indians to be dissatisfied with their dependent political status.

The most influential transcendentalist was Ralph Waldo Emerson (1803–1882). He read and was influenced by the *Bhagavad Gita* and other Indian classics. Henry David Thoreau was a younger protégé of Emerson and they spent many hours together in the exchange of ideas. He, like Emerson, drew inspiration from the *Bhagavad Gita*. Indian thought influenced four other notables—Amos Bronson Alcott (1799–1888), John Greenleaf Whittier (1807–1892), Herman Melville (1819–1890), and Walt Whitman (1819–1892).

The American Oriental Society was founded in 1812 to promote Indian philosophy, which continued through such writers as T. S. Elliott (1888–1965) and Christopher Isherwood. Thoreau's views on civil disobedience strongly influenced Mahatma Gandhi. Gandhi in turn influenced Martin Luther King, Jr., and the nonviolent tactics of the Civil Rights movement. Although there was no established Indian community, the interactional influence between India and the United States was present from colonial times and it continues to the present day.

Indians immigrating to the United States before the turn of the 19th century were primarily merchants, professionals, or educators. They came from urban India with their families and settled in urban areas, many preferring a university educational setting. They did not cluster residentially and moved to places of opportunity. Most were probably Hindu but familiar with British ways.

The first person of Indian origin to make a significant personal impact on America was Swami Vivekananda, a young monk from Calcutta. He was a devotee of Sri Ramakrishna, the great Indian saint.[2]

Swami Vivekananda had been persuaded to attend the Parliament of Religions held in Chicago in conjunction with the World's Columbian Exposition in 1895. His friends and disciples in India had raised his passage money. He arrived much too early, lost the address of his host, and did not know how to use the telephone directory. After spending a cold night in the freight yards of the windy city, Swami Vivekananda aimlessly walked around the city. He found himself in a fashionable part of the residential district without a cent. He had walked all morning and was tired and decided to sit down and leave his fate to the Supreme Being. Presently a door opened and a well-dressed lady asked, "Sir, are you a delegate to the Parliament of Religions?" In his turban, he could have hardly been there for anything else. A few minutes later he was sitting down to a delicious meal, with all his needs taken care of.

The Parliament of Religions was a turning point in Vivekananda's life as well as the influence of his faith in America. Representatives at the meetings were esteemed men of their own faith. But when this monk, who represented no established church, addressed the assembly as "Sisters and Brothers of America," people rose from their seats and cheered him. He was thrust into the role of one of the Parliament's outstanding personalities and invitations to lecture throughout the country came pouring in.

---

[2]When I visited the Ramakrishna mission in Calcutta, I was not only impressed with its cleanliness, but also the bad odors of the city seemed to be barred from entering the mission; the foul odors of the street were not present in the mission.

It was a generation after the transcendentalist movement and people were not always so receptive to Vivekananda and his message, but he remained outspoken, witty, and dynamic—often impartially representing East and West to each other. Harvard offered him the Chair of Eastern Philosophy, but being a monk, he turned it down. However, he established the American Vedanta Society of New York City and subsequently established other centers as well.

A quarter of a century later, interest in Indian culture and religion continued. Other Indian religious leaders followed and cast their influence on the American landscape. Paramahansa Yogananda established the Self-Realization Fellowship; President Woodrow Wilson's eldest daughter spent the last five years of her life at Pondicherrry, India, pursuing self-realization under the great servant and saint, Sri Aurobindo. In the meantime, the Hare Krishna movement, 3HO Foundation of Yogi Bhajan, continues to make their imprint on the American landscape.

Although the East Coast was the incubator of Eastern ideas and philosophies, it did not develop an Asian Indian community until around the 1970s. Vivekananda returned to India and established the Ramakrishna mission there. Although it isn't talked about much in the literature, at the turn of the century Indians began to attend American universities and Indians were in the States practicing their professions or business. These professionals were scattered but contributed time and money, and tried to influence American foreign policy to promote Indian independence. They also formed their own organizations, like the India League, to be more effective in their endeavors (Kamath, 1976:18–69).

West Coast: The Center of Action

The immigration history for the United States could easily give you the impression the East and West coasts are two separate countries. While the West had anti-Asian sentiment, the East was focused on prohibiting Eastern European immigration. The East was more receptive to Indian philosophy in the early period and supported the Indian independence movement. The West's anti-Asian sentiments lumped Indians with all Asians—a designation the Asian Indians would later challenge. California became the center for persecuting those seeking freedom for India and, most recently, the repository of Indian philosophy and religion. Asian Indians participated in the California Gold Rush of 1849, but substantial immigration to build a community did not start until Queen Victoria's Diamond Jubilee in 1897.

In the mid-19th century, the British classified India as having two race categories, "martial" and "non-martial." The Punjabi Sikhs fit the martial race category almost perfectly. As a people, they were big, strong, did not have caste or dietary scruples, and were willing to go anywhere. Many of them entered the British army and distinguished themselves by their bravery and loyalty. In return, the British rewarded them handsomely with jobs, land, money, and pensions.[3] Thus, they were heavily recruited into the British service in various capacities from military to police to mid-level administrators. In these capacities Sikhs along with members of other "trusted" races scattered throughout the empire in service to the queen or king.

On a side note, it has always amazed me how the British were able to instill such loyalty in the Indians they colonized. My wife's father served in the British Public

---

[3]In traveling through Punjab and Gujarat in the early 1990s, it was common to find Sikhs who were still receiving their pensions from the British government.

Health Service before independence, and for the Indian government after independence. He remained an Anglophile his entire life, often saying, "Things would not be so bad if the British were still in charge."

Some Punjabi Sikhs were members of a contingent of soldiers from Hong Kong who passed through Vancouver, British Columbia, en route to march in Queen Victoria's Diamond Jubilee in 1897. The Sikhs felt favorably received and were impressed with the tremendous economic opportunities in the region. A few stayed behind as temporary residents but many returned to Punjab and gave glowing reports of the opportunities in Vancouver. As a result, some left for the land of prosperity. During the Boxer Rebellion, Sikh soldiers interacted with Americans and learned of opportunities in the United States and Canada. Also, at the turn of the century, the Vancouver area had a paucity of labor so recruiters were sent to Hong Kong, Singapore, and Punjab to hire laborers to build the Canadian Pacific Railway. In fact, Punjab was flooded with posters and fliers extolling the opportunities in Canada.

Economic conditions in Punjab had deteriorated. Land in the canal colonies[4] became waterlogged and less productive. Land holdings became smaller as land was divided up equally among sons generation after generation. The quota for Sikh recruits in the army declined. Thus, with the economy deteriorating, Canada seemed like the land of prosperity (La Brack, 1988; Chandrasekhar, 1982).

Like many situations in human behavior, things are not as simple as they seem and that was the case in the motivation for Punjabi immigration. As McLeod (1986:23) points out, there is some correlation between the economy, land fertility, and emigration but ethnologists must consider many more factors. After living among the Punjabi immigrants, McLeod points out that family concerns, housing, marriage, family honor (*izzat* or *Mann*),[5] and perceptions are but a few of the considerations.

The Sikhs were primarily India's first substantial immigrants to Canada and subsequently the States. They started arriving in Vancouver—258 in 1904, 1,500 in 1906, and by 1907, over 2,000 Sikhs—and the "Trail of Tears" began. Anti-Asian opinion was developing on the Pacific Coast. The Sikhs, with their distinctive visibility of beards, turbans, complexion, and speech (many did not know English) easily became targets of resentment and later violence.

Being subjects of the British Empire, the Punjabis were to have all the rights and privileges as the white subjects and not be tied to the restrictions imposed on the Japanese and Chinese. However, British rulers walked a tightrope of not alienating their Indian subjects while at the same time alleviating the racist concerns of their white Canadian subjects on the Pacific Coast.

To limit immigration from India, the Canadian government passed two orders in Council to stop arrivals from India. The first required arrivals to have $200 instead of the previous $25 requirement. They also instituted the continuous voyage clause that entry of immigrants was prohibited unless they came by "continuous voyage" from their country of birth or citizenship—a requirement that no Indian could fulfill because there were no continuous voyages from India to Canada.

---

[4]Refers to land in the northwest part of South Asia developed by the British for farming by implementing a system of canals. It was initially very fertile and productive, but waterlogging due to irrigation caused a decline in productivity.

[5]*Izzat* (Hindi) and *Mann* (Punjabi) means family honor. The concept will be dealt with later in this book.

Much to the surprise of everyone, the Sikhs were willing to fight for their rights. A Sikh businessman chartered the Japanese ship *Komagata Maru* (Johnston, 1979) and with 376 aboard, each with the required $200 per person, sailed from Hong Kong on April 4, 1914—a continuous voyage—to arrive at Burrard Inlet 7 weeks before the start of World War I. Canadian authorities permitted only 22 passengers to land—those who had proof of Canadian domicile. The passengers appealed to political leaders and the public, all to no avail. They remained in the harbor without proper food, water, and sanitation facilities until their departure for Calcutta on September 27, 1914 (Johnston, 1979).

It was a turning point in Sikh/British relations, and the Sikhs began to listen to revolutionaries like Lala Lajpat Rai and Lala Har Dayal (Tinker, 1976). They had placed their trust in their colonial rulers and that trust had been betrayed. As a result of their Canadian experience, some started drifting across the border into the United States while others sailed directly to California. Some worked in the lumber industry and faced the riots targeted against them in Everett, Seattle, and Bellingham, Washington. In September 1907, one of several incidents took place in Bellingham when 600 lumberjacks herded 200 "Hindus"[6] out of town, with many immigrants suffering injuries. An anti-Asian hysteria permeated the West Coast. The Asiatic Exclusion League, newspaper articles, and magazines talked about the "tide of turbans" and the "Hindu Invasion." Even H. A. Mills, chief investigator for the Immigration Service on the Pacific Coast, reflected the widely publicized conclusions:

> The Indians were the most undesirable of all Asiatics and peoples of the Pacific states were unanimous in their desire for exclusion. (Hess, 1982:9, 10)[7]

In the meantime, Punjabis sailed directly to ports in California while Sikhs continued to cross over from Canada where they worked on and followed the railroads south to Sacramento and the rich farming regions of the "Great" Central, Sacramento, Imperial, and San Joaquin Valleys. The Asian Indians worked on farms in the summer and in the cities of Stockton, Yuba City, and El Centro in the winter. They used the traditional survival strategies their counterparts would use 60 years later in England. A Punjabi who spoke English and was familiar with American ways would persuade village mates to emigrate and get clients who spoke only Punjabi and were not familiar with life in the States. Then, he would be the gang leader and hire his men out—for a fee. The goal was to live frugally and save as much as possible. Thus, men lived in joint residence, helping each other in time of need.

The establishment of a Gurdwara in Yuba City in 1915 not only provided a religious center but also a social center for the community. It was also a governing body and representative group to the outside world. This pattern was a common one—the Sikhs building the first community Gurdwara, developing it into a multipurpose institution (including political representation and government) for the entire Asian Indian community.

As discrimination and violence developed against the Sikhs in Vancouver, more and more turned to the States to reap the benefits of the land of milk and honey. The anti-Asian hysteria culminated in the Immigration Act of 1917, or what I call the

---

[6]During this period, all South Asians were termed "Hindus" or "Hindoos."

[7]It is interesting that Gibson (1988) encountered similar opinions in her 1988 study of Sikhs in California.

"Indian Exclusion Act." The 1917 Act is not as well known as other immigration legislation, but before it was passed, Asian immigration, except those originating from
India, had been halted. The 1917 Act was a codification of previous agreements and
means of excluding Indian people. It pacified the people of the East Coast by limit-
ing Eastern Europeans by initiating a literacy requirement that is still in effect today.
It created an Asiatic Barred Zone to stop the Asian, especially the Asian Indian influx
(Helweg 1996:153–264). As a result, about 7,300 immigrants from India entered the
States between 1899 and 1920. At the turn of the century Indian students numbered
about 100. They came to the States for studies at the University of California,
University of Washington, and University of Michigan. Political activists soon
followed.

The trials the Asian Indians faced were not limited to violence. Men could not
bring their wives and children, which prohibited a normal community from developing. In the wake of the anti-Asian sentiment, Asian Indians were not allowed to
become citizens. It was based on a 1790 interpretation of legislation passed by the
first Congress that "an alien, being a free white person, could be naturalized" and was
amended in 1870 to read "aliens being free white persons, and to aliens of African
nativity, and to persons of African descent," thus barring Asians from acquiring citizenship. The Asian Indians of Punjab and the north in general are descended from
the Aryans and therefore are white. Immigration officials started challenging Asian
Indians who were citizens to get their citizenship revoked. The courts were not consistent in their verdicts but about 65 Asian Indians were stripped of their citizenship
and 45 were pending in 1927. In their fight for justice, the Indians appealed to the
British government for help but it was never forthcoming. Also, California Alien
Land Law of 1913 prohibited Punjabis from owning or leasing land because they
were not eligible for citizenship. Thus, "all we can do is common labor," one Punjabi
stated. Some Punjabis bought land and registered it in the name of a white friend,
which for some resulted in their "friend" taking everything. Also, a few married a
"white" or Mexican wife and had the land held by the spouse.

FIGHTING FOR RIGHTS IN AMERICA

The Sikhs went to court to fight for equality. One of the more famous cases was that
of the 1923 *United States v. Bhagat Singh Thind*. Bhagat Singh Thind was a Sikh Jat
from Punjab. Born in 1892, Thind arrived in the United States in 1813 and served for
6 months in the U.S. military during World War I. He studied at the University of
California Berkeley. In 1920, he was refused citizenship into the United States
because of the Asiatic Barred Zone created by the Immigration Act of 1917. With little financial or emotional backing he did the 2-year process of getting the decision
reversed. In 1921, the U.S. Supreme Court heard his case and he lost. Justice Jabez
T. Sutherland stated in the majority opinion that the "words of the statute are to be
interpreted in accordance with the understanding of the common man, from whose
vocabulary they were taken." Thus, Asians were not eligible for citizenship regardless of what race they belonged to.

The racism continued with the passage of the 1924 Immigration Act that established the quota system. It officially committed the United States to an ideology of
fostering culturally homogenous communities. Immigrants were to be thoroughly
assimilatable. However, those from India were already prohibited from entry because

of the Asiatic Barred Zone. Restrictive legislation, exclusion orders, and a falling economy all worked together to encourage Asian Indians to leave the United States. Between 1911 and 1920, about 1,500 left. Another 3,000 left during the 1920–1930 period. By 1940, only 1,476 Asian Indians lived in California—a sharp decline from the 10,000 that were there in 1914 (Helweg, 2001).

Many of those who remained behind married Mexican-American women, which gave rise to a new ethnic community, Punjabi-Mexican, although they were also called Hindus or Mexican-Hindus (Leonard, 1997:62–64, 1992). The kinship ties among this group were weaker and the influence of the Catholic Church became stronger as the influence of the mother, generally Mexican, was stronger than that of the Punjabi father. Thus, Hindu beliefs and caste ideology became weak. The strengthening of the Catholic Church became stronger because of the mother dominating that aspect of life. Also, the Church allowed Punjabis to be godparents. The godparent, or *compadrazgo* system, worked within the community and helped make it more cohesive.

World War II brought a greater appreciation for India's geopolitical position in the Pacific and the U.S. government started reconsidering its policy towards India. This shift included a change in attitude towards the immigrant community. Foreign policy and the treatment of immigrants certainly influenced each other. One result was the passage of the Luce-Celler Bill in 1946. One provision allowed Asian Indians to become citizens. Also, with this new immigration policy began a trend of liberalization that resulted in a small increase in the Indian community. Between 1947 and 1963 about 6,000 Asian Indians immigrated to the United States and between 1948 and 1965, 1,772 swore allegiance to the United States and became citizens.

With the visit of Prime Minister Nehru to the United States in 1965, Asian Indians began moving into the political mainstream. The first and only Asian Indian to take advantage of his citizenship to serve in Congress was Dilip Singh Saund (1960). He is the stereotypical success story. He came to the United States from Punjab in 1920. His family was middle class but uneducated. He subsequently earned three degrees, including a Ph.D. in mathematics from the University of California Berkeley. He married a socialite in 1928 and was first elected to Congress in 1956. During that time and before, Saund, a successful farmer, fought for Asian Indians to be eligible for citizenship.

FIGHTING FOR INDIA'S FREEDOM

The Asian Indians in America were fighting a two-front battle during this period. They were not only fighting for their rights, they were fighting for India's freedom. At the turn of the century, revolutionary fervor for independence grew in India and America was perceived as a haven for political movements. The Asian Indians in the United States maintained communications with India and tried to do their part in India's freedom struggle. For example, Taraknath Das, a Bengali student at the University of Washington in 1906, attempted to politically organize the East Indian community in the United States. In conjunction with an Irish-American publisher who hoped for Irish independence, he started publishing (editions were periodic) the *Free Hindustan* in 1908. After 3 years, the journal was suppressed due to British instigation.

It was during this time that the Ghadr Party, which took its name from the weekly newspaper *Ghadr* meaning "revolutionary" or "mutinous," was formed in San Francisco. The office, named *Yoganter Ashram,* was located at 5 Wood Street. Under the editorship of Lala Har Dayal, the paper started publishing in 1913 with the goal of promoting revolution in India. Har Dayal had come to the United States in 1911 and taught briefly at Stanford University before becoming involved in revolutionary activities. Jwala Singh, the "Potato King," a wealthy farmer of East Indian origin financed his activities.

The *Ghadr* was published in Gurmukhi, Urdu, Hindi, Bengali, and Marathi. It was distributed worldwide and contributed to the revolutionary fervor that led to the voyage of the *Komagata Maru* in 1913. The Ghadr Party was open to anyone who desired membership, but it had a more exclusive inner circle. (In principle anyone in this inner circle who betrayed party secrets was killed, but reality did not work with such deadly efficiency.) In August 1914, a group of Ghadrites sailed from San Francisco to Calcutta with the goal of staging an uprising in Punjab in February 1915. The social and political climate in India was not as supportive as they had hoped, many of their members were arrested in India, and the movement collapsed.

The revolutionary movement continued in America, but in 1917 Ghadr leaders in California were arrested for violating American neutrality laws. The court trials that followed were termed the "Hindoo Conspiracy Trials." British agents supplied much of the evidence against the Ghadrites—indeed it was probably British pressure that had brought the whole matter to the fore; for Britain wanted to halt all seditious movements concerning India. Of the 29 Asian Indians charged, 14 were convicted, and the proceedings ended in a spectacular fashion when a witness was shot to death in the courtroom—all of which contributed to giving the Asian Indians of California an overwhelmingly negative public image.

After the trial, the Ghadr leadership became exclusively Sikh and, although the paper continued under the name of *Hindustan Ghadr,* the movement lost its effectiveness and momentum. Ghadr activities ended altogether in 1947 when India gained independence; a memorial to the Ghadr Party and other Indian martyrs was established in a building containing Ghadr and related documents located in San Francisco, the site of the old newspaper office.

On the East Coast, the Home Rule League, a moderate group, had developed by 1910. Lala Lajpat Rai, a supporter of the National Congress movement, arrived in the United States in 1914, became editor of the periodical *Young India* and became leader of the League in 1917. By 1920, however, the League was challenged by the more radical Friends for the Freedom of India, which was closer to the principles of the Ghadr movement. This group, a majority of whom were Americans, led a successful campaign to thwart federal efforts to deport 14 Indians convicted of conspiracy.

The Asian Indians in the United States continued to mobilize support for India's independence movement. The Home Rule League had won many friends such as Roger Baldwin (a champion of civil liberties), J. G. Phelps Stokes, Oswald Garrison, and others. During this time, M. N. Roy illegally entered disguised as Father Martin, a Roman Catholic priest,[8] and during the 1920s, Jayaprakash Narayan, who became prime minister of India, was a student at the University of Wisconsin where he was

---

[8]Roy was in the United States from 1915 to 1917. He was unimpressed with Lajpat Rai. It was at this time that Roy married his wife Ellen. When he was indicted for illegal entry, he fled to Mexico.

active in socialist and revolutionary causes. Lajpat Rai,[9] a noted revolutionary leader in India, was in the United States less than a month in 1914 as part of a trip to the United Kingdom. Since he was banned from returning to India until February 1920, he returned to the United States in 1916 and remained there until 1920. He distanced himself, however, from pro-German activities. While living in the United States and Japan, he wrote about his life and work for Independent India (Joshi, 1965). He appeared before the U.S. Senate Foreign Relations Committee and unsuccessfully sought assistance to get representation at the Paris Peace Conference at the end of World War I. J. J. Singh, a successful businessman who had immigrated in 1926, joined the India League of America in 1939; his efforts broadened its base by opening membership to Americans and attracting considerable support. His pamphlet, *Famine in India*, was circulated to government officials, members of Congress, the State Department, and the press, thus bringing to the forefront the ravages of the 1943 famine in Bengal. His efforts resulted in the *Christian Century* and *New Republic* charging the British with poor planning and mismanagement. On November 5, 1943, the Joint Congress of Industrial Organizations and the American Federation of Labor War Relief Committee allocated $100,000 to assist the famine victims (Kamath, 1976; Singh, 1966).

East Indians in the United States took a keen interest in the affairs of their homeland and sought to influence American public opinion as well as support the social goals of their country of origin. They did not, for instance, get flustered easily when questions arose about Indian social mores that were not compatible with those of the West. One medical student of that time described how a speaker in New York handled one situation:

> I saw a sign in New York indicating that a lecture would be given by a Muslim that evening on India's quest for independence. I went to it and remember at the end of the presentation a lady in the audience asked, "Mr. Mohammed, is it true that Muslims have more than one wife?" After a moment's reflection, the speaker replied, "Madam, any man that has more than one wife deserves what he gets."

The audience roared with laughter and the speaker averted an unpleasant discussion.

A TRAIL OF HOPE

The ramifications of the Civil Rights movement in the United States were much farther reaching than providing equal access for African Americans. The movement pricked the conscience of a nation and, as a people, Americans began to look at other areas of racist inequality. One such area that was exposed for its policy based on racist ideology was U.S. immigration laws where entry was based on national origin, not on ability, qualifications, first-come-first-serve, or any other criteria. Thus, there was a movement to eliminate racism in the U.S. immigration process. Those promoting the legislation, for the most part, also assumed the immigration stream would remain eurocentric. When the 1965 bill was implemented, the economy in Europe was good, and Europeans were not predisposed to emigration. Their life was good,

[9]Lajpat Rai, a noted revolutionary leader in India, was in the United States less than a month in 1914 as part of a trip to the United Kingdom.

why should they start over? On the other hand, India had a large contingent of highly educated unemployed or underemployed individuals who were not being incorporated by India's economic and political infrastructure. The result was that this large contingent of highly educated professionals were immediately available to move to the United States to start life anew. Numbering only 7,000 in 1970, Asian Indians, along with other Asians, quickly became a prominent part of the United States immigration stream. By 1975, Asian Indians numbered 175,000; in 1980, 387,223; and by 1990, up to 815,447. In 1997 Asian Indians numbered 1.215 million and were entering the States at a rate of 850 per week, ranking third among countries providing immigrants. In the 2000 Census, Asian Indians ranked third in the Asian community behind the Chinese and Filipino populations—2001 estimates put their numbers over 2 million.

India (Figure 3.1) is currently the seventh-largest supplier of immigrants to the United States. The vast majority of the Asian Indian population came after 1965. Of the 130,000 who came between 1820 and 1976 only 17,000 came before 1965. In the 19th century only about 700 merchants, monks, and professionals entered—most were from North India. Of the 7,000 that entered between 1904 and 1923, the vast majority were agricultural workers from Punjab. However, anti-Asian hostility and restrictive immigration legislation, especially in 1917 and 1923, virtually halted Asian Indian immigration.

By 1980 the stream of high talent began to be diluted. As Asian Indians became citizens, they took advantage of the fourth preference provision of the immigration laws and brought relatives. The relatives did not have the high qualifications of their predecessors. Between the 1980 and 1990 census, there was an 85 percent increase in the Asian Pacific Islander category of the highly educated, who entered under the third and sixth preference categories. These educated and skilled people laid the basis for the immigration of relatives under the first and fifth preference categories.

The preference system attracted the highest educated and most talented people to enter the States, with East and West coasts given equal preference. The new immigrants brought with them new patterns of settlement and different skills to build the U.S. economy. They were independent of cultural brokers, because they were fluent in the English language and skilled in dealing with bureaucracies and corporate structures.

Residence patterns shifted for the Indian Americans as the Asian Indian population spilled into other states. Michigan is indicative. The Asian Indian population in Michigan exploded. In 1974 only 3,561 Asian Indians lived in Michigan. By 1980, 8,879 persons born in India lived in Michigan, and by 1990,13,286.[10] Asian Indian ancestry was claimed by 23,845, however. By 1998, Asian Indians were 0.6 percent of Michigan's population and India was the country of origin for the greatest number of foreign-born immigrants, as was the case for Pennsylvania, New Hampshire, Ohio, West Virginia, New Jersey, Mississippi, and Delaware.

The quality of this new group of immigrants can be illustrated by some statistics. Nationally, 80 percent of the Asian Indian men hold college degrees and 65 percent work in the managerial/technical/professional category. Five percent of the doctors in the United States received their primary training in India and the median of Asian

---

[10]Numbers for the Sikhs include only 30 Sikh families in 1930, 100 Sikh families in 1970, and 300 Sikh families in the Detroit area in 2003.

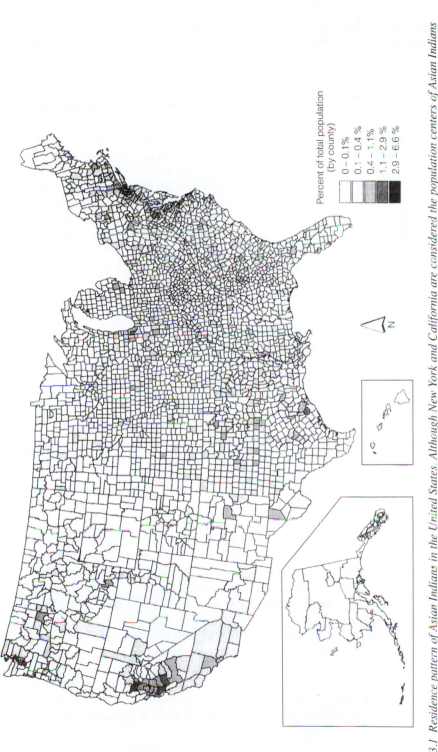

Percent of total population
(by county)

0 – 0.1%
0.1 – 0.4 %
0.4 – 1.1%
1.1 – 2.9 %
2.9 – 6.6 %

N

Figure 3.1 Residence pattern of Asian Indians in the United States. Although New York and California are considered the population centers of Asian Indians in the United States, Chicago, Texas, North Carolina, and Detroit have sizable concentrations and Indians are also dispersed throughout the country. Source: U.S. Bureau of the Census (1990).

Indian household income is 25 percent higher than that of all U.S. households. The community of only 7,000 in 1970 exploded to its present size of around 2 million in 12 years and they are still coming.

It is from these changes that the United States has and continues to gain the best brains and the highest motivated people, not only of India, but that the world has to offer. As a people, those of Indian origin residing in the United States are consistently the highest paid, highest educated ethnic community in the United States.

However, the current trail of hope has not been without its tears. In June 1982, the beating of young Vincent Chin, a Chinese American, with baseball bats on the eve before his wedding was horrific. However, when Ronald Elens and his stepson Michael Nitz did not contest the charges and never spent a night in jail for the murder, a shock went through the Asian American community. This incident made Indian Americans reconsider their identification. All this time, the Asian Indians have claimed "white" status. As of this writing, the community is not united as to whether they want to be classified in the Asian category (Shankar, Shankar, & Srikanth, 1998). But they know that divided, no group is strong enough to fight racism.

The second shocking event was the 1987 "dot-busting" incidents in New Jersey, which caused a turning point in the Asian Indian community of the New York area. The events forced the Asian Indians to deal with external racism and internal class divisions. In 1987, the Asian Indian community of Jersey City, New Jersey, became the target of racial violence. People were beaten and property was vandalized. Kaushal Sharon suffered permanent brain damage and Navroze Mody died of injuries. The attackers called themselves "dot busters" (referring to the bindi worn by Hindu women on their forehead) who vowed to drive all Asian Indians out of the area by violence.

Local officials were slow to prosecute. Some Indian community leaders blamed those in New Jersey for being clannish and different while others feared that denouncing official apathy as racism would equate them with despised minority groups.[11]

When Mody and Sharon were attacked, 15 Asian Indian students at Columbia University and Barnard College, joined later by Asian Indian students at the University of Pennsylvania, formed Indian Youth Against Racism (IYAR). In spite of being ostracized and patronized by their own elders, they helped organize demonstrations, and aided Mody's and Sharon's parents in obtaining justice and pressuring officials to prosecute. Also, during the Persian Gulf War and the invasion of Afghanistan after the September 11th crash into the World Trade Center in New York City, some Asian Indians, especially Sikhs were mistaken for having Middle Eastern origins and beaten—one Sikh was killed.

The experiences of immigrants in Silicon Valley are also shattering immigrant dreams. No matter what the computer hardware, it has to be manufactured in labor intensive situations. Unlike what news reels and advertisements show, the real world of work in Silicon Valley is anything but pleasant. Consequently, 200,000, or 20 percent, of the labor force are working in sweatshop conditions—70 percent of whom are Asian—and the percentage of South Asians is growing (Jayadev, 2002).

---

[11]All minority groups are not despised or subject to inferior treatment by the wider society. The Asian Indians do not want to become a despised minority group.

The working conditions are deplorable. The "clean" reputation is riddled with pollution, which includes surrounding neighborhoods, and is saturated with carcinogens, acids, and highly toxic wastes. Studies have shown that chemicals used in manufacturing hardware affect the brain and the immune, endocrine, and central nervous systems. These test results are only from 2 percent of the 80,000 industrial chemicals used there. Yet they have always been able to get the migrant labor to keep assembling. Mexicans were first in the area picking fruit and shifted to manufacturing when the industrial plants moved in. Ever since, corporations have been able to fill their labor needs by using disposable immigrant labor of color. The Mexicans were followed by men and women of Vietnamese, Filipino, Korean, Ethiopian, and most recently South Asian origins. For the companies it is an ideal situation where managers can live in the States while obtaining and using cheap immigrant labor—labor that is not unionized.

Jivan Nair illustrates. He came to the United States less than a year ago from Kerala. He came to the United States for a better education for his children. In the highly volatile and unstable labor market, known as the "new economy," Jivan is struggling to stay afloat in his job of low-wage electronics assembly. He is treated with rudeness where his boss's voice has the threat of violence like that of a prison guard.

As Raj Jayadev explains:

> In the Valley, low-wage assembly and manufacturing has been the not-much-talked about anchor of technological and economic growth. The labor at the bottom of the rung has been created and reserved for immigrant workers of color, and this hidden work force is subject to work in physically and mentally grueling circumstances, all for sub-livable compensation . . .
>
> There is this popular presumption about the Information Age that the technology is produced by some sort of divine intervention requiring no actual Industrial Age-type of assembling or manufacturing. Yet the fact is that every computer, printer, and other piece of technological wizardry has to be birthed in some inglorious assembly-line production site . . .
>
> Many immigrants start a job thinking of the workplace abuses as passing burdens of a transitional reality, which will end when a better job is found. But due to the paradoxical lack of "good" assembly jobs, these temporary jobs become permanent.
>
> . . . Chinese and South Asian entrepreneurs notched up US$16.8 billion in sales last year alone. The fact that there are over 20 publicly traded companies with sales in the millions founded or run by Indians in Silicon Valley, seems to buttress the "model minority"[12] paradigm, which these immigrants earn for themselves and the U.S. economy. The South Asian entrepreneurial class has even gone so far as to create high-tech industry associations like "The Indus Entrepreneur" to institutionalize their elite position and growing political weight.
>
> The model minority myth is consequently allowed to perpetuate, more so because the reality of the rest of the South Asian American existence is given a blind eye, thereby also avoiding the exposure of an embarrassingly two-faced relationship of opportunity and exploitation with high-tech industry. The loud recognition of the top-dog South Asians in

---

[12]"Model minority" is a term coined by former President Ronald Reagan in reference to the hard working and successful Asian immigrants, the inference being that other minorities should emulate the behavioral patterns of the successful Asians.

the Valley is accompanied by a strange silence about their cousins who toil at the other end of this hi-tech food chain. (Jayadev, 2002:1, 2)

Another caveat comes to the fore when one looks at New York City's taxicab industry. It pays on the average only $22,000 annually. It is a high-risk industry with the highest workplace homicides of any workplace—40 times the national average. In 1992, 90 percent of the new drivers were immigrants as were 80 percent of the existing drivers. Thirty-seven percent were college graduates while 59 percent had some college. Of the 2,500 applicants in 1991, 15.7 percent spoke Urdu and 12.7 percent spoke Punjabi (Kolsky, 2002).

The question arises as to why labor intensive jobs are being filled by such a highly educated segment of the population. The answer lies in part in the fact that the nature of the immigration stream has been changing. As the first post-1967 wave of immigrants have become citizens, they have sponsored relatives, who also sponsored relatives in a chain fashion. The overall averages look good, but in actuality, the Asian Indian population income statistics look like an hourglass. The members of the community are either rich or poor with a nonexistent middle class. The Asian Indian community is becoming only a two-tier society of only rich or poor, with no middle class. A closer look at the statistics is revealing. In 1980, the income of a full-time Asian Indian worker was $18,707, the highest among Asian Americans, almost $2,000 higher than the next highest community—the Japanese. Yet, 7.4 percent of the Asian Indian families were below the poverty line while only 4.2 percent of the Japanese families were below the poverty line. The more recent immigrants are less well off. Those who immigrated after 1975 earn much less, only $11,000 per full-time worker. One in ten post-1975 families is in poverty (Daniels, 1989:65–69).

CONCLUSION

The experience of the Asian Indians is a trail of hope and tears. Even today many come in search of a dream—for some it is fulfilled, for others it is shattered. As this chapter also shows, it is often very hard to generalize. A look at the overall statistics shows a prosperous and successful community, yet a sizable percentage are in poverty or close to it. One must go beyond statistics and impressions to understand any community in the globalizing world of today. To explain the dichotomy, the economic statistics show the Asian Indian community to be a two-tier community. This means there are large numbers of rich and poor, but very few in the middle class. Those who came first were the highest educated, most innovative, and most highly motivated, came from middle and upper class families, and made their fortunes. The community as a whole has suffered, but much has been offset by the highly qualified people who came in and immediately stepped into middle and upper class American society. Those who came later were the "poor relations" and have not done as well. In the aggregate statistics, the rich offset the poor.

Part II/A New Life in a New Land

Before the increased efficiency and ease of travel, immigration to the United States was analogous to a rebirth. The misery and loss of life on those early voyages of the sailing ships and early steamships was so great that once the voyage was made, many did not want to go through that experience again. Thus, America became the new homeland; the ideology of its being the promised land was analogous to the Jewish people crossing the Jordan to claim what God had given them.[1]

By the time the Asian Indians began arriving in substantial numbers, transportation to and from, along with communications with the homeland, had improved; however, legislation restricting further immigration, especially of family members, prevented the development of a normal community in that wives and children were not allowed to unite with the men in the United States until the passage of the Luce-Celler Act, and subsequent 1965 legislation.

To illustrate the above, Chapter 4 sets forth two life histories. The first is the story of Arjin Singh, who was the patriarch of a *split family,* that is a family where the male remained abroad while his wife and children stayed in their village. The second is of Bijoy Bhuyan, a later immigrant who was well educated and entered the United States under the post-1950s legislation. He was able to remain residentially united with his wife and children.

Chapter 5 will set forth current generalizations about the Indian American community in the United States while the following chapters will set forth ethnic issues and dynamics.

I focus on ethnicity because ethnicity is possibly the most crucial aspect in people's lives. In fact it is one of the most powerful forces influencing human behavior today (Glazier & Helweg, 2001:17). People live for it and die for it. Wars are fought over it and nations are formed around it. Again, taking my friend Jasbir Singh's example, it was imperative that he be a Punjabi. Why? Because when he was with his fellow Punjabis, he had a sense of belonging. He and his fellow Punjabis saw the world in a similar fashion. There was not a hundred percent agreement but there was

---

[1]The horrible voyage was only one factor contributing to the ideology of America being the promised land. Fleeing religious persecution and other forces had their impact.

basic agreement on judgmental criteria. Being a Punjabi, he saw himself as a hard-working, capable individual who could overcome adversity. Others had come to America and been successful, he could also. Being a Punjabi, he was a descendant of the ancient Aryan people who moved from Europe to occupy Northern India.

He had Punjabi friends he could rely on in times of need, either for advice or money. He had a family that would support him in public whether he was right or wrong; his ethnicity enabled him to make sense of the world around him. It enabled him to determine what was good, what was bad, what was right, and what was wrong. It was from his ethnicity that he got meaning and purpose in life.

It was his desire that his children follow in his ethnic footsteps. He hoped that they would believe as he did and that they would practice what he considered to be acceptable normative behaviors. He hoped that they would not violate any practices of Punjabi culture.

Jasbir did not want his children to bring shame on him or his kinsmen. In India, his family assumed that his children would become corrupt in the United States and bring shame on the family. For this reason, he and his wife were strongly advised to leave the children behind with their grandparents. Jasbir and his wife decided against this strategy. He also considered sending them to boarding school in India, but keeping the family together took precedence as far as he and his wife were concerned. So they all remained in America, with all its wealth, decadence, and impurity. They remained a family unit.

Jasbir's experience gives an idea from one individual's eyes the function of ethnicity in human behavior, but much more is involved than is set forth in this narrative for ethnicity is also a group phenomenon.

4/Two Success Stories
at Two Different Times

INTRODUCTION

The experience of immigrants who have a profession differs from those who have not completed their schooling. The stories of two Asian Indians in Michigan follow—one who came straight from his village, the other who got some education and completed his schooling in the States and obtained a degree. I hesitate to label either one typical or illustrative, but their stories give the reader an idea of the common and different experiences each encountered.[1]

IMMIGRANT WITHOUT A PROFESSION

It is not certain who were the first Asian Indians in Michigan, but people from India attended the University of Michigan by the beginning of the 20th century. Also, some Bengali Muslims married African American women. Their decedents claim to be Afro-Indians and are still present in the Detroit area.[2]

The foundations of the present community, however, started in 1924 with the arrival of Arjin Singh and five others I call the "original six."

Arjin Singh, a Sikh Jat[3] who originated from India's rural Punjab, and some of his friends moved from California to Michigan. High wages in the auto industry and educational opportunities at the University of Michigan attracted them to the area. They settled in Detroit.

Arjin Singh was born in 1896 into a landed family and studied at Khalsa College in Amritsar.[4] In 1921, he left his wife, 3-year-old son, and 1-year-old daughter in the care of his father and headed for America—he was not to see his family and friends again for 28 years.

---

[1]For two other excellent biographies of immigrants from India, see Bains and Johnston (1995) and Sharma (1971).

[2]Walbridge and Haneef (1999) write about such a Pakistani community in Detroit but I do not know if it is the same one.

[3]The Jats are an agricultural caste in India.

[4]When in the United States, he claimed he was born in 1899 so that he could work three extra years before having to retire. Like many of his contemporaries, he thought ahead to maximize his earning power.

"There was a fever to go to America," he said. "One of the attractions of the States was that you could 'earn and learn.'" This meant that you could work and go to college simultaneously.

He elaborated:

> In India my father was a landlord and I did not have to work. He had served the British as a Cavalry Officer and saw action in France in 1914. As a reward, he had a good pension and land in Punjab. I had a career, but the reputation of opportunity and prestige to go to America was great. Thus, I gave up a good easy life, and prestige to leave India for America. My father gave me financial help and I left Calcutta on January 19, 1922. I stopped in Singapore, Hong Kong, Shanghai, Kobe, Yokohama (I spent two weeks in Japan with two Sindhi friends), Hawaii, and landed in San Francisco on March 19, 1922.[5] When I arrived in California, I was given a shovel and I had to work, doing hard labor unlike anything I experienced in India.
>
> However, we did not want to shame ourselves and our families by returning after the opportunity to make our fortune in America. Thus, we remained and worked hard on the farms in the Sacramento Valley. (Arjin Singh, personal communication)

While in California, Arjin Singh worked, attended classes at the University of California, and sent money back to India.[6] In fact, he like many immigrants, worked harder in the States than he did in his own country. Yet he, like many immigrants, wanted to be perceived as successful. He sent money back home and in his communications with India stressed the positive and downplayed the negative—something most immigrants do, even today, whether rich or poor.

The automobile industry was expanding and Henry Ford was paying top wages—$5.00 a day.[7] Recruiters traveled throughout the United States, especially the rural areas, and abroad, to get workers for Michigan's exploding industry.[8] A recruiter, Mr. Mathur, was in California recruiting workers for the Ford Motor Company. As Arjin Singh relates:

> Mathur recruited Hindus or shaven Sikhs, but would not include those with beards. We had the Gurdwara[9] priest write a letter to Mr. Ford telling him that we were qualified and willing to work for him. Mr. Ford replied and asked how many Sikhs wanted to work for him. We sent a telegram saying there were 50 Sikhs ready to be employed. He had us select two representatives to meet with him in Detroit. Belvant Singh and I went, and this resulted in 25 Sikhs working for Mr. Ford.
>
> I started working for Mr. Ford in 1924 and remained with the company for 42 years— retiring in 1966. Some worked and studied at the University of Michigan. They learned agriculture so they could use their knowledge upon returning to Punjab. Western education was highly respected in India and Lal Singh, who was educated in the States, became the Minister of Agriculture.

---

[5]Sikhs are a mobile people and have Gurdwaras, places of worship, all over the world. It is there that many Sikh migrants stay as they wait to continue their journey. Gurdwaras take in people for the night and also feed them. Such benefits are not limited to the Sikhs (Helweg, 1986:6).

[6]In 1929 he posted a remittance the day before the banks closed.

[7]Word of Henry Ford's offer of $5.00 a day spread throughout the world. It is largely responsible for Michigan, especially Detroit, being the multicultural area it is.

[8]Ironically, at the preparation of this manuscript (2003) workers and professionals are being recruited from overseas to work in Michigan's research industry.

[9]Sikh place of worship: there was one in Stockton, California.

I remained with Mr. Ford. I did everything—welding, painting, and tooling. I was never laid off. During the Depression, Mrs. Ford interceded and made sure that we had work. Mr. Ford stuck up for us. He told immigration authorities that we were in training; thus we could keep our student visas. (Arjin Singh, personal communication)

In 1923 and 1924, Henry Ford wanted students from 16 nations to train and set up dealerships throughout the world. He and other manufacturers recruited and trained foreign nationals, including those from India.[10] Few returned as car dealers, but many did return.[11] Among Arjin Singh's friends, Kirpal Singh became a priest for the Gurdwara in Stockton, California, and eventually returned to India. Darbara Singh Sodhi returned and became the principal of Khalsa College in Bombay. Partap Singh Kairon attended the University of Michigan and eventually became chief minister of Punjab in January 1956 (Pettigrew, 1978:85–104).

Arjin Singh and four friends initially lived at 250 Victor Avenue in Highland Park, which is now a factory. They had the second floor of a two-story house. He lived there for 22 years, renting from a German family. When the male head of the German family died, Arjin and his friends paid the $10,000 in back taxes, thus saving the house for the widow and her nine daughters. The house was sold in 1946 and the German lady remarried, but she and her daughters still include him for birthday, Christmas, and other celebrations.

"During those early years, there was no discrimination towards us," Arjin Singh stated, then continued.

Christians, Hindus, and Sikhs all lived together like brothers. We formed the All India Brotherhood Association and I became president. Our organization entertained ambassadors from India, such as Rama Rao and Asaf Ali. We also helped new immigrants get settled by hosting them and showing them American ways. (Arjin Singh, personal communication)

Arjin Singh, like many of his compatriots, was shy about making white friends, so the Asian Indians formed their own associations and had a life within their group. They socialized over meals and at bars. As Arjin Singh says, "I am a superb cook in Western and Indian cuisine."

The Asian Indian community in Detroit maintained contact with other Asian Indians in the United States. To raise money for a Gurdwara, they solicited Sikhs all over the United States, receiving their initial $100 contribution from Bhagat Singh Thind, the same Bhagat Singh Thind who had challenged the U.S. immigration laws—he had gained a following as a holy man by then. Although the original six did not gain notoriety, the group supported India's struggle for independence; however, ties to India and communications with other revolutionaries in the United States were difficult.[12]

---

[10]The ventures never really materialized. After India's independence in 1947, the American car manufacturers were unwilling to reinvest their profits into India as demanded by the government of India. As a result, the market went to British manufacturers and indigenous enterprises.

[11]Only entrants are counted in immigration statistics. Contrary to popular opinion, many immigrants returned to their homeland. For example, between 1880 and 1930, one-fourth to one-third returned (Wyman, 1993:6).

[12]In California, the independence movement for India was much more visible where the Ghadr (revolutionary) Party was active and its newspaper, *The Ghadr,* was published and had international circulation. Activists for India's freedom from British rule were actively prosecuted, especially in the Hindu Conspiracy Trial of 1917.

Although significant immigration from India to the United States started around the turn of the 20th century, the later implementation of restrictive legislation against Asian Indians,[13] being the objects of discrimination and the Depression resulted in the Asian Indian population declining. To illustrate, 10,000 people of Indian origin lived in California in 1914. That number dropped to 1,476 by 1940 (Lal, 1999) and around 2,544 for the country as a whole. The passage of the Luce-Celler Act in 1946 resulted in 7,000 people from India entering the United States and 1,780 Asian Indians becoming citizens between 1948 and 1965.

During this restrictive period, Arjin experienced harassment from immigration officials because Asian Indians were considered Asians and not whites. Arjin Singh saved $20,000 by obtaining Canadian immigration for relatives and then having them enter the States from Canada—a loophole in the immigration laws allowed those coming from Canada to be treated as Europeans, not Asians. In 1991, Arjin Singh was directly or indirectly responsible for 50 people immigrating to the United States.

It was not easy, as Arjin Singh relates:

> Immigration authorities continually harassed us. When I brought my relatives, immigration authorities were always threatening to deport those I sponsored. Senators like Philip Hart of Michigan, Senator Cooper of Kentucky and John F. Kennedy of Massachusetts passed special legislation so my relatives, and those of other Indians, could stay in this country. That is why I and most Indians of our generation are loyal to the Democratic Party.[14] (Arjin Singh, personal communication)

Like other Asian Indians, he sent remittances back to India to build big houses, dig wells, buy tractors, obtain fertilizers, purchase new seed varieties, and make the life of his kinsmen in Punjab prosperous and prestigious. He could not return to India without forfeiting American residence until 1947, when the passage of the Luce-Celler Bill in 1946 loosened restrictions. Arjin Singh became a United States citizen in 1948 and returned to his home village for a visit in December 1950. His mother had died in 1946, but his father was still alive.

In Punjab, he saw the fruits of his remittances. There was a two-story house, more than 40 acres of highly productive land, and a prosperous family using high technology. They were yielding a bountiful harvest from Punjab's soil. His father had maintained their family's esteem in their village, and Arjin had helped make it possible. He enabled his children to have lavish weddings, relatives to have financial and political power, and kinsmen to migrate to America. These all enhanced the *izzat,* or *mann* (honor) of his family.[15] Before his death, he was able to return annually and witness the fruits of his sacrifices.

Starting in 1952, Arjin Singh sponsored relatives to America. He started with his grandchildren, posting a $6,000 bond for each. It was a good investment. Beant Singh Sandhu, one grandchild, went to Lawrence Technical School and studied engineering. He is now president of Precision Hardware Company and has 80 people

---

[13]The 1917 Immigration Act is informally called the Indian Exclusion Act because it only changed the situation for the people of Indian origin.

[14]Asian Indians today are not unified behind the Democrats like the generation of Arjin Singh. The affluent vote Republican.

[15]*Izzat* (Hindi) or *mann* (Punjabi) refers to the honor or esteem of a family as determined by the consensus of the society (Helweg, 1986:12–21).

reporting to him. Another worked at Ford until 1971. Sukhdev Singh emphasized the trades and became a locksmith and now owns a locksmith company. The owners of the small family business he worked for were pleased with his efforts and sponsored him as a skilled person in 1974. Some of his great grandchildren are in medical school.

California was the center of the Asian Indian community in the United States through the 1960s and most of the writings about Asian Indians in the United States focus on the California experience. Life in Michigan for people originating from India certainly had commonalities with those in California. Due to immigration laws, they could not bring their spouses nor could they return to their homeland, even for a visit, for fear of not being able to reenter the States. Thus, the community in Detroit, as in California, was composed of males whose orientation was their village of origin.

But immigrants in Michigan faced major differences in their situation from those of their compatriots in California. In Michigan, men worked in factories, rather than farms, so they did not build an ethnic economic base like those in California, where Asian Indians bought land and continued their traditional means of obtaining a livelihood, farming the land. Also, unlike their compatriots in California, those in Detroit did not marry Spanish women or white women to circumvent state laws that limited property ownership to United States citizens; in fact, Michigan did not have such laws, although there were some mixed marriages later.

Men like Arjin Singh sacrificed a lot. Was it worth it? Arjin Singh was adamant. His wife had been faithful to him, his family was prosperous and highly respected in Punjab, and many of his relatives had a prosperous life in America. His grandson made him give up living alone to move him into their home. "That indicates the respect and love they have for me," he says with a smile and is quick to add that he misses his independent lifestyle.

Arjin not only served his family and home village, he was a leader in Detroit. He was instrumental in the founding of the Gurdwara of Detroit in 1970. Due to his leadership, the Sikhs are planning a 37-acre complex to build a Gurdwara and subsequently, in order of priority, a retirement home for the elderly, a school for Sikh children, and social and recreational facilities for the community. The proposed Gurdwara will not just be a place of worship, but a community center for Sikhs.

For Arjin Singh, success such as he had known could only have happened in America. The pride of being a United States citizen showed on his face and a tear of joy flowed down his cheek. He blessed America for the opportunities that were provided him.

IMMIGRANT WITH A PROFESSION

Bijoy Bhuyan is the Asian Indian who is the longest Indian American resident in Kalamazoo, Michigan. He is from Cuttack in Orissa. His father was Western educated while Bijoy earned his master's degree in India. He wanted to study antibiotics and penicillin. He entered the University of Wisconsin in 1952. "In those days, our goal was to get a good education and return to India to make a contribution to the society," he stated. He entered the States on a student "J" visa, which requires students to return to their homeland for two years after earning their degrees and having sufficient on-the-job experience. He received his Ph.D. in 1956, did a postdoctorate in Wisconsin for a year, and another postdoctorate at the Prairie Regional Research Institute in Saskatoon, Canada. The work in Wisconsin enabled his wife, Janet (she is white and they met and married while students at the University of Wisconsin), to finish her degree and work in Canada while they earned their passage and settlement expenses to India. They returned to India in 1958.

His father died while he was in America. Being the eldest son, he assumed his traditional position as head of the household. "We had to get used to poverty and dust, open sewers, flies, and lack of privacy," he said. They also had to adjust to family customs and joint residence. Bijoy's younger brother's wife kept her face covered in the elder brother's presence and Bijoy did not like it; so in consultation with his mother, he stopped the practice. Bijoy did have access to the arts and entertainment—Cuttack was the commercial center of Orissa, had several colleges, and the high court.

Bijoy's father had engineering training in the United Kingdom. He had worked with the British and the family understood Westerners, their needs, and adjustment problems. Thus, Bijoy's father and family were sensitive to Janet's situation and respected her. She had one rule, which they all adhered to, if she was in her room and the door was closed, she was not to be disturbed. They made her feel welcome and although it was different, she was never bored. People were friendly and there was an excitement about India. She kept a journal and is currently writing a book about her experiences in India.

Bijoy obtained a job in Pimpri, a city near Poona. He worked as a research scientist at Hindustan Antibiotics Limited, which produced penicillin and other antibiotics. The plant had been set up with the help of the World Health Organization. The head of the research lab and many of the scientists were educated in America. Thus, the Bhuyans made friends with fellow workers and Christian missionaries in the area. They even had a Christmas tree during the proper season. The "tree" was a begonia given to Janet by a Parsee friend!

While in India they traveled third class and enjoyed life, but they realized that Bijoy would not be able to fulfill his duties as family head because he did not make enough money. They also realized that if they stayed in India longer, they would not be able to return to the States.

In 1960 Bijoy and Janet borrowed money from Janet's grandmother and returned to the United States. They stayed with her parents in Ypsilanti, Michigan, and Bijoy looked for work. He relied on friendships developed at the University of Wisconsin to provide contacts and information. A fellow Ph.D. student recommended that he try Upjohn in Kalamazoo. Even here, he had to overcome preconceived notions that Westerners had about Indians. The supervisor asked him if he was willing to work with his hands because of his misconception that all Indians had servants.

Bijoy Bhuyan returned to the States in 1970. It was under the 1965 legislation that Bijoy brought his younger brother to the United States and also sponsored him as he attended Wayne State University, where he obtained an M.A. in engineering. The brother worked for General Motors for 10 years and then returned to India. At present, he is employed by Telco in Jamshedpur, India.

Returning to India is a time to renew relationships with friends and relatives. To enhance his or her prestige, the emigrant often takes gifts to kin and friends in India; because of the gifts, a rule of thumb for travel is that it costs two dollars for every one dollar of travel expenses. It is also a time to renew the spirit of the emigrants.

The Bhuyans visit India regularly, and Janet makes an interesting point when she explains:

> When returning to India, Bijoy eats all the wrong foods. But, his high cholesterol level drops. He relaxes and the physiological effects of tensions in the West quickly recede.

CONCLUSION

The experiences of the two men share some commonalities. Both remained active family members. Arjin Singh, especially, provided for his wife and family and more than that had enhanced the *izzat* of his family. Due to him, his family held a position of high respect and wealth. Bijoy also helped his family members emigrate so they could also take advantage of the economic and educational opportunities in the States. The difference between the two is that while Bijoy's ties were to the family in India, Arjin's ties were not limited to the family but extended out to a whole community—his village.

Both relied on informal communication networks to learn about jobs and knowledge to survive in America. Arjin, like many immigrants, worked harder in the United States than he did in India. And, since he not dare return a failure, he stayed but did not tell people in his home area about his employment and wages. He, like others, added to the pool of "American Letters," that is, letters that glorified life in the States, almost to the extent that people in his home area thought the streets in America were paved with gold.

Since Bijoy was conversant in English and was familiar with Western culture, he lived independently rather than in a residential concentration of Asian Indians. He was helpful to others, as was Arjin, and he obtained a great deal of esteem for that. Equally important, each has made significant contributions to their families, communities, and countries in the United States as well as India.

5/Asian Indians
in the United States
An Overview[1]

INTRODUCTION

The information on Indian Americans is exploding. In the early 1990s, one could count on his or her fingers the number of articles and books about Asian Indians. In fact, Gary Hess (1974) titled one of his articles "The Forgotten Asian Americans: The East Indian Community in the United States." When checking the number of books Amazon.com carried in 1999, the total was around 100. By 2003, the number had increased to more than 300. This chapter synthesizes the expanding body of information concerning Asian Indians in the United States.

ORIGINS

Jasbir Singh and the immigrants in the United States who trace their ancestry to India claim a rich heritage going back to the dawn of human history. The Indus Valley civilization was one of, and possibly the first, richest, and most sophisticated civilization (2500–2700 B.C.) known to man. The antiquity of Indian culture and the wisdom of their sages is a source of pride for almost all Asian Americans. Jasbir and others are also proud of the fact that members of the South Asian Diaspora have been able to maintain their Indian culture, in spite of the adverse conditions under which they suffered—it's a tradition Jasbir and others like him want to maintain.

TRADITIONS, CUSTOMS, AND BELIEFS

Asian Indians want to maintain religious and other traditions and want their children to do the same. In fact, many maintain that they have become more religious since coming to the States. In India, they could take their faith for granted. Not so in the

---

[1]I would recommend the books listed in this footnote for further reading concerning Asian Indians in North America and throughout the world. This chapter is based primarily on the following works: Buchignani and Indra (1985), Chandrasekhar (1982), Eck (2000, 2001) Gibson (1988), Helweg and Helweg (1990), Jain (1993), Jensen (1988), Koritala (2000), Kotkin (1992), La Brack (1988), Leonard (1997), Lessinger (1995), Rangaswamy (2000), Tinker (1977). For a good annotated bibliography, see Mishra and Mohapatra (2002).

States, especially if they wanted their children to also adhere to the faith of their parents. Temples, Gurdwaras, and other worship centers are springing up across the country. They are not limited to religious functions but also are community centers that host classes in language, classical dance, religion, and culture, as well as programs for the elderly, youth, and so on.

The Sikh Gurdwaras are generally the first to be established. In the last 15 years, however, Hindu temples have increased from a few dozen to more than 400. For the Hindus, building a temple is synonymous with building a community (Eck, 2000:221).

In some respects, Hinduism had to be reinvented to fit in America. For example, they adopted a congregational style of worship so the need for feeling like one is part of a community would be fulfilled.[2] Establishing a temple also provided a center for the creation of ethnic pride.

CUISINE

Asian Indian food is as diverse as the people of South Asia. Generally the food of the south and east is based on rice while the north and west rely more on grain, lentils, and beans. Asian Indian food is generally cooked with a variety of spices like cumin, turmeric, chili powder, ginger, and garlic. South Indian food is generally more spicy than the cuisine of the north. The love for Indian food remains, but it is time consuming to prepare. Also, certain items such as roti must be freshly prepared daily. Some shortcuts are found and freezing food after making large quantities is becoming common. Also women will get extra money making roti or freezable food that the client will then thaw and use as needed. Others may cater parties. However, professional caterers are very common now.

DRESS

In daily activities, Asian Indians dress in western styles. Men wear western suits, and women prefer slacks and some gold such as earrings or necklaces. When at a party or function of Asian Indians, the women are transformed by wearing beautiful saris and heavy gold jewelry—gold jewelry symbolizes that she is deeply loved by her husband and respected by her in-laws.

DANCES AND MUSIC

Indian music comes in two varieties: classical and popular. Classical music and dance have a legacy of several thousand years with the tabula (a drum) being the basic instrument. Popular music stems primarily from the Indian cinema—the most numerous film producers in the world. There are also popular singers and groups like Apache Indian and local folk dances like the Bhangra of Punjab. The

---

[2]This is in stark contrast to India where going to the Hindu temple is at will with no congregational type gatherings.

harmonium,[3] a German invention, is also very popular and used in both secular and sacred gatherings.

RELIGIOUS HOLIDAYS AND CELEBRATIONS

Asian Indians celebrate the universal holidays such as New Years and in some ways Christmas. Independence Day (August 15) and Republic Day (January 26) are important as well as the religious holidays of *Holi* and *Diwali*. Muslims celebrate *Eid-ul-Fitr*, which is the end of Ramadan.

HEALTH AND MENTAL HEALTH ISSUES

Most Indians accept the practice of Western medicine. A few also practice Ayurvedic, which emphasizes spiritual healing along with herbs and natural ingredients such as garlic and ginger. Yoga is also very popular, and often Westerners attend yoga classes to learn how to relax.

Concerning mental health, Indians generally do not seek out counselors, psychiatrists, or psychologists. Matters are generally dealt within the family or advice sought from a knowledgeable and respected member of the community.

LANGUAGE

English is the lingua franca of India, but not its official language. Most Asian Indians speak English fluently. India, however, is a country of linguistic diversity. The initial immigrants to the United States generally spoke Punjabi. When the emigration hub developed in Gujarat, that language became prominent. As the emigration hubs are becoming more prominent in South India, Malayalam, Tamil, Telugu, and Bengali are coming to the fore.

FAMILY AND COMMUNITY DYNAMICS

The Asian Indians who are mostly professional also follow the pattern of American white professionals. They remain dispersed, that is, they generally live far enough away so fellow Indians would not be able to see things that would lead to gossip or a bad reputation.[4] They generally maintain a nuclear family although constant visitors from India and long stays by relatives and friends seem to cast doubt on that practice.

Parents do not like their children, especially girls, to date. Peer pressure is forcing change on some of these norms, however. On the other hand, education is highly valued and families often ensure their children are in their rooms by 8:00 P.M. every

---

[3]The harmonium is a 2 foot by 1 foot rectangular box-shaped instrument with a piano style keyboard on one side and a bellows on the other. When played, the artist sits on the floor with the instrument and pumps the bellows with one hand and plays the keyboard with the other.

[4]Generally, those who are professional or well educated have the skills to live well in the United States and so they want to remain apart so as not to be closely scrutinized. Those from rural India, who may not be well educated or familiar with American ways, often need advice or help and want to live in a place where there are other Indians who will help in a time of need. It is not uncommon to have parents with their sons or brothers living in close proximity if employment location permits.

weekday evening studying. The practice of using tutors is not practiced in the States like it is in India.

WEDDINGS

Weddings are a joyous time, especially when held in India. Relatives will come from all over the world to take part in the week-long festivities of singing, dancing, play acting, good food, jokes, and merriment. Whether held in the States, or India, it is a time of establishing family pride, unity, renewal, and family honor or *izzat*.

RELIGIONS

The multiple faiths of India are represented in the States. Zoroastrianism is followed by the Parsees with temples in Los Angeles. Jains, Buddhists, Christians, and Muslims are also present, but the Sikhs and Hindus dominate.

Although the first Hindu temple was built in San Francisco in 1920, it wasn't until 1950 that Sikh and Hindu temples started springing up. Some temples are quite famous, like the Sri Venkateswara Temple in Pittsburgh or the Ganesha Temple in Flushing, Queens. The Flushing temple had workers come from India to do the stonecutting and the building was financed in part from monetary contributions from India (Eck, 2000).

Hinduism is not organized to the degree Christians and Sikhs are. People have meetings informally in their homes, and women often have a small shelf with figurines of deities where they and other family members offer a quick prayer, often in passing on the way to work.

The Sikhs, noted by their beards and turbans, were the first to come and the best organized. Their temple is a religious/political/governing/social service institution for Sikh and non-Sikh alike. It is a multifunctional institution around which the local community builds (Mann, 2000).

ECONOMY AND EMPLOYMENT

As mentioned in previous chapters, Asian Indians first came as unskilled field laborers but after 1965 as professionals, mainly medical and engineers. Those who cannot practice their profession in the States have gone into financing, small business, or consulting. Also, Asian Indians have a higher representation in management than any other community. If the above was not success enough, they generally are on the average the highest paid, highest educated ethnic group in the United States (see Appendixes A and B).

Due to the family reunification emphasis in American immigration policy, Asian Indian immigrants are becoming citizens and can sponsor family members who do not have the education and training of the initial immigrants. These lesser educated people tend to go into service occupations or partner with their more affluent sponsors in small businesses such as convenience stores. As mentioned, the economic profile of the Asian Indian community is like an hourglass shape—the rich and the poor with only a few in the middle class. Nevertheless, there are three distinct segments to the Asian Indian population. One is the initial post-1968 immigrants, primarily professional men who brought their wives later, but the wives did not work

G. S. Grewal

Singh Development Company in Detroit is a superb place where employees are treated humanely, with respect and with dignity. During their tenure in Detroit, they have created 2,448 permanent jobs, generated $80 million in revenues as well as being involved in community services.

outside the home. The second segment is also professionals who brought their wives with them, but the wives have taken up careers. The third segment is generally relatives of previous immigrants; they are uneducated, generally taking service jobs.

The orientations of the three groups differ. One segment is primarily concerned with getting a good marriage for their children and is looking towards retirement. Another segment is more concerned about their children getting a good college education and establishing themselves. The third segment is the young newly married couples who are starting careers and working to build a surplus for the future.

GLOBALIZATION

As the world economy becomes more globalized,[5] Asian Indians also change their perspective. They become more transnational in their perspectives and behavior. For example, the function of national boundaries changes as kinsmen and friends travel the globe visiting each other or communicate instantaneously over the Internet. Concepts like citizenship take on a different meaning. When emigrants become U.S. citizens, they swear not to have allegiance to any other ruler or potentate. How can that be done when India recognizes dual citizenship?

Now, money crosses national boundaries with electronic rapidity. Partnerships can be formed with participants from various cultures, races, and nationalities, each

---

[5]Globalization is the process by which the world is developing a single economy, which is less influenced by nations or their boundaries.

G. S. Grewal

Although their numbers are still small, their skill in politics is beneficial to them, even in the U.S. Thus active support of politicians and being so recognized is a prominent part of Asian Indian behavior in America.

residing in a different country, speaking a different language, working under different laws and behaving according to different customs.[6]

POLITICS

During the early part of the 20th century, Asian Indians in the United States fought for their rights in the States as well as supported the movement for India's independence from British rule. India got its independence in 1947 and by the late 1950s Asian Indians were not very active in the United States—they looked more to Indian politics than America.

Around 1980, there was a noticeable change. The people of Indian origin in the States raised money for their favorite candidates and got recognition as a separate ethnic category on the census forms. Since they are residentially dispersed, they do not form powerful voting blocs. They, however, use their campaign contributions very wisely and effectively to get the desired results. Also, Asian Indians are more noticeable in Washington, DC, working on staff and raising money.

RELATIONS WITH INDIA

Asian Indians in the United States maintain an interest in Indian politics. They make monetary contributions to their favorite candidates and advertise and promote their views as if they were in India.

---

[6]Johanna Lessinger (1995) explains globalism and transnationalism and its behavioral ramifications very well.

ACCOMPLISHMENTS AND CONTRIBUTIONS

A good perusal of Appendixes A and B shows some of the social and cultural dynamics that may not be evident.

The list of contributions and accomplishments of Asian Indians as individuals, groups, and an overall community are too numerous to adequately list here. They hold prominent positions at prestigious universities. Also, Indian names are prominent in art, literature, film, politics, journalism, literature, music, and space and technology. Indian representation in the professions is very good; no wonder that Asian Indians in the United States are so affluent. For example, in a diversified economy like Kalamazoo, their high level of education makes them more marketable.

Looking at the language and citizenship profiles reveal a very diverse community with a variety of experiences. This raises the question of how a unity can be maintained with such an ethnically diverse population.

COMMUNITY DYNAMICS

Appendixes A and B also reveal a great deal about the Indian American community in the United States, both on the local and national level. Although the appendixes are not an exhaustive list, some things are worthy of note. People of Indian origin constitute the fastest growing Asian community. Between the 1990 U.S. census and the 2000 U.S. census, they jumped from the fourth to the third largest Asian group in the United States. As a community, they are largely professionals who are well educated, high achievers, and earn good salaries.

The community is more ethnically and economically diverse than it was a decade ago and the quality of the skills that immigrants bring is declining—but they still claim the highest educated and income-producing community in the United States. However, they continue to maintain close ties with India and contrary to popular stereotypes, the second generation is following in the footsteps of their parents. At least parents can instill the value of hard work into their children.

THE STUDENT EXPERIENCE

Asian Indians have a long history of participating and influencing and being influenced by higher education in the United States. The exchange on the higher education level exploded with the implementation of the Fulbright program. In 1946, just 30 days after the United States dropped two nuclear bombs on Japan and amid a climate that "We must not let this happen again," the bill was passed.

It was in this atmosphere of international awareness that Senator J. William Fulbright of Arkansas proposed the biggest educational cooperation scheme the world has ever known. As Senator Fulbright later stated for the *New York Times:*

> The program . . . is based on the assumption that human beings are capable of reason. . . . Not that they always use it, but they're capable of it and let's try and get them to use it.
>
> The cost of this program from the beginning would not amount to one-third the cost of a submarine. . . . [It is a program of] enlightened self-interest.
>
> It's not the intention to make all the world American. It's to give Americans primarily an understanding of the rest of the world so that they can bring some wisdom to America about how the world operates.

People of Indian origin, especially Sikhs, have a reputation in community involvement. This is especially true for the Sikhs in Detroit, Michigan who are noted for their inputs concerning a soup kitchen for the poor, painting and remodeling inner-city housing, conducting blood drives, serving on the PTA and many other activities.

By 1950, an agreement was reached with India to establish the United States Educational Foundation in India (USEFI). Between 1950 and 1975, more than 5,000 Indian and American scholars crossed the oceans to take part in exchange professorships and research projects.[7] This exchange developed a cadre of American supporters for India. These same American scholars have been ardent proponents of American aid programs and foreign policy direction because they have an understanding of Indian culture, aims and aspirations.

Initially, the intent was to go back to India and many who did still hold prominent positions in government, education, and industry where they continue to make contributions to their homeland.[8]

The new students and their situation is different. The number of Indian students in the United Stated increased as immigration expanded in the 1980s, and there were corresponding changes in obtaining visas also. An Indian who could gain admittance and financial backing to study in the United States had no guarantee that a visa would be granted. If the officer at the embassy was not convinced that the student would return to India, he or she did not have to award the visa, and this caused the Indians to feel discriminated against. I recall sitting in the Gujarat home of one distinguished professor who asked us, "Why is America discriminating against our Indian students

[7]The program spawned 156,000 exchanges over the last 40 years and at present annually aids 10,000 students from 27 countries.

[8]See Helweg and Helweg (1990) and Kamath (1976) for a more detailed account of this early period.

and not letting them attend American schools when they are qualified and have admittance to a reputable university there? Is that fair?" This was a difficult question to answer because I knew that many students going to the United States in the 1980s had no intention of returning. Therefore, it was no surprise that immigration officers were becoming more stringent in granting visas.

There are ways to circumvent the regulations successfully. I found out from the foreign student office at Western Michigan University that the American consulate in India was not issuing visas to students who did not have scholarships. Foreign student offices are helpful to families wanting to sponsor a relative. Dr. Joshi, a university professor, wanted to bring his niece to America to study and was very unhappy when he found that she could not get a visa. So he gave the money earmarked for her expenses to the university, which in turn set up a scholarship in such a way that his niece was the only one who could qualify for it. She later was granted a visa.

Budgetary constraints in the United States currently mean less emphasis on education. The whole program of educational exchange might have collapsed if it had not been for the efforts of American scholars who pressured their representatives to maintain the programs. In spite of these efforts, however, foreign study and exchange programs are decreasing. Whereas in the past the mutual exchange enriched education in both countries, communication is now maintained by the scholars who had been part of earlier programs.

The new type of Indian student coming to America is represented by Manju Bhandari, who is from Punjab and graduated in home economics from Lady Shri Ram College in New Delhi. She obtained a Rotary scholarship to study child development at Boston University. After completing her master's degree she returned to India for a year. She obtained another Rotary scholarship to attend Western Michigan University to do further studies in child psychology. She had made close friends among the international student community at Boston University but did not become involved with the Indian association. She explained:

> I wanted to get to know something else besides my own culture. Besides, they impose many restrictions on their members. By associating with others, I was able to make friends without having to be subject to continuous scrutiny and pressures by people of my own society. As a result, I became a broader person.

Indian students opt for relationships outside the Indian groups or among their peers according to their individual circumstances. Most settled immigrants opt to be part of the Indian associations whereas some Indians may behave like Manju. Young students are under subtle pressure from their parents to be part of the Indian community because elders feel that their children will be less subject to the bad influences of American culture. Most Indian students, however, are under time constraints to finish their studies and do not have the time to seek out the Indian society. If they do socialize, they do so with other students who will show them the new culture.

Manju and the new type of students coming from India have already been exposed to American society. As Manju noted, "When I arrived in the States there were few surprises." Manju came from New Delhi; her father is a prominent medical doctor with many American friends and is a member of the Rotary Club, which made it possible for Manju to get the scholarship. Therefore, coming to America was not as traumatic for Manju as it had been for her predecessors.

Simran Singh was very impressed with her experience at Stanford (Helweg & Singh, 1982). She talked about the following:

> . . . centrally heated conference-type rooms, the professor being dressed casually in an open-necked T-shirt. He lectures perched on his desk, his chin on his knee. He insists that his students call him by his first name. I found it stimulating to be so relaxed with some of the best known specialists in their fields.

She expanded on the freedom students had to ask questions, and mentioned the "Honor Code that all Stanford students are required to sign, which morally binds them not to cheat." She was impressed with the time professors took in correcting and commenting on student work and by the fact that students could hold part-time jobs. She continued:

> It is unbelievably easy to support oneself—job opportunities are many and the average pay is approximately four dollars an hour. And with the secondhand turnover, you can buy a TV for 10 dollars, a bike for 25, and a car for 250. An Indian student can probably get much more out of Stanford than an American because there is much less that he takes for granted.

She then described computer, video, library, and other opportunities.

> The workload at Stanford was heavy, so recreation was possible only during weekends. Some students had social concerns as they fought to alleviate hunger in the third world, and places like the Hammarskjold House at Stanford provided a forum for the debate of third world issues.

In their profiles of Indian students in America today, Pais (1989) and Pais, McCord, and Dutt (1989) describe a community that is less politically active in causes having to do with India, and generally less politically active than student groups from places like the Middle East. Asian Indian associations do, however, debate social issues such as nuclear proliferation, and become involved in Indian affairs. They often have Diwali and Independence Day celebrations and some, like Kumar Gupta of Columbia University, started a FM radio program of Indian music; Gurinder Singh Mann, a doctoral student at Columbia, is trying to unite and involve the Sikh and Indian community through university programs.

In general, the Asian Indian associations tend to be inward looking and concerned with immediate gratification. One individual noticed by the press in the 1980s is Harmeet Dhillon, a student at Dartmouth University, editor-in-chief of the *Dartmouth Review* and an outspoken conservative. She and Dinesh D'Souza (who, at the age of 26 was named a domestic policy advisor to Reagan's White House) have been the leaders of conservative movement among Asian students. In 1986 she campaigned against Dartmouth's distribution of safe-sex kits, and when fellow Indian Rejiv Menon led a group to put up shanties to protest apartheid, she fought him, charging that the action was "blatantly anti-American. If he hated America and what it stood for, why did he come here?" She felt that some Indians disliked the United States but immigrated there when the opportunity presented itself.

The relations between those who come from India to study and those who come to reside in the United States are sometimes strained. Geeta Anand stated the feelings of many:

I don't mind if they are Communists and leftists, if they pay their way through. . . . But 90 percent of them come here on scholarships, assistantships, and so on, and they proceed to bad-mouth America, bad-mouth Dartmouth, and bad-mouth the very system that is making their education possible. That is nothing but profiteering and exploitation.

Many like Rajin Sethi disagree. As he states:

The whites colonized our land for over 200 years and exploited our people and resources and transformed our very prosperous India into a human wasteland. Tell me, who is exploiting whom.

Like in other countries, Asian Indian students are thinking more globally; students do not plan to stay in any one country or any one business for their career path. They plan to go where the opportunities are, which likely means changing countries of residence.

By 1998, educational opportunities had opened up in Australia, Canada, and Europe, but the United States remained the preferred place for advanced studies. A staggering 311,000 entered the United States for advanced studies over the last decade, making India one of the leading suppliers of foreign students to the United States. During the 1997–98 academic year alone 34,000 of the 480,000 foreign students in the United States were from India. During the 1998–99 academic year India was fourth in supplying foreign students to the United States, behind Japan (47,000), China (46,000), and Korea (43,000).

During the 1990s, the U.S. share of the foreign student market dropped from 40 percent to 30 percent, but the students from India continued to come at a rate of 35,000 per year from 25,000 annually during the 1980s. Most studied in the science and engineering fields (Rajghatta, 1998).[9]

With the Indian government's emphasis on technology, Indian students want to study in United States where they can get the type of education needed to advance in India. The first stage brought Indian students to the United States with the ambition of returning to India to have a prestigious position and make a strong contribution to India's development; a large number did return and many now occupy positions of influence in government and the private sector. They have been able to influence their country's future, as they had expected. It was a time of excitement for they knew that they would be in positions to mold India into the kind of society and country that would be best for all. For some this dream was never realized, as in the experience of Jagdish Sharma; returning home did not automatically grant him the position of power and prestige he sought.

The goal of the Indian students in the United States has shifted from wanting to return to India to becoming very successful in their profession, that is, making a lot of money and remaining in the United States. The earlier idealism to mold India's future has faded and the new type of Indian student in America aspires for career enhancement and money. These Indians are knowledgeable about life in the United States, and so their adjustment is easier and they face fewer problems than their predecessors.

---

[9]In India, engineering is the most prestigious field, over medicine and sciences.

CONCLUSION

The Asian Indians, like other groups, had to deal with the changing communities and situations. They had to organize themselves and be a viable political, economic, and social unit. They did this in order to maintain their unity and power in their new abode.

It was a time of rapid change and need for mutual help. They came to a land that was not so strange as was experienced by their European counterparts at the turn of the century. Problems were different and qualifications were more stringent.

6/Ethnicity in the New World

With New People

DYNAMICS OF ETHNICITY

Like many concepts in human behavior, ethnicity is often treated as if it is something changeless or immutable. Nothing could be farther from the truth. One's ethnicity is a dynamic process and always changing. Kathleen Conzens in her 1990 address to the American History Society likened ethnicity to a river. A river is always moving. Some places it moves fast and other places it moves slow. Sometimes rivers merge with other rivers and sometimes they bifurcate. They have a beginning and an end (Conzens, 1991).

History is replete with examples of ethnic groups being created and eliminated. Even if a group keeps the same name, what that name or label means is always changing. It must be kept in mind that membership in a group, or ethnicity, can be ascribed by the wider society or it can be by choice, depending on the cultural context in which a people find themselves. To illustrate, I can choose or reject being an American, but one is an Asian Indian by birth—no choice is involved. Choosing to be an American can be a political or ethnic choice—can be either or both.

The Asian Indian experience is indicative of what I am talking about. When Asian Indians first came to the West Coast, people called them derogatory names like "Hindoos" or "Hindus." They claimed to be Aryan, white, or Caucasian; but to the wider white community they were Asian and not fit for American citizenship.

During and shortly after the World War II, the people from India were termed Indians. The problem with that term was it often confused with the Native people of North America. Thus, the person from India would often say, "I am an Indian from India, I am not an Indian like you have in America."

To eliminate the confusion they started calling themselves East Indians, but this term caused more confusion by classifying them with the people of the East Indies, many of whom were of African origins or stereotyped as such. Since the late 1980s, they have adopted the term Asian Indian. It is not perfect because they do not consider themselves Asian. However, as the Asian community has coalesced under the pan-Asian umbrella to be sufficiently strong, the Asian Indians have had to deal with the fact that as a community, their numbers were not enough to be a viable political force to gain or maintain their rights and access to resources. They might face injustices like the Chinese did when the Vincent Chin incident took place—the attackers never served a day in jail for using baseball bats to bludgeon a Chinese man to death on the night before his wedding. Yet, people debate as to whether there is enough cultural compatibility of the people from India with the people of East Asia to include Asian Indians in the pan-Asian Movement.[1] Most recently, South Asianists have coined the terms South Asian Americans or Pakistani Americans or Bangladeshi Americans. The people of India have followed their lead and coined the term Indian American. They are still officially classified on the U.S. census forms as Asian Indians, but Indian American is gaining popular usage.

In the late 1990s, academics started lumping the people of India, Pakistan, and Bangladesh together under the term "South Asian Diaspora." Whenever I talk to an immigrant from South Asia, he or she generally responds with disdain at the merging of the three groups. It is one reason I kept the South Asian out of the title of this study. It is not what I would consider an agreed on categorization by the people being written about; thus it was or is not a valid category from my point of view. Also, to lump India and Pakistan into the same ethnic category when the two countries are continually at hostilities does not seem valid. Nevertheless, "South Asian Diaspora" is increasingly being used (Shankar & Srikanth, 1988).

The brief account of the Asian Indians' search for an appropriate label illustrates Conzens's river analogy. The identity and the terminology describing Asian Indians has changed from the early derogatory labels to the point where they have some input into what that label may be. They felt themselves distinct from African Americans, Native Americans, East Indians, and Asians, and the labels of identification reflect those perceptions. These same people have changed over time to better define themselves within the North American context.

Ethnicity is a person's identification or membership in an ethnic group. An ethnic group is a community of people with a real or fictitious shared tradition and agreed on set of values. It exists within the pluralism of the modern nation-state, which distinguishes it from a tribe, band, or village (Glazier, 2001:2–4).

An ethnic community generally sees itself as having a heritage going back to the beginning of time, thus giving the members a "tie to the eternal" where they can obtain meaning in life by using their life to make things better for those who follow. "Tie to the eternal" is belonging to a people who have existed from the beginning of time and will continue to exist for eternity. This connection is important for it means that the contribution a person makes to his or her ethnic community will have a lasting and permanent impact. In essence, a person's ethnicity builds on and modifies what has developed from the past to make life better for offspring or decedents.

BUILDING CONCEPTS OF ETHNICITY

To understand the ethnic process, I modify the work of Jack Glazier (2001:1–16) and Benedict Anderson (1993). From what I see, there are four major foundations to ethnicity: (1) land, (2) language, (3) history, and (4) culture, which includes religion and mythology.

---

[1]See Shankar and Srikanth (1988) for a more detailed discussion of the debate as to whether the people of India should identify with Asians or not.

Land

The land or homeland is very important to any group. It is a place where one belongs, can relax, assures survival, and provides a tie to the eternal, that is, claim to existence from almost the beginning of time. How this plays out in actual experience is illustrated by the American experience. As discussed earlier, the crossing of the Atlantic Ocean was such a horrible experience that it became perceived as the "promised land." Since World War II, however, transportation and communications have become so efficient that it is not necessary to leave one's homeland behind. One can maintain a dual residence, one in the homeland and one in America.

The above may seem very academic and irrelevant but nothing could be farther from the case. For example, for most emigrants from India, they do not claim India as their homeland, they claim their ethnic region as their homeland, that is, Punjabis see Punjab as their homeland, Gujaratis claim Gujarat, Bengalis claim Bengal, and so on. Second, in most of the world, homeland and ethnic membership is determined by blood; in the United States is it is by residence and choice. To illustrate, I can move to Punjab and live there the rest of my life. I can buy land, worship, and speak the language fluently, but I will never be a Punjabi because my kinship origins are from England. On the other hand, I can move to America and claim it as my homeland regardless of the location of my ancestral origins.[2] Or, I can be a Punjabi and never have set foot in the region and not be able to speak the language. Membership is based on the place of origin of my ancestors or my blood factor.

Language

I was sitting at a party in New York talking to an elderly Punjabi lady. During our conversation she began to register her displeasure at the fact that the children were not learning Punjabi. She emphasized her concern:

> Our children in this country lose out because they are not taught the Punjabi language. Language is like the trunk of a tree, from it comes the root and branches. So it is with our language. If we Punjabi people are to survive in this country, our Punjabi children must learn the Punjabi language.

The lady, with her uneducated background, knew what she was talking about.

Language is important for two reasons: it provides a tie to the eternal and it is a communication system configured to that particular culture. In the case of the Punjabi language, it is considered an Indo-European Language, which traces it back to the origins of mankind. Thus, its use reinforces the self-perception of the Punjabi people and Punjabi culture existing during the dawn of human existence. Consequently, to the Punjabi, they are an eternal people who have always existed and always will.

Next, the Punjabi language is configured to Punjabi culture. Terms like *Mann* are not directly translatable into English. Earlier on, I have translated *Mann* as family honor, but even that does not do justice to the concept.

---

[2]As a caveat, the Canadian General McKenzie, the first Commander of UN forces in Yugoslavia stated, "I have never seen such vicious ethnic fighting in my life." He was correct for there they are fighting to keep their homeland for ethnic survival; in North America, the conflict is over access to resources—a big difference.

People like the lady I talked to feel that the Punjabi culture will die out in America because the language will die out. One thing is sure, as Punjabis remain in the States and do not maintain their language, traits will be forgotten or modified so as to be explainable in the English language and compatible with American culture.

History

History, like language, has a two-pronged function. Like language, it provides a tie to the eternal, but the second function is different, it reinforces existing cultural values, beliefs, and perceptions. As a tie to the eternal, history relates the drama of a people to the beginning of time, which again reinforces the ideology that one belongs to a community that has its origins at the beginning of time and will continue on forever.

Unlike popular opinion would have you believe, history is not something immutable or unchangeable; history is always being rewritten to reinforce the values and beliefs of a people of that time. Martyrdom is emphasized in Sikh history because dying for one's faith or a just cause is a prominent tenet of the Sikh faith. Sikhs and Hindus have lived side by side for hundreds of years while Sikhs were heavily persecuted by Muslim rulers and invaders. Sikhs are also proud of their martial qualities that make good soldiers. Yet when Indira Gandhi had the Indian Army invade the Sikh Golden Temple in Amritsar, Sikh history was suddenly seen in a different light. Hindus were talked about as being eternal enemies and the "strong tie of Sikhs and Muslims" was emphasized. Past massacres by Muslims to Sikhs were suddenly forgotten. Sikh soldiers deserted from their regiments. The militaristic tradition was suddenly set aside.

Sikhism is usually viewed in the West as a young religion that started with Guru Nanak in the middle 15th century. Khazan Singh, however, argues that the teachings of the gurus were just a return to the pure faith that had been corrupted over the centuries by the Brahmans. Thus, Sikhism is an older, more pure faith than that practiced by the Brahmans of the present day (Singh, 1914a and 1914b).

Culture

Culture involves many more components than land, language, or history. In addition, the cultural components cannot be seen, but exert a very powerful influence on human behavior.

In order to understand the kinds of cultural conflicts that Isaacs (1958) talks about and the situation faced by both Americans and Indians as a result of the immigration process, it is helpful to look at the cultural frameworks of both groups—the beliefs, values, and interpretations people use to determine life goals and interpret the world around them (Kroeber & Parsons, 1958:583–84). Virtually all people feel some sense of superiority about their own culture. When new ideas are introduced, they may feel threatened. If new ideas are adopted, they often have to face the fact that earlier ones were wrong, and the possibility that the new ones may be so as well. For Indian immigrants, these feelings are intensified when their children challenge parental values and choose a different belief system. The concern for these parents is important because their success in life lies largely in their progeny. If the children reject the culture of their parents, they are telling their parents that the elders are wrong, a bitter fact to deal with. There are also practical considerations. If the second generation adopts the American concept of individualism, the elders will not be cared for in their old age—they will be relegated to "living graves" or old-age homes. Conflict arises for immigrant youngsters because they often have to deal with two (and sometimes more) incompatible systems—Western individualism and Indian collectivism.

Knowing the culture of a people provides a framework for understanding that society, but culture within a group varies: how the framework influences actual behavior is difficult to determine. Henry Murray (1986) of Harvard says, "In some ways, all people are alike. In some ways some people are like some other people. In some ways all people are unique." There are always exceptions to generalizations; in this chapter I deal only with cultural tendencies and principles backed by literature on both Indian and American culture (Mandelbaum, 1972a, 1972b; de Tocqueville, 1840; Bellah, Madsen, Sullivan, Swidler, & Tipton, 1985).

For any community to survive, there must be some agreement concerning beliefs, meanings, values and norms; otherwise there would be chaos as to how people should behave, what is right and wrong, and how to communicate. The difference between what people say and what they do is a crucial factor. Some Americans think of themselves as sensitive and sympathetic but do not hesitate to fire economically destitute workers to maximize profits: their self-perception of care and compassion does not reflect actual calculating and materialistic behavior. People do not always obey their cultural rules. They may deviate from "altruistic" norms when it is in their own interest, or form "exclusivist" norms when moved by compassion. Knowing a group's values, meanings, and beliefs nevertheless helps an outsider understand the basis on which group members evaluate, interpret, and perceive themselves and their situation.

Many studies address American and Indian culture in far greater detail than is intended here. I highlight some prominent themes to give the reader an idea of the conflicts faced by both communities in terms of their values, beliefs, and perceptions.

As you read the comparisons below, keep in mind that Indian cultural patterns change as immigrants stay in America. A dynamic process is going on with Americans and Indians continually influencing each other.

AMERICAN AND INDIAN CULTURES COMPARED

Upon arrival in America, Jasbir Singh and other immigrants quickly became aware of themes in American life that have been grouped under labels like the "Protestant Ethic" and "Frontier Spirit." Although the nature and impact of these themes have varied over time, both have influenced and provided principles that guide American actions and perceptions (Stewart, 1985).

The Protestant Ethic

The "Protestant Ethic" was identified in the work of Max Weber, who observed that many prominent 18th and 19th century capitalists were Protestants. He examined this phenomenon and (among other things) delineated two of many principles the early Puritans settling in North America adhered to: interpretation of success as a sign of God's election and predestination, that God has chosen those to be saved before they were born. Weber concluded that Calvinists looked for signs they were destined for salvation; the visible judgment factor was that "God blessed his own." Thus, a group that prospered and advanced was blessed by God. Individualism, then, developed because salvation was an individual matter and the circumstances of birth had nothing to do with admittance into God's kingdom.

These principles, the belief in predestination combined with the business-mindedness of the Puritans, had profound effects on the thoughts and perceptions of both the individual and corporate America as a whole. Although many Americans probably do not credit divine intervention for their success, there is a strong tendency to identify a growing or prospering group or organization as virtuous. Growth is crucial. As one corporate executive put it: "Either you grow or you die." Progress is demonstrated by statistics that may show monetary gains or increased membership. As a result, emphasis is on short-term accomplishments.[3] Long-term goals are important only so long as they do not cause short-term retrenchment. Americans tend to think in terms of "good old fashioned American ingenuity" or "American knowhow" or "hard work," assuming that the less prosperous are not working hard.[4]

The above criterion can also be applied on the individual level. Studs Terkel's conclusions suggests that many Americans believe that if they work hard and are good, they will prosper.[5] Consequently, the unemployed are encouraged with remarks like "You can't keep a good person down. You will find something," implying that if you succeed, you are good and deserving of success—if you do not succeed, something in you is lacking. In other words, Americans tend to believe that the world is just, with each person reaping a reward according to what he or she deserves.

Caste Ideology

Asian Indians, like Americans, feel that their way of life is best. If Americans justify their position by their prosperity and world dominance,[6] Indians do so by their pure, devout, and holy living according to rituals and prescribed codes of behavior. Indians generally do not see the world in terms of black and white or right and wrong; they emphasize compromise and believe that many paths lead to the same goal.

The Indian concept of superiority has it roots in caste ideology; outsiders to the caste system are considered polluted or the farthest away from God. Indeed, in the past, people who traveled abroad were considered to be defiled and had to undergo a ritual of purification to reenter the Hindu system. Although not all Indians obey these strictures today, the idea that Indians are more spiritual and pure than others does persist. Indians view emigrants with a degree of suspicion as to whether they have upheld their faith and maintained their purity.

Many of the immigrants in this study had come from positions of esteem in India. They were from caste status and had many family members working for British

---

[3]Many argue that the declining competitiveness of American business is due to its short-term thinking. John Naisbitt, however, argues that long-term considerations are becoming more prominent (Naisbitt, 1982).

[4]These sentiments are more prominent in the rural Midwest and South than on the East Coast or in university communities (Naisbitt, 1982).

[5]Studs Terkel also encountered many bitter people for whom the "American Dream" was a farce (Terkel, 1980).

[6]Here the philosophy of Social Darwinism coupled with the view of the Protestant Ethic is influential. Both justify the perception that success is synonymous with being right.

administrators, a fact that lent them a still greater sense of superiority. Furthermore, most came from an educational system that was modeled after Britain's and which instilled in its students the conviction that their training was superior. Nevertheless, Asian Indians have a great respect for the power, wealth, and success of Americans. Often, their attitude toward the United States is one of contradiction; the Indian feels his abilities are superior, but he cannot achieve his maximum potential unless he associates himself with the "inferior" West, which, in turn, degrades his superiority or purity. It is a dilemma the Indian emigrant continually tries to cope with but finds difficult to resolve.

The Individual versus the Group

Generally, individual rather than group considerations guide American behavior and perceptions; Americans see the world as centering on the individual. The axiom "Only I am responsible for and influenced by my actions," aptly fits such thinking. Americans are taught that enhancing the individual is an important goal. American children are encouraged to go into careers that are compatible with their aspirations and talents. "Do your own thing" is a commonly repeated maxim, and individual satisfaction is often given priority over parental desires. Pursuing a career is valued over looking after one's elders. Old people in the way of one's happiness or career development may be placed in homes for senior citizens or become wards of the state; legally a child is not responsible for the welfare of his parents. For many Americans, the self-esteem of an individual is in his or her own accomplishments. Credit is taken for the advancements made in one's career and not for the success of siblings.

Indians interpret the American emphasis on individualism as selfishness, for Indians think of themselves in terms of the group, especially the family. Neither choice of career nor spouse are individual matters; the former must enhance the family and the latter must fit into the kin group. One's esteem is determined by the *izzat,* or honor, of the family unit. If a brother does well, all members of the family take credit for his accomplishments because it was not an individual effort but a family endeavor. According to this system, a person who looks after his or her elders will be blessed and will enhance the family honor.

In Indian culture, the concept of individuality is almost nonexistent; one does not think of individual enhancement, but of the effect on the kin group. Will it provide contacts? Is it prestigious? Will it help obtain a suitable marriage for oneself and one's siblings? Will it give pleasure and honor to the parents? Not only is the family included in decisions, but family members are part of the decision-making process. Kinsmen discuss options around the family table and consider everyone's input. Maintaining family *izzat* guides much of the behavior. *Izzat* is the "social credit" (Mandelbaum, 1972b:168), the extremely favorable appraisal placed by the society on individuals, families, or groups when their behavior is in accordance with the critically preferred standards (Helweg, 1986:12–26).

Thus, not only do Indians usually think in terms of the group, but they are sensitive to the perceptions of the wider community that evaluates them and determines their social ranking. For example, the criteria of social evaluation for village-dwelling Punjabis include such factors as *muhabbat* (love toward friends), *khidmat* (hospitality toward others), *seva* (service to others), *varna* (place in the caste system), *robh* (power in the community), *jaidad* (wealth), *zamindarid* (ownership), and *pirhi* (prestige according to family history) (Helweg, 1986: 12–21). Since this study focuses on urban Indians, the criteria for determining family *izzat* depends more on *robh, pirhi,* and a form of *muhabbat* different from that of rural Indians. *Robh* may be obtained by securing a leadership role in an Indian association or in another prominent organization in the United States. The esteem of the organization's leaders increases with the prestige of the association. In this way, the host community has some influence in this evaluation, for the organization's success in representing the Indian view gains prominence in the eyes of both the Indian and American communities.

For *pirhi* evaluated in its traditional way, a person who comes from a family of leaders is proud of the accomplishments of the group. Even in America, those families of high *pirhi* receive respect from their fellow Indians. Those whose family gained prominence in East Africa are also highly acclaimed by the community in the United States. The efficient communication networks allow news of accomplishments to travel, thus giving esteem to prominent expatriates from other places such as Toronto or London.

Muhabbat for urban Indians focuses on how the family behaves, both within its group and towards the outside world: A family that lovingly looks after its own members is highly regarded. A brother who helps his younger brother to obtain employment or a loan; an uncle who aids a nephew in finding a job; the kin group that maintains a united front without revealing family disagreements to outsiders. Another good example is Jasbir's sister who not only helped Jasbir but many others migrate to the United States. For these efforts, she and her parents were held in high esteem in India and by the Asian Indian community in the United States. All exhibit traits that add prestige.

A communal summation of family behavior determines *izzat. Izzat* may be enhanced when the Indian emigrant uses wealth and prestige to gain recognition in India. This takes various forms, from gifts for family members in India to heading a project that helps the home community. *Izzat* evaluation can be from either the immigrant community abroad, the home society in India, or both.

Izzat also has certain ramifications for the behavior of Indians in America. It reinforces the sense of superiority of their own culture, first, because individuality is equated with selfishness. Indians tend to look down on Americans who do not take responsibility for their elders and extended family. Second, *izzat* helps Asian Indians adapt to life in America because they are very much aware of social evaluation—thus, they are observant of American behavior and sensitive to criticism. They adopt the manners of upper class Americans in the way they decorate their homes, practice social graces, and dress. Indeed, to many Americans, an Indian may appear to have adopted American culture because his or her dress, social graces, and behavior in the workplace are Westernized.[7] It is accordingly difficult for most Americans to understand an Indian from a high caste or high *izzat* family who feels superior to those with wealth or political power.

---

[7]There is generally a difference in appearance between immigrant Punjabis and Gujaratis: Punjabis tend to look more Western, Gujaratis seem to adhere more to their own symbols. There are also stereotypes according to caste. Brahmans are considered pugnaciously intellectual; Kshatryas and warrior castes swashbuckling; Banias crafty, miserly, and cowardly; Jats, dense and unrefined; . . . Gollas (cowherders) litigious and full of vice; Kasais (butchers) liars; and so on (Tyler, 1974:5).

Group identity is reinforced in a culture like India's because support of the kin group is needed to survive. One needs family financing to start a business or parental support to get a start in life. Individualism and self-interest may thus gradually penetrate into immigrant Indian perceptions, because family help is no longer as crucial as it was in India.

Social Hierarchy

As can be seen from the above, Indian culture is built on different beliefs and assumptions than American culture. More emphasis is placed on birth and communal membership, and living for the group.

> Social ranking in Indian culture is based on one's position of birth, which is determined by how the individual lived in a previous life, how one lives according to the present station in this life, and how one has fulfilled that station. Ideally, if a person is born as a carpenter, the goal in life is to be the best carpenter (that is, fulfill his *dharma*), and thus assure his birth into a higher position in the next life. This progression is dictated by the social position of one's birth according to *varna,* or caste principles. (Dumont & Pocock, 1957, 1958a, 1958b and Dumont, 1966)

Westerners frequently misinterpret these concepts as evidence that Indians are only concerned with the next world and not in trying to better their positions in this life. But Indians do like amenities and wealth, and even though their status may be based on birth, this fact does not deter them from working for creature comforts in this life. M. N. Srinivas (1969:6) describes these aspirations well in his concept of "Sanskritization," the process by which a "low" Hindu caste, tribal, or other group, changes its customs, ritual, ideology, and way of life in the direction of a high, and frequently, "twice-born" caste. Generally such changes are followed by a claim to a higher position in the caste hierarchy than that traditionally conceded to the claimant caste by the local community.

Such behavior is not unique to people from India, for almost all people emulate members of the highest social strata (Lynch, 1969). However, Indians who have already developed observational astuteness are particularly inclined to emulate prestigious traits when they enter the United States.

Unlike India, America considers itself to be an egalitarian society. A sense of social hierarchy is present, but most people do not like to admit that they adhere to inequality. Thus, bosses may be on a first-name basis with their subordinates and treat their employees with courtesy. It is difficult for Indians to adjust to treating tradespeople, blue-collar workers, or lower-echelon people in a respectful manner, for Indian immigrants come from a hierarchical society where servants and peons are kept in their place. When Indians carry that attitude over to their workplaces in America, they risk incurring the wrath of subordinates for treating them with disdain.

"The Frontier Spirit"

Significantly, American culture has its foundation in the "frontier spirit" of the pioneers, who moved westward across North America to conquer what they considered to be a hostile but boundless land. The implications of this "frontier spirit" instills the idea that almost any obstacles can be overcome and goals achieved, a view further reflected in militaristic ideology and terminology such as "capturing the market" or "beating the competition." Coupled with a competitive spirit is the belief in unlimited potential, which holds that anyone can succeed depending on how hard he or she works; so it is difficult to deal with cultures like India's that emphasize an ascribed hierarchical ranking.

Indian culture values harmony with one's environment, and maintains that social and physical surroundings are not just to be conquered. Indians can be highly competitive, but they use different tactics than Americans. They believe in working within the system rather than fighting or changing it. In keeping with the concept of harmony, the Indian worker attempts to get ahead by developing friendships in high places. So he or she carefully observes how things work and evaluates how he or she can work within that framework. Indian culture teaches the importance of having the support of those in power and authority, so Indian workers cultivate these patron-client relationships.

Concepts of Privacy

Privacy and space are very important to Americans. Communal or joint residence patterns are almost impossible for the average American to cope with. Those in urban areas desire to spend time in the country, a luxury they can afford because of the vast amounts of available land and open spaces. Privacy is not valued in much of Indian society because of the high density of the population; Indians are used to living in joint residences with many people around them. Therefore, many Indian immigrants feel a sense of isolation in America and describe life there as lonely.

Many Indian immigrants find that Americans are friendly, but only to a certain point. Dropping unannounced into people's homes is generally not done in America to the degree it is in India, where houses are open and neighbors freely drop in to see each other. Not having the freedom to visit others unannounced makes the new immigrants feel isolated, so they quickly try to develop networks and socialize among themselves.

CONCLUSION

Indians of South Asia's agricultural and industrializing communities entered America with different cultural concepts and their own form of cultural superiority. They differed from Americans in many ways: their sense of worth depended on the group, not the individual; their social rank was based on birth, not earned wealth; and their society imposed different strictures and controls on its members.

Life was not without its challenges for these new immigrants moving from one cultural system to another. Their life goals and morality would be challenged by the second generation. This new generation had to find a belief and value system in a context not compatible with the cultural framework of the initial settlers.

Like other immigrants, Indians came into a culture where the game of life was played by a different set of rules. Much of this tension was never manifest to the casual observer because it emerged only in the confines of the family. Indeed, many immigrants have not fully dealt with these problems and are still facing them today.

7/Academic Scholarship and Sikhism
Conflict or Legitimization

INTRODUCTION

To the casual reader, in the previous chapter the topic of ethnicity may seem like an academic concept. Nothing could be further from the truth. The cultural or symbolic system guiding people's lives is difficult to understand because it is not something one can see, feel, or quantify. Thus, as this chapter will show, cross-cultural interaction can easily cause misunderstanding and conflict.

In his controversial book *Imagining India,* Ronald Inden (1990) argues that because of Western methodological biases and assumptions, a valid history of India has not been presented. As he states:

> If we shift the major presuppositions and assumptions of Ideological discourse, it is possible, I argue, to construct a picture of Hindu India that differs greatly from the ones we have inherited. Such a shift of presuppositions need not, cannot, be confined to the study of India by South Asian specialists. The theory of human agency I am trying to articulate in this book also extends to the study of other regions of the world (1990:3).

As the following case shows, having different presuppositions and assumptions—in other words a different culture—can cause conflict and misunderstanding at the most basic level.

Over the past decade disagreement has developed within the Sikh community of North America. One group supports the goals and results of Sikh scholarship and studies in the universities of Canada and the United States. The other feels that current university scholarship is undermining their faith.[1] The debate has taken on inter-

---

[1]It is hard to label these two groups because both comprise university professors, conservatives, liberals, people on the right, and people on the left. However, those who attack Sikh studies at the universities are generally technically trained, that is, medical people, scientists, and engineers. Thus, unlike the Culture Wars, this conflict is not so easy to label.

Most recently the anti-university element has focused their attack on, among others, the works of Oberoi (1994) and McLeod (1980, 1988). See Mann and Saraon (1988) and Mann, Sandhu, Sidhu, Singh, and Sodhi (nd) who present the position attacking Sikh studies scholars in American universities.

national proportions where Sikhs in England and India are also becoming involved. In fact, some scholars in Sikh faith have been summoned by, appeared before, and tried by the *Akal Takht*[2] in Amritsar.[3] It has taken on the nature of a Culture War (Hunter, 1991) where, on the part of some, reason and the search for truth has been replaced by dogma.[4]

To those who feel Sikh studies programs in universities are undermining their faith, their vehemence is understandable. Because they perceive, among other things that (1) some of these programs financed by private contributions from the Sikh community have not been supporting their faith, (2) recommendations from the Sikh community have not been followed, even though they were given an advisory role in the development and implementation of these programs, (3) their children will lose their Sikh faith, and (4) Sikhism in general will be discredited. On the other hand, those for university Sikh studies feel that academic freedom and honesty must be maintained—that trustworthy scholarship should be promoted, no matter what a group believes.

I will argue that underlying this conflict is an older issue that has plagued South Asia from the time the West colonized the region: What criteria should be used to validate a belief system? This problem has been an issue in South Asia ever since Western philosophy, religion, and scientific methodology challenged the religious and philosophical systems of the subcontinent. I will analyze the current Sikh dissension in North America from a social science perspective. In essence, I will argue that the two groups of people are interacting in a context with each behaving and perceiving the situation from different cultural systems. Each is evaluating the other by different criteria, and thus perceiving the other in a derogatory manner, because each is using what they perceive is the true framework for judging the other.

CULTURE

To understand the current tensions within the North American Sikh community it is imperative to comprehend the nature of culture. Culture (Kroeber & Parsons, 1958; Schneider, 1968:1–18) is an abstract symbolic system that is composed of values, meanings, and beliefs.[5] Beliefs may well be the most important element for they are the basic concepts—the foundation on which people interpret the world around them,

---

[2]The *Akal Takht* is a multistoried building in the Sikh Golden Temple of Amritsar, Punjab. It is one of the five seats of authority for the Sikh faith, *takht*. Its *jathedar* (leader) is considered to have authority over the other four, and is the final arbiter in matters relating to the path. See Cole and Sambhi (1990:35) and Harbans Singh (1983:56–60) for a more complete description.

[3]There are many references dealing with the above issue. See *The World Sikh News*, which frequently reported on this issue, and *The Sikh Reformer, Number 5* for a concise summary of the debate. See also Mann and Saraon (1988) for a position challenging the university scholarship in America focusing on Sikh studies.

[4]Social scientists realize that it is virtually impossible for an individual to be completely objective. I am not a Sikh. Also, I have a high respect for the scholarship of McLeod, Oberoi, and Pashaura Singh. Although I feel I am giving a fair and impartial analysis, I feel the reader should know possible biases I might have.

[5]See Schneider (1968) for a more complete treatment of the concept of culture, on which this chapter is based.

evaluate themselves, judge others, and develop priorities in their lives. Yet, beliefs are concepts that cannot be proved right or wrong. When thinking of beliefs, religion immediately comes to mind, but concepts like capitalism and the free market can be equally influential.

Culture also assigns meanings to symbols, provides for a common language, and enables members to interact according to the configurations of their particular culture. However, the same symbols may have different contexts at different times. Some people of the Middle East felt their practice of keeping women isolated was based on high esteem for the female gender and their crucial role in maintaining family honor (Helweg, 1986:12–15). To the feminists of the West, this was oppressing or enslaving. The concept "human rights" meant different things in different cultural contexts. In war, many soldiers have sacrificed their lives to keep a national flag flying. In actuality, the flag is a piece of colored cloth. In another place or context, the same cloth may be used for a rag.

Values help establish priorities. When a person is selling a product, that item may have its good and bad points. The salesperson, in describing the product to a potential customer, has the option of being honest and possibly losing the sale. Making money and being honest are both values, and he or she must make a choice. The culture sets forth a guide to follow, usually to be honest. The members of a group agree on how values should be prioritized. Thus, people generally see themselves in ideal terms, such as being honest; but when faced with the actual choice they may behave otherwise and opt for maximizing profit. How people perceive themselves is known as "ideal culture," but how others see them is "real culture." People generally see themselves in terms of ideal culture and others see them in terms of real culture.

Cultural Conflict

One example of cultural conflict is the different way baseball is played in Japan and the United States.[6] The concept of being fair is one of many differences. An American baseball player in Japan, doing very well, will face the "expanding strike zone." In such a situation, umpires call strikes that are outside the normal range. They believe Americans are big, strong, and experienced at hitting the ball, while Japanese are not as big, strong, or experienced. From the Japanese perspective, fairness demands that the strength of the American be compensated to make things equal. To the Japanese, this practice is fair and helps adjust for differences in size and experience. Americans view the changes in rules as unfair and putting them at a disadvantage.

Similarly, the game of life is being played by some Sikhs in America according to their cultural beliefs, rules, and interpretations; and these differ from the cultural framework on which some universities operate. Because both groups behave differently, each considers the other as being unethical or not living up to their commitments.

---

[6]See Whiting (1989) for the study on which this analysis is based.

Contrasting Cultural Concepts

In the current Sikh studies conflict, two sets of opposing systems are involved: (1) religion/science and (2) East (Sikh)/West (Judeo-Christian). The following will show that they are not only different systems, but one system is being used to attempt to validate or disprove the other.

Religion/Science

Religion and science[7] are in essence two different systems operating under very different goals and means. First, the purpose of religion is to tell "why," the purpose of science is to explain "how." Religion tells people why they are here and why they should live the way they are taught. Science tells people how humanity developed and how the natural world operates. A holy book teaches beliefs and why people should behave in a certain manner. A science book teaches laws and regularities that are found in the dynamics of the natural world.

Second, religious beliefs cannot be proved right or wrong. Evidence may be collected to support a belief, but the belief cannot be proved or disproved. The scientific method is different. Science operates from the assumption of unbroken regularity in the universe. It leaves no room for miracles or divine intervention. Religion allows for miracles and divine intervention. Moreover, scientists observe, and make hypotheses, so that phenomena can be predicted. This brings me to the third point, namely, that the hypothesis must be falsifiable. In other words, the scientific hypothesis must be stated in such a way that if it is wrong, it can be so shown (Ruse, nd). Religions allow for miracles and are not formulated in a falsifiable manner. The point is that religion and science operate according to completely different assumptions and goals. One cannot be used to verify the other.

East (Sikh)/West (Judeo-Christian)

Many concepts have the same name in Eastern and Western contexts, but different meanings. To illustrate, I will explore three of these many concepts. As I set forth the concepts, within each tradition there is variation. The purpose is not to set forth a theological discourse, but to illustrate a process that is taking place. The three concepts are the notion of deity; the method of achieving goals prescribed by the religion; and the idea of truth.

Deity

Many Christians perceive of their god or deity as a personality, a supreme being that has created man in his own image. Among many Christians, it is a "he" and the relationship is like that of a father to a child. For some, it is a strict father who judges and punishes, for others it is a kind and loving father who helps and guides, sometimes with pain, to improve one's character.

---

[7]When I use the terms "religion" and "science" here, they are the concepts as set forth in the Western tradition. I do this because the Sikh studies conflict is taking place primarily in the West and argued primarily by Western-oriented and Western-trained people.

On the other hand, for many South Asians, and Sikhs, the deity they worship is an all-pervasive force uniting all things of the universe. The purpose of the Guru is to enable one to establish a oneness or relation with the deity. All are united because God is in everyone. Thus, harming others also harms oneself, not because it destroys a person's individual character or because the person is committing a sin; but because one is part of the other, and harming the other is harming oneself. Therefore, one Sikh goal in life is to become sensitive to the deity that is inside everyone.[8]

Method

Considering the deity concept for some Christians, they achieve piety in the same way one establishes a relationship with a friend—communicating, which allows one to maintain his or her individuality. Communicating is one aspect of prayer, to talk to God on a personal basis. Also, some Christians believe a person achieves piety by obeying rules and helping people in this life. The purpose of ritual and worship is to learn or receive encouragement so one will live a correct life in this world. In other words, one's piety is partly determined by the way one lives his or her life—which means that one is judged by individual achievement.

For many South Asians and some Sikhs, the goal is to lose one's individuality and become one with God. To use an analogy, a glass of water is a distinct entity. If that water is poured into a lake, the water is still there, but it is indistinguishable from the larger body of water, or lake. Very often what the Sikh and South Asian are trying to do is lose their individuality and become one with God via the Guru. To do this, they want to lose their individuality by becoming one with the spirit. This is often done with the guidance of a guru or *sant*. For the Sikh, meditation on the divine Name (*nam*) in the morning is to lose the individual self and become part of the whole.[9] Sikhism is not other-worldly to the degree of Hinduism. Guru Nanak was specific about teaching that his followers are to work, do well, and help others in this world. Also, Guru Gobind Singh, in his admonition to take up the sword for justice, also implies the concern of Sikhs with the world.

Truth

The nature of Truth[10] is fundamentally different in South Asian and Western cultures and also a major source of the conflict on which I am focusing. In the West, Truth is found outside a person and is absolute. Often Westerners validate by measuring, touching, or applying a code or criteria to the situation. Often Westerners feel that the methodology of science can be applied to validate everything, including religious beliefs. In Western Christianity, one learns Truth by reading scriptures and listening to preachers. These scriptures set forth absolute laws or rules that many perceive as immutable. Again, they are outside the individual.

For the Sikh, and many South Asians, Truth is found inside a person. One learns or achieves it by becoming one with the deity through the guidance of the Guru. The

---

[8]I have only focused on a few relevant points here. For a more complete explanation, see Cole and Sambhi (1990:68–9) and Kohli (1973:16–21, 1972a:9–14, 1972b:121–2).

[9]See Kohli (1972a:61–71) for a fuller explanation.

[10]I am not using "truth" meaning deity; I am focusing on determining the validity of one's beliefs or ascertaining proper behavior.

Guru and scriptures are certainly important, but in the end, for the Sikh, it is one's relationship with the deity and Guru that reveal Truth. Second, Truth for the Sikh is not necessarily absolute. Truth has many levels and is dependent on context and circumstances.

The experience of the Muslim saint Kabir illustrates the difference. The story goes that one night Kabir heard a knock at his door. When he opened it, there was a thief who said, "I am being chased by the police for stealing this bread, will you hide me?" Kabir replied, "Yes, go and lie in bed with my daughter." Soon, there was a knock on the door and the police standing there said, "We saw the thief we were chasing enter your house, we have come to apprehend him." Kabir replied, "Come in and see for yourself, in bed is my wife and in the other bed is my daughter and her husband." The police left because no man would allow a stranger to be in the same bed with his daughter.

In analyzing the story, the question that becomes crucial is: Did Kabir do the right thing by hiding the thief and disobeying the law? From the Western perspective, the answer is "no" because the law is an absolute, always to be obeyed. For Kabir, this is not the case. He was in tune or close to the deity that is inside him and the feeling he had was that he should help the thief. Who knows, maybe this was God's way of revealing Truth to the thief. One does not always know the "higher plan," so to speak; however, those who are one with the deity or the Guru are instruments of it and not subject to earthly laws. Truth or right action for Kabir was relative. At another time in another context, it may not be correct to help a thief. But the only way one can tell is by being in tune with the deity that is within all people.

In thinking through the concepts of deity, method, and truth, implications on the cultural level become clear. Both communities, East and West, Christian and Sikh, are evaluating and living life according to different rules and concepts. And although the same words are used, their meanings are different. Thus, each evaluates the other in its own terms of cultural reference. This results in misunderstanding that each perceives the behavior of the other as negative. For example, to some Christians, meditation has little value. To a South Asian, the Christian concept of prayer often does not produce what is important. Many Christians consider their faith the only truth. Most Sikhs see their beliefs as being the best, but not the only way.

Sikhs and Christians may believe they are worshiping the same deity. But what that means differs and how it is done is based on their beliefs, which cannot be proved either right or wrong. Each may collect evidence or make arguments to support their view, but neither can prove their way, or the other, right or wrong. Yet these values, meanings, and beliefs influence behavior, perceptions, and evaluation of themselves, others, and the world around them. To use the terms of a game analogy, each community of people is playing the game of life according to different cultural rules and concepts; and each is evaluating the other on the basis of its own rules or cultural system.

SIKH/UNIVERSITY CONFLICT

Returning to the basic issue of the chapter: Why do some Sikhs feel that certain Sikh scholars and Sikh studies programs have not upheld their commitment and are not doing proper scholarship? The debate and issues are not only old ones in South Asia, but also for religions, such as fundamentalist Christianity, which have had to deal with conflict-perceiving scholarship as challenging the validity of their faith.

The debate has been emotional and people have been martyred and careers destroyed on both sides of the issue. The process will probably go on, because what is at the heart of the conflict are beliefs; and, it is beliefs, as I pointed out earlier, that are the principles on which people build their lives, whether in religion or scholarship. Thus, I will argue three basic points: (1) misunderstanding arose because American universities and certain Sikh groups are operating within two different cultural systems, (2) the validation of the Sikh faith can only be done within an Asian or Sikh cultural system, not that of Western science, and (3) developing a university program in Sikh studies gives their religion legitimacy in Western society.

Conflict of Two Cultural Systems

Religion and science operate under two systems of orientation. As I mentioned above, religion explains the "why" and science the "how." To use one to validate the other is like using oranges to comprehend apples. Each is different in structure and outcome. Although people do not like to admit it, beliefs are not subject to validation by scientific evidence. How can one prove that capitalism is the best for everyone? Westerners think it is best because it is the system they operate by in their culture. But what criteria should be used? Scientific methods only validate scientific theory and processes. Scientific method cannot validate the "why" of life, only the "how." When Sikh scriptures are subjected to study or Sikh history is examined, all that can be determined is a "how" never a "why." Understanding the "how" will never invalidate a belief.

Universities, especially publicly funded universities in the United States, operate under the principle of separation of church and state, as set forth by the Constitution of the United States. This means that publicly funded universities are committed to scientific methodology and not to the validation of any religious belief. In fact, it is unlawful for anyone in the United States, in a publicly funded institution to advocate a particular religious ideology using state resources. Of course, the courts are continually defining what this means and hearing challenges, but separation of church and state is a guiding principle. If a religious community wants to proselytize or set forth a religious ideology, they can do so under the auspices of a privately funded institution.

The state university is obligated to hire a person judged to be the best qualified scholar to serve in the position. In the case of Sikh programs, there may have been an agreement that members of the Sikh community would be an advisory body but that advice does not have to be followed. The final decision lies with the university, and they must ensure that the scholar hired has the complete freedom to pursue scholarship in a manner consistent with the practices of his or her disciplines, whether it be a science, social science, or humanities. In other words, publicly funded universities must follow scientific principles, not religious dogma.

Validation of Sikhism

As Sikh programs have been established at several universities, Sikh scriptures and society have been subjected to textual, historical, philosophical, social, and scholarly evaluation. The outcome has not always been what Sikhs would desire. In fact, some feel that the very institutions to which they have contributed significant financial resources have undermined the validity of their faith.

The basic issue comes down to the validation of a religion. I would argue that a belief system is validated by its own cultural system. In the case of the Sikhs, the South Asian cultural system defines Truth subjectively and relatively—Kabir knew he was doing the correct thing in aiding the thief because he felt it was proper in these circumstances. Conversely, what should validate Sikhism for a Sikh is not Western science and scholarship but criteria according to their own culture—the experience of reciting the *gurbani* or meditating on the morning *nam*. Because the spirit of the deity is inside a person, according to Sikh teachings, one goal is to become tuned to that internal spirit. It is by such a method that validation takes place. Western scholarship and methodology does not, and it cannot, validate or disprove Sikh beliefs.

Some Sikhs argue that Sikh studies professors do not show what it is like to be a believer from the perspective of the followers of the Gurus. In the past, social sciences have felt that their methodology should follow the physical sciences and be detached and objective. However, current thinking abandons that position and considers the subjective perspective of a Sikh or a member of another ethnic group or culture. The limitation is accepted, but the purpose is to analyze and understand, not convert.

One might ask, "Why did or do South Asians feel threatened by Western scholarship? They have a history of accomplishment from which to be proud." One cause was the development of a *colonial mentality* under British rule that set forth the Western philosophical and religious challenge in South Asia. Second, as one looks at the list of Sikhs who feel that their faith is being eroded by university scholarship, the vast majority are trained in Western science of engineering fields. Thus, it is no wonder that they think in terms of Truth being outside themselves and Truth being absolute, rather than Truth being inside a person and relative. People tend to think in terms of their training. Many who are upset with the treatment of Sikhism by academics are challenging the system using the philosophical criteria of the physical sciences rather than the social sciences or humanities.

Legitimizing Sikhism Abroad

Thus, comes the final issue. Should Sikhs invest in universities to establish Sikh studies program? The answer to that question depends on the desired goal. If the goal is to teach and validate the faith then the Sikhs would be better off creating religious universities as many of the Christian denominations have done. I feel that this is an option that should be taken very seriously.

On the other hand, there are very distinct advantages in establishing Sikh studies programs in state universities. First, it gives legitimacy in the public perception of Westerners that will never be achieved otherwise. Without being part of the university curriculum, chances are that Sikhism will remain a strange and exotic creed for most Americans and not taken seriously.

Related to the above, the establishment of Sikh studies programs will make Sikhs an established and recognized feature of the American and Western landscape; and that recognition will be present because it offers itself to be challenged by scholarship. Scholarship, again, will not validate or disprove the faith, but by its presence at a university, Sikhism will be legitimized and established in the perception of the general public.

CONCLUSION

I have tried to show that much of the tension in creating Sikh studies programs in American universities and colleges has resulted in conflicting perceptions between donors and recipients. Two groups of people are living and evaluating the other according to different cultural systems. As a result, severe misunderstandings develop. Unfortunately, the people most hurt have been the scholars hired to do what they are supposed to do. This is not the fault of any particular people or group, but misperceptions caused by two groups of people dealing with each other on the basis of two cultural systems. As a result, each had different expectations, and evaluations by each of the other lead to misunderstanding and conflict. More care should be taken in the future on both sides to know exactly the conditions under which money will be given or received for the establishment of Sikh studies.

Second, Sikhs should learn their culture and look to it to validate their faith. They ought to use the South Asian and Punjabi concept of Truth to evaluate their beliefs, not Western science and methodology. Also, Sikhs have nothing to fear by allowing scholars to examine their faith and history. No amount of scholarship can discredit their beliefs. The purpose of the scholarship is to determine how, not understand why; and, beliefs cannot be proved or disproved. If past history is valid, being subject to scholarship will result in a much stronger Sikh community.

Part III/Life in America
Asian Indian Style

In spite of the common origins and cultural precepts, modifications take place as Asian Indians adapt to their new abode. Even in countries where they are *preadapted*, such as the United States, Canada, and Great Britain, a comparison will show marked differences in the communities.[1] Consequently, the global and transnational perspective must be maintained while still setting forth the distinctively local character of the Asian Indian community.

Some of the processes set forth may be unique to the American experience, some may not. The goal is to show how Asian Indians have adjusted to life in America, not to make them unique.

[1] For example, compare Helweg (1986) with Helweg and Helweg (1990).

8/Getting Organized

INTRODUCTION

Although this study is about the Asian Indian Diaspora, with a special focus on those living in the United States, that group is not a homogeneous community. As I pointed out in the beginning of this work, India is a land of diversity. It comprises 16 major and distinct language groups and hundreds of dialects. India has at least four major religious communities and numerous smaller groups. Some of the religions, such as Christianity and the Muslin faith, seem mutually irreconcilable. Religious practices vary from organized standard ritual to individualistic and animistic beliefs. In fact, some argue that Hinduism is not a religion but is a collection of diverse and numerous belief systems under the Hindu umbrella.

Even the caste system is not applied in a standard manner. For example, in Kerala, the untouchables are more numerous and powerful than the twice-born or more pure elements. The Sikhs claim to not consider caste affiliation, but do. As Lushman Singh put it, "In the Gurdwara we are all equal. When we walk out of the Gurdwara, he knows and I know I am better than him."

ESTABLISHING UNITY IN DIVERSITY

The questions are consequently raised: How can a community of such diversity achieve and maintain the tribal like unity described in Part I of this book? How can two religious communities work together while in other cultures and context they have a tradition of animosity? The answer is complicated, but I have some ideas that may contribute to finding an answer. My ideas concern (1) the absorbing nature of Hindu culture, (2) criteria and agreement on component of identity, (3) being a part-society, (4) kinship networks, (5) associations, and (6) networks and networking.

Absorbing Nature of Hinduism

All religions of South Asia or India are not Hindu, but the Hindu influence is all pervasive all the same. One aspect that is relevant here is that Hinduism is an absorbing religion, not a proselytizing one. Therefore, there is not the conflict of religious groups like there is in Western and Middle Eastern cultures. Western missionaries always were frustrated when the people of India would accept Jesus Christ and worship Him along side Krishna or other deities. The converts in India could not grasp the concept of the exclusivity of the Christian or Muslim message.

This absorbing concept is a crucial component in maintaining unity, for one strong element causing division is eliminated as new people are absorbed into the community. This absorption quality is seen in Indian family businesses—they treat crucial and capable employees so well and in such a manner that they are almost part of the family. The benefits are not just in salary and perks. As J. S. Grewal of Singh Inc., put it, "it's a matter of treating people with respect." Grewal not only makes sure that his workers are paid well and have proper perks, but they are invited to Indian functions and family celebrations. They become more than employees, they become surrogate family members. They are absorbed into the family firm. Employment for these select is not just a job; there is a sense of loyalty and belonging that goes beyond doing a good job—it's being part of a family.

Components of Identity

In spite of the diversity among the people of India and South Asia, there is a great deal of cultural agreement at a higher level of abstraction. For example, the people of Kerala and Punjab may practice the caste system differently, but the fact that they both practice it contributes to their ethnic unity. Pakistan may be a Muslim country, but the caste system is practiced there, as it is in Burma, Sri Lanka, and Bangladesh. In the case of the Asian Indian population, the fact that they originate from the same political entity gives them an ethnic commonality, as it does for Pakistanis and other groups of South Asian origin. Among the Asian Indians, there is an agreement on belonging to a common diaspora.

Recently the term "South Asian Diaspora" is being used to treat the people from South Asia as a unit. I suspect this is an academic construct rather than a unit of identity among the South Asian community; for whenever I talk to an Asian Indian regarding a South Asian identity, they look at me in displeasure.

In the past, being South Asian was enough to have a sense of ethnic affinity. As the community has grown, however, associations have become more region specific—Punjabis associate primarily with Punjabis, Bengalis with Bengalis, and so on. With this trend towards regionalism, India has still remained a unit of identity. I have not seen or experienced South Asia as a unit of identity, although it is used frequently in the literature. This may change if the communities unite to obtain more political clout in the future, especially if the Asian Indians do not become part of the pan-Asian movement.

Part-Society

India was never a united country politically until the British took over the region. It took a neutral, powerful, and an external ruler to forge a united India out of the many disparate groups of the region. English is the uniting language of India. The work of the national government is done in English. After independence, when the country tried to switch over to Hindi, the rioting and social disruption was so great that the changeover was ignored, even though it was written into the constitution. It took and still takes an external and neutral governing body to maintain a united India.

Being a part-society, the various places hosting the Indian Diaspora are also external and neutral forces molding unity in the Indian Diaspora. Being a part-society, the Indians of India are categorized and treated as a unit. The people of Indian origin need to maintain unity if they are going to have political influence and access to resources. Also, being governed by a neutral power, no particular group feels threatened. For these and possibly other reasons, overseas Indians, being a part-society helps forge and maintain a cohesive community outside of their homeland.

Kinship

It is usual for an Asian Indian family to be scattered throughout the globe. I saw the potential of this when visiting Vijay Patel in Sydney, Australia. He was a doctor but had two brothers in Fiji who ran an export-import business there. He had another brother who dealt in real estate in the United States and another brother who looked after the ancestral land in Gujarat. Following the advice of his brothers, he has invested in the U.S. real estate market. He has bought land in India and invested in Fiji. In essence, the brothers are running an international holding company.

There are countless informally kin-based investment firms among the Asian Indian Diaspora. Such networks are generally more efficient and reliable than the commercial firms because information is reliable and free. Decisions are discussed on an informal basis. Time and costs are more efficient when decisions are informal. Also, within the family, one knows who has reliable information and who does not. These informal kinship networks are not discussed much in the literature and certainly are not noticed like the large conglomerates with their public relations specialists and fancy logos. Also, if someone help you make money without your having to pay him or her, that is going to bring you closer. I hypothesize, however, that these small but numerous family kinship networks are a much greater producer of diaspora wealth than is currently recognized.

Associations

At the turn of the century and early 20th century, many immigrant ethnic groups formed societies or associations to promote a social unity, to transmit their culture to the next generation, to look after the welfare of their own and be a political force. In those days, the welfare function of the ethnic association was most important because they looked after widows whose husbands had been injured or killed, helped the disabled, and were a political force for workers' rights.

In the United States, when the federal government took over the welfare function, some ethnic organizations privatized to become recognized by insurance companies. Among the post-1968 Asian Indian immigrants, the function of the association had changed. Associations now sponsor functions to promote cohesion in the ethnic community and entertainment. In the case of Kalamazoo, a communal dinner was the ritual for *Diwali* with local dignitaries invited to show off the community. The diverse interests and goals of an Asian Indian community such as Kalamazoo negate the idea that this group will vote in a bloc, and agents handle many of the entertainers and holy men from India. Thus, its type and local requirements largely determine an association's function. In spite of the diversity, I have classified associations networks as follows: international, pan-Asian, pan-Indian, local, and specific purpose.

A good example of an international association is the Global Organization of People of Indian Origin (GOPIO) that was described earlier. They have sponsored several conventions that have had panels dealing with everything from child rearing to business tactics. Asians Indians from all over the world are found at GOPIO and other international conventions, and it helps promote a sense of identity and pride, even for those who do not attend but read about it in *India Abroad* or other newspapers. Such organizations promote pride in the diaspora, a sense of unity, and are a political force.

An example of an association is a pan-Asian Indian organization like the Association of Indian Associations (AIA), which attempts to unify the diverse Asian Indian community in the United States. They also have national conferences with panels, resolutions, and political action. There has been a pan-Asian movement but the Asian Indian community has not been unified in joining it. Its inception was to ensure justice, equal rights, and to fight discrimination against Asians in the United States. Outsiders generally consider Asian Indians Asian because of the title, but members of the Asian Indian community do not necessarily agree (Fisher, 1980:5, 109, 114).

Other Indian organizations are national in scope but more specialized in their purpose or parochial in their vision. An example of what I call a "parochial association" is the World Sikh Organization (WSO), which focuses on Sikh interests in the United States and India; when there is turmoil in the state of Punjab, the WSO publicizes its point of view and tries to influence American officials and representatives of congress. Similarly, the Hindu Temple Society of North America obtains contributions and craftsmen from India to build Hindu temples, and Indian university and college alumni groups throughout the United States raise money to support their alma maters in India. Although parochial associations are limited and deal only with a particular religious or cultural group, membership in a parochial association does not exclude involvement in pan-Indian immigrant issues and organizations.

There are also many "specific-purpose" associations in the pan-Indian association. A good example is the Chicago-based India Development Service (IDS). Its members have worked to promote intermediate technology for India and sponsored an economic development project involving 13 villages in Karnataka. They financed an Indian to return, live in the region, and channel the expertise of Indians in the United States to develop the region. There are many other national specific-purpose organizations like the India Abroad Foundation, which has an annual fund drive to raise money for welfare agencies in India.

In the 1980s, organizations addressing women's issues developed rapidly. Working for women's rights was not new to South Asian women. The area has been one of the most progressive in the world in establishing equal rights. When the Equal Remuneration Act was passed in 1976, India became a leader in women's rights, in some ways even ahead of the United States. In the United States, however, Asian Indian women were few in number until after the 1965 liberalization of immigration rules, so it was not until the 1980s that organizations like the Committee on South Asian Women began to develop. Some groups organized on university campuses and spread from there; others like the Club of Indian Women in Chicago started as a social club and then became more active. (The club started an Indo Crisis Line in

1983 when they realized that Asian Indians were being abused; it started the Network of Professional and Self-Employed Women.)

Initially, the general Indian community shunned such organizations and denied the existence of any problems. But as groups such as the Association of Indian Women in America began receiving distress calls, people began to realize that women's problems could not be ignored.

Local Community Associations

The local community association usually forms around the local India association. For example, the India Association of Kalamazoo formed in 1960 to integrate the South Asian community—Pakistani, Sinhalese, Punjabi, Gujarati, Sikh, Hindu, and Jain. Being South Asian was a sufficient cultural bond to unite. They held celebrations to commemorate occasions like *Diwali,* Independence Day, and Republic Day: they rented a hall, the women cooked delicious Indian dishes, and they invited their white neighbors and friends to get a taste of Indian culture. In 1970, the once-a-month, one-dollar-a-head Indian movie was added to the program: the India association rented Indian movies from a distributor in Chicago and showed them at a Western Michigan University auditorium. Families, friends, and children filled the 300-seat hall to capacity. By 1980, however, the video cassette recorder (VCR) revolution made the custom obsolete.

Friendship Associations

This group is important for people like Ashok and Meena Mehra because it replaces their family; they do not have other relatives living in the area, so their network has become a surrogate kin group. In Indian culture, kinsmen come first and are not taken for granted. Thus, Meena's friend Saroj Advani would like to be part of the social group but cannot: she lives with her husband's parents, and family obligations prohibit her from being part of the Mehra group.

When family or friends visit the United States, the Mehras must treat them well to maintain family honor or *izzat*. If a family friend returns and complains that Ashok and Meena did not treat them well, the family honor is demeaned. For those living in large cities like New York and Chicago, visitors from India can become a problem.

Looking at the Indian community in the United States, one can see that it is composed of social networks like that of Ashok and Meena Mehra. Levi-Strauss distinguished "tribal" communities from "industrial" societies;[1] the social networks of Asian Indians across the United States, too, have characteristics of tribal societies for they are egalitarian, governed by consensus, try to minimize friction, stress uniformity, and emphasize reciprocity. The friendship group of Ashok and Meena Mehra is typical in that even though the members are dispersed residentially, social pressure and the need to belong keep the group unified. Having decisions made by consensus promotes this unity (Bailey, 1965). If any one member becomes autocratic, he or she will be ostracized—which would be disastrous for those who do not have family nearby.[2] Each member is careful not to cause friction—conversations center around

---

[1]In essence, I mean a group of people whose decisions are by consensus, where leadership is informally recognized, and there is minimal hierarchy in the relationships (Charbonnier, 1961).

[2]All members of an Asian Indian network generally feel a need to be part of the group. I never witnessed anyone being ostracized; however, the fear of that possibility is frequently felt.

neutral topics. Dress, house decorations, and behavior are geared to be part of the group; there is always the pressure to "keep up with the Joneses" without being too different. Additionally, gift giving is one important means of establishing and maintaining relationships (Mauss, 1967; Sahlins, 1965).

Friendships in the United States, especially in large cities, are often developed and maintained from India. For Ashok and Meena, people in India referred their initial friends to them. It is imperative for them to treat visitors from India well, for the esteem of their family and friends in India depends on it. If they are not proper hosts, the *izzat* of their kinsmen in India could be harmed; they do not want to be responsible for shaming their parents and friends.

To understand any community, it is important to know how the members associalionalize their lives. It is easy to generalize about a group's behavior, but a group's actions vary according to their context; as Leach (1976) points out the meaning of behavior and resulting symbols depends on the context in which they occur. Success and favorable recognition in the pan-Indian association involves giving the appearance of being American and being able to deal with the American political system, whereas the same behavior in the local community association or friendship association may bring disdain and condemnation—individual members may only desire role models that emulate the culture of origin in its most conservative form.

To be successful in the pan-Indian association, one needs skills in dealing with bureaucracies and national and urban politics. People from rural origins are not likely to have such skills and thus the worldly type of immigrant that is coming to the United States today is better equipped for success. Those who operate in the pan-Indian association gain meaning and success by obtaining bureaucratic or political changes that benefit the Asian Indian community—goals gained by what some would call Westernized behavior. In contrast, those in the local community associations gain meaning and success by promoting or preserving their ethnic distinctness from the host society—in other words promoting Sanskritized, or traditional Indian behavior.[3] It is in the local community that the process of identity formation becomes apparent. In the case of the Asian Indians, community unity was based first on being South Asian, but, as the community grows, identification becomes narrower—from "Indian" to "Punjabi" to a specific religion. Claims and levels of identity change over time according to circumstances. Also, the same person may operate in different associations so behavior will vary according to which association he or she is in at a particular time.

Of course developing and joining associations is not unique to Asian Indians in America. Bellah (Bellah, Madsen, Sullivan, Swidler, Tipton, 1985) describes similar behavior in traditional American society, but it is a factor in promoting unity.

CONCLUSION

As political and geographic barriers become less important and communications and travel efficiency become better, international organizations like GOPIO become more influential as do kinship and other networks. The social structure, context, and cultural unity are all in place; the Indian Diaspora now has to capitalize on the rapidly developing globalization and transnationalism to become a more significant political and economic force in today's world.

[3]The meaning of Indian or Sanskrit may vary from group to group.

9/Issues

INTRODUCTION

South Asians Main Targets of Sept. 11 Backlash. By Bala Murali Krishna

> The first major study of bias crimes in the U.S. after Sept. 11 terrorist attacks found that 96 percent of 243 incidents of violence that were documented targeted South Asians.
>
> In more than half of the incidents, the targets were Sikhs, whose men wear beards and turbans in accordance with their religious beliefs, making them similar in appearance to terrorist leader Osama bin Laden.
>
> The study, "Backlash: When Americans Turned on Its Own," by the National Asian Pacific American Legal Consortium, said one of two murders documented in the study was that of a Sikh man in Mesa, Arizona.

In spite of the successes and contributions of the Asian Indian community to America and their homeland, all is not perfect in the land of milk and honey. Some of the problems Indians face are shared with all immigrants, while others are unique to the Asians or Asian Indians. There is not agreement on all the issues either. Perceptions differ according to class and location. Some issues may even be created or exaggerated by the press while others may be ignored while being a real concern of the community. Keep in mind the complexity in dealing with the topics at hand.

People react according to their perceptions, not necessarily reality. Thus, perceptions have to be dealt with whether they conform to reality or not. Put in practical terms, if a person feels discriminated against, it is those feelings and perceptions that also have to be dealt with, regardless of the facts. For example, one of the misperceptions during the conflicts with Iraq is that Indian Americans are from the Middle East or are Asians—neither of which would they classify themselves.

PERCEPTIONS

The Asian Indians, like almost all immigrants today, have to deal with a phenomena called the "American Letters." Whether one's origins were Swede or Finn, Czech or French, the tales communicated back to the homeland were highly exaggerated. Old letters of pioneers told that all one had to do is hold a pan by a creek or lake and a fish would immediately jump into it. Others claimed that all one had to do is point a gun in the air and shoot it and flocks of birds would fall down. Many who came literally believed the streets were paved with gold.

The following letter from a Swede illustrates:

> Here in America, you do not have to go without work if you want something. I never had to look for work. I got it anyway. So there is certainly a difference between here and Sweden, where you have to bow and be humble and ask everywhere and still don't get work anyway.
>
> I have it quite good now. . . . I have the highest position in the company. If you aren't born here, you can't get in with folks the way you would like.
>
> You know those who were born here believe they are better than those who came from another country.
>
> There probably isn't another country in the world that has as much graft as America.
>
> You can't imagine how hard it was to leave again, but I also thought it was good to get away from all the oppression and all I would have to do if I stayed in Sweden. Here you are in any event, a free man in a free country (Helweg 2001:44).

The facts may have changed but the American Letters syndrome still exists. The immigrant writes back glorifying his or her life in the States exaggerating the good, especially about overcoming prejudice and discrimination to succeed.

All immigrants are generally surprised at how hard life in America is: people frequently not only work at the office from 8:00 A.M. to 5:00 P.M., but have to spend at least two additional hours commuting. When their high expectations of an easy way of life do not materialize, they became disillusioned.

Jagdish Sharma taught political science at a mid-level state university in 1970. Before coming to the United States, he heard exaggerated success stories about Indians in America and when he obtained a position at the school, he assumed that he would be a vice president within 2 years. Since he was doing well in India and had also studied at the University of London, he reasoned that the Americans would be anxious to use his talents. Unfortunately, his dreams did not materialize in 2 years, and he became very disappointed.

Part of the problem, as Jagdish's example shows, was the idea perpetuated in India that Indian degrees were equal or superior to those of American institutions. As people talk in India, they seem to have the impression that they are so superior that success is automatic in the States for all Indians. Thus, the Indian who comes to the United States, even if he or she attended a poor university in India, expects his or her credentials to be accepted as on a par with any American school. Furthermore, those who attended British schools consider themselves superior and consider it demeaning to have to prove themselves first before they can aspire to top-paying jobs.

Indian returnees also frequently brag about their accomplishments and high positions in the United States. They drop names of high officials as if they were close friends. A young Indian boasted at his wedding, "I will have my congressman get my bride her visa so she will not have to wait." Such statements are often true, but also leave the impression that the recognition and prestige of Indians in the United States is great. This is not always the case.

Immigrant women often came from families with servants, so they were spared the menial tasks of cooking, laundry, and general house cleaning (they especially abhor cleaning bathrooms). They had *ayahs* (maids) to care for the children and *malis* (gardeners) to look after the yard. Their role was to do interior decoration and flower arrangements and manage the household staff. Nandani Saigal had a rude awakening when she came to Los Angeles to attend her daughter after the birth of her first grandchild. She complained a week later, "I have to do all of the things I have never had to do in my life. I have to cook, wash, and clean house. I have always had someone else do these chores for me in India. I do not think I ever want to live here." In 1962, as a new bride in the United States, Vimla Prakash wrote home and proudly told them how she was cooking all the meals, cleaning the house, and washing and ironing her husband's clothes. Her grandfather wrote back in horror for he did not think his granddaughter should be a cook, sweeper, or *dhoban.*

DISCRIMINATION

Discrimination is a hard topic to deal with because of its reliance on qualitative and subjective data. Also, the situation is different from place to place and person to person. Does discrimination against Asian Indians exist in the United States? Of course, the answer is in the affirmative. But if you ask people if they have been discriminated against, a successful professional in Kalamazoo is likely to say, "no" while the New York City taxi driver with a college degree is likely to say, "yes."

In 1976, the India League of America held a meeting in Chicago and were surprised to learn from their surveys that 44 percent of the Indians in America claimed that they had suffered discrimination (Elkhanialy & Nicholas, 1976:5; Howe, 1986:19). Mohapatra (1979) states that his data "suggest that in general most Indians are probably discriminated against in the job market"—60 percent in the administrative category and 45 percent in the technical category. Periodicals like *India Abroad* and *India West* continue to present the theme of prejudice against Indians quite prominently (Sikri, 1987; Hudson, 1987; Gune, 1986). The possibility of inequality seems puzzling, coming from a community that claims the highest education and income level of any group in the United States.

A study completed by the U.S. Commission on Civil Rights complicates matters further. James Cunningham, of the Commission's office stated, "We know there is discrimination against Asian Americans—that is a given." The report, in fact, revealed that American-born Asian Indians were worse off than their foreign-born counterparts.[1] Other statistics reveal that between 1966 and 1980, 95 percent of Indians entering the United States were from professional backgrounds and 80 percent were English speaking.[2] Of these first-generation Indian immigrants, 73 percent had 16 or more years of schooling, as compared to only 35 percent among the American-born Indians. The average income of the foreign-born first-generation Indians was $23,600 as compared to the average of $16,300 for the American-born; the American-born Asian Indians also have the highest level of poverty (20.2 percent or five times that of any other group), which may be caused by labor-market discrimination.

---

[1]The report was titled "The Economic Status of Americans of Asian Descent" and was not released because the commissioners did not agree with the methods and conclusions (Assisi, 1988).

[2]In contrast, 74 percent of the non-Hispanic whites, 64 percent of the Filipinos, 38 percent of the Chinese, 30 percent of the Koreans, and 21 percent of the Vietnamese spoke English when they entered the country.

The assumption in India is that their people are discriminated against in the United States. Indians read American publications such as *Time* magazine that report racism and discrimination in American society, and automatically assume it includes them. (There is also a carryover from Britain where Indians are considered black or colored.) As I walked down Fifth Avenue in Manhattan, Uma Jain told me that she had been discriminated against. When I probed further, she replied, "All Indians in the United States are discriminated against. Since I am an Indian, I have been discriminated against." It was her assumption that because she was an Indian in America she must be discriminated against.

Even though a significant number of Indians succeed and their advancements far exceed that of the average American, they still feel discriminated against because "I could never be president of Ford Motor Company."[3] Ram Hiremath, who has extremely good qualifications, was very bitter and felt discriminated against when a person with lesser qualifications became the head of his division. He assumed that he did not get the job because he was an Indian.

In North Carolina, neighbors resisted the attempts of an Indian to open a Montessori school in the area. The Indian sponsors immediately cried discrimination rather than seeing the inconvenience and financial loss such actions would have on the neighborhood. It must be kept in mind that any church or school may face similar opposition, but when the Indians face rejection, they feel they are being discriminated against.

Monoranjan Dutta (1982) argues that when the median income of Asian Indian families is adjusted by considering age, education, and experience, the Asian Indian median family income is 15 percent less than that of the white family. Dutta makes the assumption that Indian credentials and experience are equal and should be given immediate acceptance in the United States.

Some Indians may have accents that are hard to understand, as in the case of Karnail Singh who had a bachelor's degree in English and education from Punjab University. His spoken English was poor and most Americans could not understand his accent. Yet, when he was not hired as an English teacher at one of the local public schools, he felt discriminated against. Ramgopal Chaudhary claimed that his degree from Agra University was equal to one from Delhi or Harvard.[4] The fact that some universities are not admitting every Asian who is better qualified than competitors from other ethnic groups may be a case in point. At present, however, research can be found to support either side of the argument. The above information seems to indicate two things: First, some Asian Indians, like other groups, use the discrimination argument to maximize their opportunities. Second, and more important, like the general Asian population in America (Hu, 1989), a split is developing

---

[3]It is interesting to note that Indians have moved into top positions. Bhaskar Menon is chief executive officer of Capitol-EMI Music North America, and Ajay Singh Mehta is president of Alfred A. Knopf publishing house. Others include Behari Gobind Lal, Pulitzer Prize–winning journalist; Amin Bhatia, Hollywood composer; Joy Cherian, Equal Employment Opportunity Commissioner; Zubin Mehta, the music director of the New York Philharmonic; Ved Mehta, staff writer for the *New Yorker* magazine; Manindra Kumar Mohapatra, dean of the Graduate School of Public Administration at Kentucky State University; and, many Asian Indians are deans and department chairs at American universities. However, Monoranjan Dutta argues that the numbers are few compared to the pool of Indian scientists and social scientists available in America (Pais & McCord, 1989).

[4]Margaret Gibson (1988) writes about more blatant discrimination recently suffered by Asian Indians; however her focus was not the educated professional (who form the focus of this book), but people of rural origins.

in the community between the very rich and very poor, in spite of the appearance of general prosperity indicated by the statistics.[5]

GLASS CEILING

Practically all Asians face the "glass ceiling," a term used to indicate " those artificial barriers based on attitudinal or organizational bias that prevent qualified individuals from advancing upward in their organization into management level positions" (Jafrey, 2002). The term was initially used to depict the blocked promotion opportunities of women in corporations, it was later expanded to include ethnic minorities of which Asian Indians are a part. In fact, the Federal Glass Ceiling Commission examined the artificial barriers faced by minority men and all women in advancing into management and decision positions in corporate America. Their 1998 report concluded that Asian Americans encountered an "impenetrable glass ceiling" (Helweg, 1993:570–75)

The glass ceiling is determined by comparing the promotion of and managerial level positions of ethnic minorities with the white population—whites being the benchmark for comparison. Educated Asian Indian American males experience a net disadvantage in rising to and obtaining management positions, although for some, their economic returns are commensurate with whites after they are at the management level. U.S.-born Asian Indian males are also at a disadvantage but not as much as the foreign born.

A typical example is one cited by Irfan Jafrey (2002:2) where an Asian Indian testified:

> When I left the company after 5 years, I was doing functions of level 4 (the highest level to which a senior engineer can progress), but they did not given me a raise in salary or acknowledgment, or recognition deserved. I was static in level 2 of the organization chart.

Why does this happen? Some argue that upper management is predominantly white and wants to keep white control. Although, I do not see a white conspiracy to keep Asian Indians down, there are certainly negative perceptions that foreign trained are not as competent as American trained, in spite of much evidence to the contrary. In a year that one Indian applied, there were 50,000 applicants for 1,800 places in Indian universities. In 2000, there were 150,000 applicants for 1,800 places. In this highly competitive environment, it is no wonder that among recruiters and knowledgeable people, degrees from India's IITs have equal stature as engineering degrees from Stanford University and the Massachusetts Institute of Technology (MIT).

Sometimes, Asian Indians are not properly evaluated because of communications skills or cultural differences. For example, self-promotion may be interpreted as defensiveness or feelings of inferiority. Not playing golf or knowing about American

[5]Arthur Hu (1989) puts the argument very well when writing about the Asian community in America. He shows that in 1980, when Asians were only 1.5 percent of the population, they comprised 5 percent of the engineers, 8 percent of all doctors, and generated more revenues than any other minority group. In college admissions in 1987, Asian Americans were 13 percent of the freshmen at Harvard, 25 percent at the University of California-Berkeley and 30 percent of the entering women at MIT. However, per capita and per person incomes are 10 percent lower than white households and many recent Asian immigrants are impoverished refugees. Their average earnings are over $50,000 a year, 50 percent greater than white families; yet their poverty level is also 38 percent greater than whites.

sports may keep them out of the network so they are not noticed nor in the informal information network.

Responses to discrimination have been varied. After a while, some start up their own business. New companies like InfoSpace.com, Imandi.com, and AskMecorp.com have paved the way for others to follow. In Silicon Valley, Indian engineers have grouped together to help each other. In Washington's Puget Sound, Mjay Vashee, a 49-year Asian Indian has helped over 200 of the Asian Indian Diaspora find jobs. At Microsoft they joke about the IM (Indian Mafia) network. Naveen Jain and Raghav Kher are two of about 10 Asian Indian engineers at Microsoft who help create web startups.

In their quest to come to the United States and gain economic security, the Asian Indians like other immigrant groups have developed a "refugee mentality," where due to their experience of harsh conditions and realities experienced in America, they have an insatiable quest for success. Or put another way, "failure is not an option." Mr. Bafna, dean of a Midwestern university engineering school, put it this way. "I tell my students from India that they must work seven times as hard as a white to even think of getting equal rewards."

One big question always arises: are they taking jobs away from Americans? Not at all—software companies need from 190,000 to 350,000 skilled information and technology workers above what the domestic labor force can supply.

H1B VISA

The H1B visa is designed to fulfill manpower needs of the United States, especially on the technical professional level, without granting permanent residency—the individual has to leave after he or she is no longer needed. How this works is that someone from outside the United States contacts or is contacted to perform the needed skill or trade until their time period is up and they are no longer needed. Then the visa holder must return to his or her homeland. The problem that bothers the Asian Indians and other immigrant groups is that this places a lot of pressure on the visa holder to find a new sponsor or some way to legitimize an extension of his or her stay or obtain permanent residency. Otherwise, the visa holder must return to his or her homeland. This creates two problems: (1) the emotional pressure on the visa holder is almost unbearable. If a visa holder returns home, he or she will be seen as a failure and probably will not be able to get a job commensurate with his or her abilities. The person will be perceived in general as a failure. (2) This gives the employer almost life or death power over the visa holder that can lead to exploitation. The visa holder has to do as told, or he or she will be forced to leave and not be allowed back into the United States.

MODEL MINORITY

Since President Reagan first used the term "Model Minority" to refer to the successes and ideal behavior of the Asian community or certain subgroups within the Asian community, the model minority syndrome has been one of controversy. People still question Reagan's motivation. Was he just praising the Asians? Was he trying to create animosity between the Asians and the African Americans—a sort of British style "divide and rule"?

As can be inferred from above, the Asian Indians are proud of their accomplishments in the States and downplay their failings or mistakes. If they openly ascribe to President Reagan's categorization, they become split off from the other minority groups and not only isolated, but hated, resented and the targets of violence. On the other hand, if they do not ascribe to President Reagan's analysis, they will lose their position of professional respect they have obtained in the eyes of the host society. It is a double-bind situation they find themselves in.

GOVERNMENT RESPONSIBILITY— BASED ON BLOOD OR RESIDENCE?

Generally identity is determined by blood or residence. For example, one can become an American after living in the geographical boundaries of the United States. However, my family and I can live in Japan for centuries and not be Japanese. Yet, Japanese can live in the United States for generations and still remain Japanese— they were also Americans.

This brings us to the issue of who is responsible for the diasporic Indians? The government of India has not been consistent on this issue. In my opinion, both sides talk loyalty but practice expediency. Those in India see India as the spiritual homeland, the place where those abroad look to for spiritual strength and sustenance. The Indian temples of the south have been especially supportive in providing money, artisans, and priests to support the overseas religious community.

The government has not been so consistent. In the 1950s through the 1970s, the admonitions from Delhi were for NRIs to become good citizens of their country of residence. For those areas where the PIOs were being discriminated against, the government of India did not feel responsible. The attitude seemed to be "you overseas Indians have made a choice, now live with it. Don't expect the Indian government to bail you out."

Starting in the late 1970s and early 1980s, various state governments, like Punjab and Gujarat, followed by the national government of India, began to realize that they could make money by getting overseas Indians to invest and/or return to their homeland with their money.

Gujarat's INDEXb was a good example. The organization provided individualized investment portfolios with analysis on markets and investment opportunities. It also got the returnees many privileges, such as jumping the wait-list to obtain immediate telephone connections, admission to good schools for one's children, and purchases of motor scooters or cars.

The central government had such schemes as giving NRIs preferential treatment in buying the apartments built and used for the ASIA games India hosted. However, granting dual citizenship was a major Indian government shift in policy and indicates an acceptance of responsibility for taking care of the PIOs scattered throughout the world.

INVISIBILITY VERSUS VISIBILITY

The American press is an important ingredient in informing, influencing, educating, and shaping public opinion. Thus, when Matthew Shepherd, a student at the University of Wyoming, was beaten because of his sexual orientation, it made national headlines and resulted in demonstrations and restitution. The incident of Reginald Denny being pulled from his truck during the Los Angeles riots is still prominent in many minds. Yet, in Queens, New York, when Rishi Maharaj, was beaten by three white youths using baseball bats and shouting racist slurs and statements, the press did not take notice.

Geo George, a student, notices that crimes against foreign nationals, like South Asians, go relatively unnoticed by the press. They are an invisible minority. George argues that the "invisibles" need to ban together to obtain national attention and to be noticed, considered, and to be treated fairly (George, 2001).

The South Asian community has become noticed because of their ability in business. Initially it was their success in reviving the nationwide motel industry and dominating the newsstand kiosks in New York City. More recently the business press such as *Business Week* and the *Wall Street Journal* have brought the business acumen of the Asian Indians to the fore. But, they face a dilemma, the more they are noticed the more likely it is that they will lose benefits of disadvantaged minority status. As a colleague put it: "Why should the Asian Indians with their high incomes get the benefits designed to help disadvantaged African Americans?"

MARRIAGE

Asian Indians in the United States want their children to marry within the Indian community because they want to ensure that they will be cared for in their old age. Indian immigrants often assume that white girls are not loyal, that they are sexually promiscuous, and that they believe in divorce. This places a strain on the relationship of a culturally mixed marriage: the non-Indian spouse senses a lack of trust which in turn leads to friction between the husband and wife.[6]

CARE FOR THE ELDERLY

Care of the elderly is a primary concern. Indian parents do not like the concept of nursing homes for the aged. According to them, Americans do not take care of old people and are not concerned for them when they are feeble. Since India does not have a state-controlled, comprehensive social security system, parents have had to rely on their children, especially the eldest son for their care. Even Indian parents who have lived in the States for several decades fear old age. Accordingly, they try to find an Indian spouse for their son to ensure his loyalty.

WHAT ABOUT OUR CHILDREN?

Surprises

During my research in India during the early 1980s, my wife and I were at the Welham School for girls talking with a group of teenagers who were born in the States. As the conversation progressed, my wife asked, "What do you think about arranged marriages?"

---

[6]It has been my experience that this is not true. Generally, the white women that Indian men do marry have a strong loyalty to the kin group and are very kind to elders.

One girl spoke for the group when she said, "We agree with the practice. Our parents are older and wiser and can make a much better decision than we can. They are much better in determining what is compatible with our personality."

Ethnicity 2000

The Asian Indian students at the University of Michigan held a conference and invited me to make a presentation. When I arrived, many things impressed me. It was possibly the best-organized conference I had ever attended. They had a special folder prepared for me with all the relevant information as well as someone assigned to assist me in any way needed. Their direction was clear—the major goal was success in business, at least that was my initial impression; yet, when it came for evening recreation, they enjoyed doing Bangra-type dancing and Bollywood[7]-type singing and dancing. They knew the latest hit tunes from India and when someone on stage entertained, their voices, facial expressions, and body movements exactly mimicked popular films from India.

Were these students blending East and West? No, that was not the case. What was evident to me was that they were compartmentalizing their lives.[8] When dealing with the Westerners, they wore blue or pinstriped suites and spoke perfect English, but their Indian culture came through in their consideration of invited and respected guests. I received a thoughtful handwritten note of appreciation, which does not happen all that often in my experience. I would not say that the Indian students were blending East with West or Asian Indian culture with American culture. What they did do, however, was compartmentalize their lives and seemed to accept or reject Western or Asian Indian traits or blocks with little or no modification.

Misperceptions

To an outsider, it is easy to come to a superficial conclusion that the second generation is casting off their Indian heritage—eating beef at McDonald's or being sucked into American commercialism (Mishra & Mohapatra, 2002:17–19). But such a conclusion only leads to misinterpretations as to what is really happening.

What is not happening is their copying of Western culture or rejecting Indian culture, or vice versa. What is happening is that the second generation is creating something new. It's not an amalgamation but a new creation.

Asian Indian Youth Culture

The beliefs that unite the Asian Indian students can be quickly identified and can be surprising. What follows is not an exhaustive list, but some ideas that I see, but there is much more. What I see may not be universal, for Asian Indians in different contexts (cultural, political, and geographical) yield different results.

First, Asian Indians are taught that they are *discriminated against,* that there is a *glass ceiling* prohibiting their advancement into upper management positions. To

---

[7]"Bollywood" is the term used for the Bombay Cinema industry—the producer of the largest number of films annually in the world.

[8]Compartmentalization is a social process first identified by Milton Singer in his travels in India (Singer, 1972). It's a process by which people divide their lives up into spheres. By doing this they can avoid cultural and social conflict (Helweg & Helweg, 1990).

G. S. Grewal

Much has and is still being written about the loss of identity for Asian Indians in North America. However, this nationally recognized Bhangra Dance Troupe have a strong grasp of their identity and pass it on.

cope with this situation, they have to be somewhere between two or three times as good as any white person to maintain an equality with whites as they rise up the corporate ladder. This engenders a feeling of accomplishment and as a result there is a sense of superiority that if a white person can do something, the Indian can do it better. He or she may not get the recognition he or she deserves, but is capable and can and does better quality work.

Second, Asian Indians take *pride* in being Asian Indian in America. Whether they go to India, or remain in the States, they have money and are treated with respect. In the States, many have a sense of superiority because their academic record is high and accomplishments are numerous.

In American culture, a child is likely to get the greatest notoriety in sports. One need only read Asian Indian on newspapers, such as *India Abroad* to see that the Asian Indian community gives greater *emphasis to scholarship*. Being good in sports has its advantages, but it also is kept in its place.

In spite of what may seem like a generation gap, Asian Indians still have an underlying respect for parents and elders. Literature is starting to come out concerning the disrespect Asians Indians have for their elders. It occurs, but not to the degree the media leads people to believe. Elders live with their children, and some go into business with their offspring. The point is that elders are still part of the family network.

Like any immigrant, the influx of people from the country of origin as well as close communication with the country of origin tends to promote the beliefs and values of the sending community. New immigrants not only promote the values and beliefs of the sending society but good communication help reassert the traditional social mechanisms that promote and inhibit behaviors. Emigration does not stop the gossip network or other mechanisms from having their impact on the new immigrant.

G. S. Grewal

This is Darshan S. Grewal and his uncle, Gurmale S. Grewal on the night they both received awards from the BIA, Building Industry Association Awards in 2001. Darshan received the "Young Builder of the Year" award. He was particularly praised for the home designs he originated. Gurmale S. Grewal received the "Developer of the Year" award.

No matter how well parents and children relate, the end result is that parents and children must compromise sufficiently to maintain family unity. Often, Indian children are not averse to an arranged marriage and the parents find spouses. If they cannot find someone in the United States, they spread the word in India. The children may meet a potential spouse at a group like an Indian student association and then the parents arrange the marriage with a person of their child's choosing.

In spite of the worry and heartache parents experience, the Asian Indian children generally develop pride in their cultural heritage. Asha's parents worried about her growing up in America and forsaking her heritage. However, when she went to the university, she associated with other Indian students and developed a strong commitment toward India. As Indian children become adults, they may not have the same ideology as their counterparts in India, but the degree of rebelliousness that many elders fear does not materialize. Most Asian Indian children grow up with a tendency towards a healthy compromise and absorbing the best of both worlds.

As husbands, wives, and parents have problems with the changing roles required in America, so do children. Jagir Singh typifies these feelings:

> My parents exposed me to the world and its many opportunities. I learned how to deal with life and its many ramifications. They gave me every opportunity. Now they expect me to be a docile and obedient son when I have all this energy inside me wanting to go out and experience what life has to offer.

Giving children a broad experience creates an entrepreneurial mentality that is not compatible with docile obedience and unquestioning acceptance to the dictates of elders. Also, with the influence of Western ideas, a "culturally split family" develops where the children start living with a different set of values, beliefs, and interpretations from their parents. These conflicts, however, are often solved by the children, who compartmentalize their lives just as their parents do.[9]

With the increased globalization and transnational perception of the Asian Indians, along with the well-defined identity of the next generation, it is likely that that India and its diaspora are likely to become viable political, social, and economic forces both in India and their countries of residence.

[9]See Helweg and Helweg (1990).

Epilogue

The nature, composition, and processes of human capital on the global level have changed considerably since the days when Christopher Columbus tried to enslave native Americans. Economic considerations have always been there, but the nature of their institutions and factors making forced change seem voluntary, have made strong inroads. It was the quest for new products that played a significant role in the emigration from mother India. Due to abusers in the system, the quest, even now, often turns out to be a hollow dream.

Asian Indian emigration to America seemed to be the fulfillment of everyone's desires but it also turned into disaster. Now with the new immigration, movement may be based on reliable information with streams of people using their brains over their brawn. However, the future is hard to predict. One thing is certain, we as scholars still continue to use antiquated theoretical designs for antiquated social processes.

Nationalism, citizenship, commerce, and world-wide frameworks are demanding new methodologies and new concepts to better understand this new immigration that is sweeping the globe. As this study has shown, approaches to the situations have varied in the past and continue to do so in the present. This is partly due to the great variety of institutions and situations now faced by mobile men crossing the globe to gain sufficient employment. Even localized situations seem to have international consequence. A Sikh has to do penance in Punjab for a miscalculation in California. Filling labor needs in America provides capital for relatives in a home village to pay taxes. Now, the smallest infraction can have international consequences. However, processes like the globalization of capital have yet to be incorporated into our research frameworks.

The Asian Indians of this drama have developed various ways to deal with the new economy. Various kinds of associations and family units have been significant and vital contributors to the growth of capital. These family units on the other side of the globe are the beneficiaries, not necessarily the country from which the resources are being extracted, nor those who are supplying for their families and villages first. The important point to remember is that actions on one part of the globe have ramifications for the other side and if we are not mindful and do not give credence to the complexities of the mobile human capital of today's world, many lose in capital and or human life.

The United States claims to be a land of immigrants. I believe that it is these immigrants that have enabled the United States to exist in various times of prosperity and poverty. A look at the Asian Indians living in the United States today shows that they have been tremendous contributors and foundation builders to enable the United States to maintain its present position of world leadership.

During the depression, Michigan was holding a writer's workshop. During those days, discussions arose as to how to develop an identity for the Great Lakes State. Suggestions came from all regions of the economy: lumbering, iron ore extraction, manufacturing and so on. Suddenly, one of the individuals in their group had a flash of insight. He began to reveal something that none had considered. The wealth and identity of Michigan was in her people, not in technology, products or exploitation. It is a lesson many never learned. If we are going to understand the world economy, power structure, and mobile human capital, we are going to have to understand the people first. Unfortunately, we have not learned that lesson, but a review of the material presented here will bring the reader to the same conclusions.

Appendix A
Profile of the Asian Indian
Community in Kalamazoo, Michigan,
1990–2000

LANGUAGE PROFILE

	1990		2000	
Native Language	**Number**	**Percent**	**Number**	**Percent**
Gujarati	66	25.88	108	34.06
Punjabi	40	15.69	30	9.46
Hindi	24	9.41	56	17.66
English	22	8.63	3	0.94
Telugu	18	7.06	17	5.36
Kannada	18	7.06	21	6.62
Marathi	14	5.49	20	6.30
Sindhi	13	5.10		
Malayalam	12	4.71	8	2.30
Tamil	9	3.53	26	8.20
Urdu	5	1.96	18	5.67
Marawari	4	1.57	1	0.31
Hausa	2	0.78		
Arabic	2	0.78		
Pushto	2	0.78		
Filipino	1	0.39		
Konkani	1	0.39	4	1.26
Oriya	1	0.39	1	0.31
Kanuri	1	0.39		
Nepali	1	0.39	1	0.31
Bengali	1	0.39	3	0.31
Total	**317**		**317**	

RELIGION PROFILE

	1990		2000	
Religious Affiliation	**Number**	**Percent**	**Number**	**Percent**
Hinduism	167	65.49	249	77.50
Christianity	33	12.94	15	4.67
Jainism	18	7.06	21	6.54
Islam	16	6.27	18	5.60
Sikhism	13	5.10	13	4.04
None	4	1.57	3	0.93
Judaism	2	0.78		
Undisclosed	2	0.78		
Zoroastrianism	2	0.62	2	0.62
Total	**321**		**321**	

CITIZENSHIP PROFILE

Country of Citizenship	1990		2000	
	Number	Percent	Number	Percent
India	146	57.25	91	30.03
United States	82	32.16	206	67.98
Canada	5	1.96	3	0.99
Germany			1	0.33
Sweden			2	0.66
Pakistan	4	1.57		
United Kingdom	3	1.18		
Nigeria	3	1.18		
Guyana	3	1.18		
Kenya	2	0.78		
Oman	1	0.39		
Abu-Dhabi	1	0.39		
Malaysia	1	0.39		
Israel	1	0.39		
Undisclosed	3	1.18		
Total	**303**		**303**	

OCCUPATIONS PROFILE

Occupation	1990		2000	
	Number	Percent	Number	Percent
Engineers			31	10.40
IT Engineer			1	0.33
Biochemists			1	0.33
Chemists, Biologists, Scientists, Technologists, Architects, Pharmacists	52	19.61		
Medical doctors			44	14.86
Dentists	36	14.12		
Students	35	13.73		
Teachers, professors	16	6.27		
Teachers			4	1.35
Housewives	71	27.84	1	0.33
Horticulturist			1	0.33
Cashiers, clerks, secretaries	8	3.14		
Clerical			16	5.40
Business (owners)	5	1.96	39	13.10
Business analyst			1	0.33
Data management specialist			1	0.33
Managers, administrators	5	1.96		
Managers, store			1	0.33
Pilot			1	0.33
Chemists			3	1.01
Managers			4	1.39
Nurses	4	1.57		
Salesmen, marketing	3	1.18		
Controllers, accountants	3	1.18		
Librarians	3	1.18	1	0.33
Veterinarians	3	1.18		
Foremen, factory workers	3	1.18		
Computer operators	2	0.78		
Computer software			5	1.68

(*continued*)

OCCUPATIONS PROFILE (*continued*)

Occupation	1990		2000	
	Number	**Percent**	**Number**	**Percent**
Computer engineer			1	0.33
Medical technologist	1	0.39		
Mechanic	1	0.39		
Cinematographer	1	0.39		
Technical			3	1.01
Professors			16	5.40
Administration			3	1.61
Retired			23	7.77
Physical therapist			7	2.36
Electrical supervisor			1	0.33
Financial assistant			1	0.33
Financial administrator			1	0.33
Research scientist			3	1.01
Dental hygienists			1	0.33
Production, television			1	0.33
Esthetician			1	0.33
Pharmacist			6	2.02
Accountant			1	0.33
Food technician			1	0.33
Data processor			1	0.33
Artists			1	0.33
Students			6	2.02
Undisclosed	1	0.39		
Total of Sample	**255**		**232**	

Source: V. Mehta, Chairman of the Kalamazoo India Association.

Appendix B
Profile of Asian Indian Population
in the United States

DEMOGRAPHICS

- Based on the count of the 2000 Census, there are 1.7 million people in the United States who identify themselves as Asian Indians or Indian Americans—first- and second-generation immigrants or those whose ancestors migrated to the United States from India. They reflect the multi-ethnic, multi-religious and multilingual society of India.
- Indian Americans are represented in many fields including academics and entrepreneurs, doctors and lawyers, engineers and financiers.
- The Asian Indian population in the United States has recorded a phenomenal growth of 106 percent in the past decade, the highest among all Asian origin groups.
- The Asian Indian population has risen more than twofold in 2000, growing to 1.7 million, or 0.6 percent of the total U.S. population, from 815,447, or 0.3 percent of the total population in 1990.
- The Indian population has risen to become the third largest Asian American community in the United States, after the Chinese and Filipinos.

ACHIEVEMENTS

Medical

- Five percent of all physicians in the United States obtained their primary degree from India.*

Education

- More than 87 percent of Indians in America have completed high school while at least 62 percent have some college education.
- As much as 58 percent of Indian Americans over the age of 25 hold a bachelor's degree or higher. Eighty percent of the men have college degrees.
- High levels of education have also enabled Indian Americans to become a productive segment of the U.S. population, with 72.3 percent participating in the work force. Of these work force participants, 43.6 percent are employed in managerial and professional specialties.
- Technical, sales, and administrative support occupations constitute another 33.2 percent of the work force. The remaining 23.3 percent of the population works in other areas, such as operators, fabricators, laborers, and precision production.
- More than 5,000 Indian Americans today serve as faculty members in institutions of higher education in the United States.

- Of the 16,873 American-born second generation, between ages 18 and 24, 14,776 graduated from high school and 10,965 received a college education.

High-Tech/Silicon Valley

- According to University of California, Berkeley Study, about one-third of the engineers in Silicon Valley are of Indian descent, while 7 percent of the valley's high-tech firms are led by Indian CEOs. Some successes are well known, such as Vinod Khosla, cofounder of Sun Microsystems, and Sabeer Bhatia, who founded Hotmail and sold it to Microsoft for $400 million.
- About 300,000 Indian Americans work in technology firms in California's Silicon Valley.
- Indian Americans account for more than 15 percent of high-tech startups in that region. The median income of Indian Americans in that region is estimated to be $125,000 (average $200,000) a year.
- Indians started four out of ten startups in Silicon Valley, and they account for 15 percent of employees in technology firms.

Notable Asian Indians

- Massachusetts' Guru Deshpande, cofounder of a number of network-technology companies is worth between $4 billion and $6 billion.
- Two Indian Americans—Har Gobind Khorana of the Massachusetts Institute of Technology and the late Subrahmanyan Chandrasekhar of the University of Chicago—have been awarded the Nobel Prize, in medicine and physics respectively.
- NASA's premier X-ray observatory was named the Chandra X-ray Observatory in honor of the late Subrahmanyan Chandrasekhar. Known to the world as Chandra, he was widely regarded as one of the foremost astrophysicists of the 20th century. The observatory was launched into space in July 1999.
- Dr. Kalpana Chawla added a new chapter to the history of the Indian American community. In 1997, she became the first Indian or Indian American to fly in a U.S. shuttle. She was part of the space shuttle *Columbia* flight STS-87.
- Walt Disney Corporation paid Mannoj Night Shyamalan $2.5 million for the screenplay of the movie *The Sixth Sense*.

Visas

- Fifty percent of H1B visas issued each year go to Indians. The U.S. consulate in Chennai (India) issues the highest number of visas in the world.

Economics

- Forty-five percent of the women in the Asian Indian community are employed outside the home.*
- Fifty percent of the Asian Indian community owns their own homes.*
- The estimated annual buying power of Indian Americans in the United States is around $20 billion.
- The median family income of Indian households is 25 percent higher than for all U.S. households.

- Indian Americans own 30 percent of all motels and hotels in the United States.*
- The number of Indian American new economy millionaires is in the thousands.
- Indians are running Fortune 500 companies. Rono Dutta is president of United Airlines, and Rakkesh Gangwal is president and CEO US Airways. Calcutta-born Rajat Gupta, a member of the American Indian Foundation is managing director of consulting giant McKinsey & Co.
- Forty percent of Indian immigrants have taken up U.S. citizenship.*
- Indicates fact was based on 1990 census; other statements are based on later figures.

*Sources: Embassy of India. 2001. Indian American Community Story of Achievements. India Business Relations, Washington: Embassy of India. Indians in USA, wysiwyg://www.geocities.com//kheduvora/indians_in_usa.htm. Tinseltown. 2003: Tinseltown.TV: Mediapack, http:www.tinseltownonline.com/mediapack.Asians__pop.html

ASIAN INDIANS VERSUS AVERAGE AMERICANS (1998)

	Indian	Average American
Professional jobs	30%	13%
Average annual household income	$88,000	$51,000
Graduates	57%	20%
Educated Internet savvy	57%	20%
Online	69%	43%

U.S. ASIAN POPULATION, 2000

National Origin	Population	Percent
Total	11,898,828	100.0
Asian Indian	1,899,599	16.0
Bangladeshi	57,412	0.5
Bhutanese	212	
Burmese	16,720	0.1
Cambodian	206,052	1.7
Chinese, except Taiwanese	2,734,841	23.0
Filipino	2,364,815	19.9
Hmong	186,310	1.6
Indochinese	199	
Indonesian	63,073	0.5
Iwo Jiman	78	
Japanese	1,148,932	9.7
Korean	1,228,427	10.3
Laotian	198,203	1.7
Malaysian	18,566	0.2
Maldivian	51	
Nepalese	9,399	0.1
Okinawan	10,599	0.1
Pakistani	204,309	1.7
Singaporean	2,394	
Sri Lankan	24,587	0.2
Taiwanese	144,795	1.2
Thai	150,283	1.3
Vietnamese	1,223,736	10.3
Other Asian, not specified	369,430	3.1

Asian Indian U.S. Geographic Residence, by State, 1990 and 2000

State	1990	2000	State	1990	2000
Alabama	4,348	6,900 (0.2%)	Nebraska	1,218	3,273 (0.2%)
Alaska	472	723 (0.1%)	Nevada	1,825	5,535 (0.3%)
Arizona	5,663	14,741 (0.3%)	New Hampshire	1,697	3,873 (0.3%)
California	159,973	314,819 (0.9%)	New Jersey	79,440	169,180 (2.0%)
Colorado	3,836	11,720 (0.3%)	New Mexico	1,593	3,104 (0.2%)
Connecticut	11,755	23,662 (0.7%)	New York	140,985	251,724 (1.3%)
Delaware	2,183	5,280 (0.7%)	North Carolina	9,847	26,197 (0.3%)
Dist. of Columbia	1,601	2,845 (0.5%)	North Dakota	482	822 (0.1%)
Florida	29,117	70,740 (0.4%)	Ohio	20,848	38,752 (0.3%)
Georgia	13,926	46,132 (0.6%)	Oklahoma	4,546	8,502 (0.2%)
Hawaii	1,015	1,441 (0.1%)	Oregon	3,508	9,575 (0.3%)
Idaho	473	1,289 (0.1%)	Pennsylvania	28,396	57,241 (0.5%)
Illinois	64,200	124,723 (1.0%)	Rhode Island	1,975	2,942 (0.3%)
Indiana	7,095	14,685 (0.2%)	South Carolina	3,900	8,356 (0.2%)
Iowa	3,021	5,641 (0.2%)	South Dakota	287	611 (0.1%)
Kansas	3,956	8,153 (0.3%)	Tennessee	5,911	12,835 (0.2%)
Kentucky	2,922	6,711 (0.2%)	Texas	55,795	129,365 (0.6%)
Louisiana	5,083	8,280 (0.2%)	Utah	1,557	3,065 (0.1%)
Maine	607	1,021 (0.1%)	Vermont	529	858 (0.1%)
Maryland	28,330	49,909 (0.9%)	Virginia	20,494	48,815 (0.7%)
Massachusetts	19,719	43,801 (0.7%)	Washington	8,205	23,992 (0.4%)
Michigan	23,845	54,631 (0.5%)	West Virginia	2,154	2,856 (0.2%)
Minnesota	8,234	12,169 (0.2%)	Wisconsin	6,914	12,665 (0.2%)
Missouri	6,111	12,169 (0.2%)	Wyoming	240	355 (0.1%)
Montana	248	379 (—)			

STATISTICAL PROFILE OF ASIAN INDIAN ACHIEVEMENTS IN UNITED STATES

Population

1920s	5,000 (estimate)
1960	5,000 (estimate)
1970	350,000
1990	815,477
1997	1.215 million
2000	1.7 million

	Growth	*Growth Rate*
1980–1990	8.5%	103%
1990–1997	55%	
1990–2000		105.87%
2000	Third largest Asian ethnic group behind Chinese and Filipinos.	

Undocumented

1988	15,000
1992	28,000

Place of Residence

- Largest portion reside in California, New York, New Jersey, Texas, Florida, and Illinois, in that order.
- Each has over 60,000. But every state has sizable Indian population.

Education

- 85 percent have attained high school level.
- 20 percent have attained bachelor's degree or higher.

Participation in Work Force

- 72.3 percent of total
- 84 percent of men
- 43.6 percent managerial/professional
- 33.2 percent technical sales and administrative support
- 22.2 percent other areas, that is, fabricators, laborers, and precision production

Income

- $17,777 per capita (national per capita is $14,143)
- $56,143 mean household earnings in 1989
- 9.7 percent poverty rate (13 percent is national average)
- $20 billion annual buying power

Family

- 3.83 average size
- 89.2 percent married couples

Organizations

- Over 1,000 nationally, some of which belong to unifying groups.

Professionalism

- 55,000 or more teaching in American universities
- 4,000 members of Asian Indian Hotel Owners Association (AIHOA)
- 50 percent of the lodging sector of the economy, which is about 640,000 rooms
- 12,500 motels with a market value of $31 billion are owned by AIHOA members.
- American Association of Physicians from India is a powerful force and the only Asian Indian association to have a legislative office in Washington.

Second Generation

- 14,778 of 16,873 between ages 18–24 have graduated from high school and 10,965 have completed a college education.

- 65 percent of 18–24 age group have some college education.
- Pursuing wider educational interests—first generation focused on science and technology, second generation includes social science, liberal arts, and traditional science.

Politics

- Becoming a voting force
- Influences through campaign contributions
- A few have obtained public office.
- Individuals and associations have influenced U.S. policy towards India.

Appendix C
Milestones in the History of Asian Indians in North America

1820 Recorded entry of one Indian immigrant.

1901 First significant immigration of Sikhs to the West Coast.

1907 First major outbreaks of violence against Indian immigrants in Washington State.

1910 East Indians declared eligible for citizenship in *United States v. Balsara.*

1917 Congress enacts law barring East Indians and other Asians from becoming citizens.

1923 The Supreme Court rules in *United States v. Bhagat Singh Thind* that East Indians are not eligible for citizenship because they are not white according to a 1790 naturalization law that restricted citizenship only to "free white" people.

1926 An Indian lawyer, Sakaram Ganesh Pandit, successfully argues that East Indians are Aryans (hence white) and is allowed to retain his American citizenship.

1946 Congress enacts law allowing East Indians citizenship and allots India an annual immigration quota of 100 people.

1956 Dilip Singh Saund becomes the first South Asian to be elected to Congress.

1965 New immigration laws enacted to allow Indians—and every nationality—equal immigration rights and to give preferential treatment to professionals and relatives of citizens and permanent residents.

1982 Move to reform immigration law is launched in Congress. Asian Indians lobby against proposals that seek to deny immigration rights to certain categories of relatives.

1985 India relaxes currency restrictions to provide a greater incentive for non-resident Indians (NRIs) to invest and become involved in collaborative and technological transfer schemes that promote India's development.

1986 Asian Indian community mobilizes to influence U.S. immigration legislation, supporting family reunification and the relaxation of restrictions on foreign medical graduates (FMGs). The Immigration Reform and Control Act provides amnesty for undocumented aliens who had been in the United States since before 1982 (the program began on May 5, 1987).

1987 The Immigration Act of 1987 is introduced, making visas easier to obtain for independent immigrants (people who do not have immediate family connections in the United States). Organized racial violence against Asian Indians by groups calling themselves "dot busters" erupts in Jersey City.

1988 Asian Indians take a prominent role in the United States presidential election.

1989   Asian Indians are denied affirmative action preferences by the city of San Francisco, Asian Indians, along with other Asian groups, react against the "model minority" label given them by President Reagan. First global convention of people of Indian origin was held in New York City.

Appendix D
History of Immigration Legislation

Outlined below are thumbnail sketches of immigration-related legislation adopted between 1790 and 1990.

1790   In an area previously controlled by individual states, an act was adopted that established a uniform rule for naturalization by setting the residency requirement at 2 years.

1819   Congress enacted the first significant federal legislation relating specifically to immigration. Among its provisions it (1) established the continuing reporting of immigration to the United States and (2) set specific maintenance rules for passengers of ships leaving U.S. ports for Europe.

1864   Congress first centralized control over immigration under the secretary of state with a commissioner. The importation of contract laborers was legalized in this legislation.

1875   Direct federal regulation of immigration was established by a law that prohibited entry of prostitutes and convicts.

1882   The Chinese exclusion law curbed Chinese immigration. Also excluded were persons convicted of political offences, lunatics, idiots, and persons likely to become public charges. The law placed a head tax on each immigrant.

1885   Admission of contract laborers was banned.

1888   Physicians were arrested—the first since 1798—to provide for expulsion of aliens.

1891   The U.S. government established the Bureau of Immigration under the Treasury Department to federally administer all immigration laws (except the Chinese Exclusion Act).

1903   Immigration law was consolidated. Polygamists and political radicals were added to the exclusion list.

1906   Procedural safeguards for naturalization were enacted. Knowledge of English was made a basic requirement.

1907   A bill increased the head tax on immigrants, and added people with physical or mental defects or tuberculosis and children unaccompanied by parents to the exclusion list. Japanese immigration became restricted.

1917   Added to the exclusion list were illiterates, persons of psychopathic inferiority, men as well as women entering for immoral purposes, alcoholics, stowaways, and vagrants.

1921   The first quantitative immigration law was adopted. It set temporary annual quotas according to nationality.

1924   The first permanent immigration quota law established a preference quota system, non-quota status, and consular control system. It also established the border patrol.

1929   The annual quotas of the 1924 Act were made permanent.

1943   Legislation provided for the importation of agriculture workers from North, South, and Central America—the basis of the "Bracero Program." At the same time the Chinese exclusion laws were repealed.

1946   Procedures were adopted to facilitate immigration of foreign-born wives, fiancé(e)s, husbands, and children of U.S. armed forces personnel.

1948   The first U.S. policy was adopted to facilitate immigration of persons fleeing persecution. It permitted 205,000 refugees to enter the United States over 2 years (later increased to 415,000).

1950   The grounds for exclusion and deportation of subversives were expanded. All aliens were required to report their address annually.

1952   The multiple laws that governed immigration and naturalization to that time were brought into one comprehensive statute. It (1) reaffirmed the national quota system, (2) limited immigration from the Eastern hemisphere while leaving the Western hemisphere unrestricted, (3) reestablished preference for skilled workers and relatives of U.S. citizens and permanent resident aliens, and (4) tightened security and screening standards and procedures.

1953   The 1948 law was increased to admit over 200,000 refugees above the existing limit.

1965   The national origins quota system was abolished. But still maintained was the principle of numerical restriction by establishing 170,000 hemispheric and 20,000 per country ceilings and a seven-category preference system (favoring close relatives of U.S. citizens and permanent resident aliens), and tightening security and screening standards and procedures.

1976   The 20,000 per-country immigration ceilings and the preference system became applied to Western hemisphere countries. The separate hemispheric ceilings were maintained.

1980   The Refugee Act removed refugees as a preference category and established clear criteria and procedures for their admission. It also reduced the worldwide ceiling for immigrants from 290,000 to 270,000.

1986   The Immigration Reform and Control Act (IRAC) was a comprehensive reform effort. It (1) legalized aliens who had resided in the United States in an unlawful status since January 1, 1982; (2) established sanctions prohibiting employers from hiring, recruiting, or referring for a fee aliens known to be unauthorized to work in the United States; (3) created a new classification of temporary agricultural worker and provided for the legalization of certain such workers; and (4) established a visa waiver pilot program allowing the admission of certain nonimmigrants without visas.

   Separate legislation stipulated that immigrants whose status was based on a marriage be conditional for 2 years, and that they must apply for permanent status within 90 days after their second year anniversary.

1989   A bill adjusted from temporary to permanent status certain nonimmigrants who were employed in United States as registered nurses for at least 3 years and met established certification standards.

1990   Comprehensive immigration legislation provided for (1) increased total immigration under an overall flexible cap of 675,000 immigrants beginning in fiscal year 1995, preceded by a 700,000 level during fiscal years 1992 through 1994; (2) created separate admission categories for family-sponsored, employment-based, and diversity immigrants; (3) revised all grounds for exclusion and deportation, significantly rewriting the political and ideological grounds and repealing some grounds for exclusion; (4) authorized the Attorney General to grant temporary protection to undocumented alien nationals of designated countries subject to armed conflict or natural disasters and designated such status for Salvadorans; (5) revised and established new nonimmigrant admission categories; (6) revised and extended through fiscal year 1994 the Visa Waiver Program; (7) revised naturalization authority and requirements; and (8) revised enforcement activities.

Sources: "History of Immigration Legislation." FAIR. Jan. 1999. http://www.fairus.org.html/ 03003604.htm.

Appendix E
A Chronology of Some Events
Related to India and Indians
in the United States

1492   Columbus sailed westward on his way to India. He reached an island he named San Salvador after the Holy Savior and called the people *Indos,* thinking he was in India.

EIGHTEENTH CENTURY

1719–1796   Several indentured servants or slaves of Indian origin were brought to the United States via England.
1790   An unnamed "man from Madras" was seen on the streets of Salem, Massachusetts, by Rev. William Bently.

NINETEENTH CENTURY

1820   Ram Mohan Roy published *The Precepts of Jesus,* which was reprinted in the United States in 1825 and 1828. It contained Roy's interpretation of Christianity, which became the object of discussion among the intelligentsia and commented on in the American religious publications.
1830–1855   New England Transcendentalists' Club flourished in Concord, Massachusetts, with Ralph Waldo Emerson (1803–1882) and Henry David Thoreau (1817–1862) as prominent members. Indian philosophy and scriptures played an important role and were of much interest.
1836   Isaac Nordheimer (1809–1842) was one of the earliest to teach Sanskrit in an American institution of higher learning. He taught at the City University of New York on Wednesdays and Fridays in 1841. Edward E. Salisbury was appointed Professor of Sanskrit and Arabic at Yale University.
1855   American Unitarian Missionary, Rev. Charles Dall arrived at Calcutta.
1858   Joguth Chandler Gungoolly (b. 1834), after being baptized, was sent by Rev. Dall to Boston for missionary training.
1874   Pratap Chandra Mazumdar (1849–1905), a Brahmo Samaj leader came on a lecture tour to the United States in 1883 (2nd visit), 1893 (3rd visit) to attend World's Parliament of Religion, and 1900 (last visit).
1883   Anandibai Joshee (1865–1887) came to the Women's Medical College of Pennsylvania to study medicine.
1893   Vivekananda (1862–1902), the Vedantic missionary came to Chicago to attend the World's Parliament of Religion. His second visit to the United States was in 1896.

TWENTIETH CENTURY

1904   Sudhindranath Bose (1883–1946) came to study at the University of Illinois, Champaign, and later, after being established, participated in the Indian Independence movement.

1906   Taraknath Das (1884–1858) was a Bengali political activist, after leaving India a year before to avoid political prosecution and passing via Japan, landed in Seattle.

1906   P. Mukerji (1884–1982) came to study at the University of Pittsburgh, became a metallurgical engineer, and later participated in the Indian Independence movement.

1911   Har Dayal (d. 1939), the prominent leader at the early stage of the *ghar* movement, came to the United States in1914 and later left for Switzerland.

1912   Rabindranath Tagore (1861–1941) the Nobel Laureate poet was on his first U.S. visit and lecture tour during his stay in Illinois, when he was awarded the 1913 Nobel Prize for literature. In 1906, he had his second U.S. visit, 1921 his third visit, and 1930 his last U.S. visit.

1917   Srilendranath Ghosh (d. 1949) a Bengali political activist sailed for Philadelphia under a disguise to avoid political persecution and participated in the Indian Independence movement. In 1936, he returned to India.

1917   Ananda Kentish Coomaraswamy (1877–1947), art-historian and philosopher, came to the Boston Museum of Fine Arts.

1917   Goobindran Jamandas Watumi (1891–1959), businessman and philanthropist, came to Honolulu.

1920   Sharat K. Roy (1897–1962), paleontologist and explorer, came to study at the University of Illinois.

1920   Haridas Muzumdar (1898–1973), Gandhian pioneer and sociologist, came as a student to New York.

1920   Dilip Singh Saund (1899–1972), Congressman, came to study at the University of California, Berkeley.

1920   Paramhansa Yogananda (1893–1952), missionary (self-realization fellowship) came to Boston to attend an international congress of religious liberals.

1922   Jiddu Krishnamurti (1895–1986), philosopher and world teacher, left Europe for California to live in the Ojai Valley.

1923   Yellapragada Subbarow (1895–1948), medical researcher, reached Harvard University for postgraduate study and research.

1935   Subrahmanyan Chandrasekhar (1910–1995), astrophysicist and Nobel Laureate, came to Harvard College Observatory as a lecturer in "Cosmic Physics."

1946   President Truman signed the Indian Immigration Bill permitting one hundred Indian families to immigrate to the United States.

1949   Raj Chandra Bose (1931–1987), statistician and member of the National Academy of Science (NAS) came to the University of North Carolina as a Professor in Statistics.

1951   Haridas Chaudhuri (1913–1975), philosopher and Aurobindo devotee, came to the Association of Asian Studies in San Francisco as the Professor of Indian Philosophy and Comparative Religion.

1950 Maharishi Mahesh Yogi (b. 1911), the Guru of the Western world and preacher of TM, traveled to the United States, stopping in Hawaii and San Francisco. In 1961, he visited Los Angeles for the second time.

1965 Bhaktivedanta Swami Prabhupada (1896–1977), initiator and organizer of the Hare Krishna Movement and the International Society of Krishna Consciousness (ISCON), arrived in Brooklyn.

1981 Bhagwan Shree Rajneesh (1932–1990), promoter of Dynamics Meditation, arrived in New Jersey and later moved to Oregon.

Sources: Sachin N. Pradhan. 1996. *India in the United States: Contributions of India and Indians in the United States of America.* Bethesda: SP Press International, pp. xiii–xv.

Appendix F
An Immigrant Success Story

The Grewal brothers of Detroit descend from one the original six Asian Indians to settle in Detroit. Their grandfather, Sarwan Singh Grewal, left Punjab in 1921 and after a year-plus stay in California traveled to Detroit with the group that included Arjun Singh. Sarwan Singh Grewal was a Sikh Jat from the village of Sahouli located in the Ludhiana District of India's Punjab. He learned about the opportunities in California from his cousin, Ishar Singh Dhillon, who was studying at the University of California, Berkeley.

With reluctance, Sarwan's father gave him passage money. Sarwan obtained his passport in Lahore and took the train to Calcutta, where he boarded a freighter for Hong Kong. After nine days in Hong Kong he boarded a steamer for the month long trip to California. In California, he and his companions initially worked for 20 cents an hour; Sarwan Singh and some of his friends realized that they could not survive on such a low wage and turned to contract farming.[1] After a few years they bought a car and drove East. After a month in Chicago, they continued on to Detroit where they settled in 1924.

Sarwan Singh worked with his Congressman and had a bill passed in Congress enabling him to bring his grandsons, Tahil, Lushman, Jeat, and Gurmale, the four Grewal brothers, to America.[2] Thus, at the tender age of 13, the youngest brother, Gurmale Singh Grewal, began a new life in a new country.

The Detroit riots in 1967 were devastating for the Grewals. The value of their real estate holdings dropped drastically and the family suffered the untimely death of their grandfather in 1968. Young Gurmale Singh Grewal, at the age of 19, took on the responsibility for renovating the family-owned Wolverine Hotel for the city. The project and its success turned into the Singh Development Company with the following Mission Statement:

> Develop high quality real estate properties that will meet market needs, enhance the communities they serve, and improve the quality of life of the people who live and work in them.

With each brother heading key sections of the company, the Singh Development Company has grown to being one of the top five development companies in Michigan. Qualified and capable family members work in the firm. Nonfamily but capable individuals are treated with respect, paid well, and are loyal to the firm.

Gurmale attributes much of the firm's success to being sensitive to the desires of his clients as well as treating his employees with dignity and respect. Thus, turnover is low. Also, having brothers and family members in key positions of the company has added to its efficiency, for family members take a greater interest in the business

---

[1]They learned early on that working for an hourly wage did not yield enough to live on.

[2]Mandeep Kaur Grewal. "The Sikh Diaspora: A Century of Sikh Struggles in the United States" (unpublished, 2000).

and communications among them are more informal and efficient. Also those non-family employees in key positions are treated so well they do not want to leave, and are "adopted" into the family.

The Grewal brothers set aside every Friday evening for a family dinner, a ritual which promotes unity and a cohesiveness. It also provides a setting where business and other family matters can be dealt with informally.

The brothers have kept one foot in India and the other in Detroit so to speak. They have been a tremendous asset to Detroit and their home village of Sahouli. Through the company in Detroit, they have created 2,448 permanent jobs, generated $80 million in wages, and $4 million in tax revenues.[3] Gurmale, the CEO,[4] is active in the Democratic Party and respected and consulted by officials and representatives from both the United States and India.

Gurmale, like his brothers, has not forgotten his village. He set up a computer center in the village that is tied to the Internet. Through his brothers and family members in India, he has also invested in land as well being involved in the internal and external affairs of Sahouli. He visits Sahouli about twice a year, and more often if needed. The Grewal brothers, like many immigrants from India, are making very positive contributions to their communities in Michigan as well as their region of origin. In fact, they were honored in 2001 by capturing two Building Industry Association Awards. Gurmale Singh Grewal, CEO of Singh Development Company, received the Developer of the Year award from the Building Industry Association (BIA) of Southwestern Michigan. Singh Development builds premier apartment communities, commercial office buildings, luxury single-family subdivisions, and senior living communities.

The other recipient was Darshan Singh Grewal, president of Singh Homes, a division of Singh Development Corporation that specializes in luxury single-family homes.

[3]These figures do not include employees, assets, taxes, or revenues of the Singh Development Corporation.

[4]As one watches the Singh brothers operate, consensus and listening are practiced. No one seems to have authority over the others. Decisions are generally by consensus and all are listened to.

Appendix G
Remittances to India by Region
of Origin and U.S. Dollar Equivalents

Year	U.S. Dollars (in millions)	Year	U.S. Dollars (in millions)
1972–1973	134	1985–1986	2,219
1973–1974	182	1986–1987	2,340
1974–1975	277	1987–1988	2,725
1975–1976	490	1988–1989	2,669
1976–1977	698	1989–1990	2,297
1977–1978	1,071	1990–1991	2,021
1978–1979	1,151	1991–1992	3,848
1979–1980	1,817	1992–1993	2,651
1980–1981	2,692	1993–1994	3,617
1981–1982	2,322	1994–1995	8,113
1982–1983	2,524		
1983–1984	2,561		

Year	North America	Western Europe	Britain and Australia	Middle East
1970–1971	284	114	223	37
1971–1972	312	194	38	307
1972–1973	391	159	275	46
1973–1974	432	189	442	74
1974–1975	670	349	448	259
1975–1976	1,105	502	620	1,316
1976–1977	1,651	664	590	2,704
1977–1978	1,382	785	1,026	4,868
1978–1979	1,566	949	1,013	4,813
1979–1980	2,210	1,192	1,631	17,904
1980–1981	2,100	1,684	2,548	12,194
1981–1982	3,355	1,866	2,195	10,975
1982–1983	3,363	1,828	2,494	1,378
1983–1984	3,871	2,119	2,460	15,000
1984–1985	4,589	2,220	2,550	17,140
1985–1986	4,803	2,578	3,224	13,884
1986–1987	5,323	2,617	3,675	15,368
1987–1988	6,245	3,705	3,740	18,058
1988–1989	12,955	3,943	3,236	15,463
1989–1990	7,998	5,434	3,488	17,753
1990–1991	2,645	4,633	4,844	14,499
1991–1992	36,270	9,464	7,901	34,023
1992–1993	20,740	13,603	8,964	32,139
1993–1994	28,700	12,940	13,252	49,486
1994–1995	73,559	23,900	30,106	107,763
1995–1996	86,385	28,561	33,617	117,961

References

Preface

Khadria, Binod. 1999. *The Migration of Knowledge Workers: Second-Generation Effects of India's Brain Drain.* New Delhi: Sage.

Potts, Lydia. 1990. *The World Labour Market—A History of Migration.* London: Zed.

Shukla, Sandhya. 2001. Nations for South Asian Diasporas. In *Annual Review of Anthropology, Vol. 30.* Palo Alto: Annual Reviews.

Introduction

Barth, Fredrik (ed.). 1963. *The Role of the Entrepreneur in Social Change in Northern Norway.* Oslo: Universitetsforlaget.

Benedict, Burton. 1968. Family Firms and Economic Development. *Southwestern Journal of Anthropology. XX.V.* 1.

Bryce-Laporte, Roy Simon. 1978. *Sourcebook on the New Immigration: Implications for the United States and the International Community.* New Brunswick, NJ: Transaction.

Daniels, Roger. 1990. *Coming to America: A History of Ethnicity in American Life.* New York: HarperCollins.

Dinnerstein, Leonard, and David Reimers. 1988. *Ethnic Americans: A History of Immigration.* New York: Harper & Row.

Glazer, Nathan, and Daniel P. Moynihan. 1963. *Beyond the Melting Pot.* Cambridge, MA: MIT Press. Second edition published 1970.

Graves, Nancy, and Theodore Graves. 1974. Adaptive Strategies in Urban Migration. In *Annual Reviews of Anthropology.* Benard J. Siegel (ed.). Palo Alto: Annual Reviews.

Helweg, Arthur W. 1979. *Sikhs in England: The Development of a Migrant Community.* New Delhi: Oxford University Press.

Hirschman, Charles, Philip Kasinitz, and Josh DeWind. 1999. Part II. In *The Handbook of International Migration: The American Experience.* New York: Russell Sage Foundation.

Kasdan, Leonard (ed.). 1970. Introduction. *Migration and Anthropology.* Seattle: American Ethnological Society, University of Washington Press.

Keely, Charles B. 1971. Effects of the Immigration Act of 1965 on Selected Population: Characteristics of Immigrants to the United States. *Demography VIII:*157–169.

———. 1980. Immigration Policy and the New Immigration, 1965–1976. In *New Immigration: Implications for the United States and the International Community.* Roy Simon Bryce-Laporte (ed.). New Brunswick, NJ: Transaction Books.

Jackson, J. A. 1968. *Migration.* Cambridge: Cambridge University Press.

Jansen, Clifford J. (ed.). 1970. Readings in the Study of Migration. London: Pergamon.

Lewin, Kurt. 1952. *Field Theory in the Social Sciences: Selected Theoretical Papers by Kurt Lewin.* Dorwin Cartwright (ed.). London: Tavistock.

Park, Robert Ezra. 1928. Human Migration and the Marginal Man. *American Journal of Sociology 33*:6, pp. 881–893.

———. 1950. *Race and Culture.* Glencoe, IL: Free Press.

Shaw, R. Paul. 1975. *Migration: Theory and Fact.* Philadelphia: Regional Science Research Institute.

Wyman, Mark. 1993. *Round-Trip to America: The Immigrants Return to Europe.* Ithaca, NY: Cornell University Press.

PART I

Barth, Fredrik. 1961. *The Role of the Entrepreneur in Social Change in Northern Norway.* Oslo: Universitetsforlaget.

————. 1963. Economic Spheres of the Darfur. In *Themes in Economic Anthropology. ASA Monograph 6.* Michael Banton (ed.). London: Tavistock.

Benedict, Burton. 1968. Family Firms and Economic Development. *Southwestern Journal of Anthropology 24*:1.

Bhachu, Parminder. 1985. *Twice Migrants: East African Sikh Settlers in Britain.* London: Tavistock.

Greenfield, Sidney M., and Arnold Strickon. 1986. Introduction. In *Entrepreneurship and Social Change: Monographs in Economic Anthropology No. 8.* Sidney M. Greenfield and Arnold Strickon (eds.). Society for Economic Anthropology and University Press of America.

Helweg, Arthur. 2002. *Entrepreneurs and Entrepreneurial Networks of South Asia.* Unpublished paper presented at the 12th World Economic History Conference.

Lessinger, Johanna. 1995. *From the Ganges to the Hudson: Indian Immigrants in New York City, Boston, London, Toronto, Sydney, Tokyo, and Singapore.* Boston: Allyn & Bacon.

Lockwood, Douglas. 1963. *We the Aboriginal.* Melbourne: Cossell.

Redfield, Robert. 1960. *The Little Community/Peasant Society and Culture.* Chicago: Phoenix.

Chapter 1

Abraham, Thomas. 1999. NRI/PIO—A Perspective. New York: An Address to the Global Organization of People of Indian Origin Conference.

Ashcroft, Bill, Gareth Griffiths, and Helen Tiffin. 1968. *Key Concepts in Post-Colonial Studies.* London: Routledge, pp. 68–70.

Barrier, N. Gerald, and Verne A. Dusenbery. 1989. *The Sikh Diaspora: Migration and the Experience beyond Punjab.* Columbia, MO: South Asia Publications.

Barth, Fredrik. 1961. *The Role of the Entrepreneur in Social Change in Northern Norway.* Oslo: Universitetsforlaget.

————. 1963. Economic Spheres of the Darfur. In *Themes in Economic Anthropology. ASA Monograph 6.* Michael Banton (ed.). London: Tavistock.

Benedict, Burton. 1968. Family Firms and Economic Development. *Southwestern Journal of Anthropology, xxiv:*1.

Buchignani, Norman, and Doreen M. Indra, with Ram Srivastiva. 1985. *Continuous Journey: A Social History of South Asians in Canada.* Toronto: McClelland and Stewart, Ltd.

Cohen, Robin. 1997. *Global Diaspora: An Introduction.* Seattle: University of Washington Press.

Gordon, Paul, and Anne Newland. 1986. *Different Worlds: Racism Discrimination in Britain.* London: Runnymede Trust.

Greenfield, Sidney M., and Arnold Strickon. 1986. Introduction. In *Entrepreneurship and Social Change, Monographs in Economic Anthropology.* New York: The University Press of America for the Society of Economic Anthropology.

Helweg, Arthur W., and Usha M. Helweg. 1990. *An Immigrant Success Story: East Indians in North America.* Philadelphia: University of Pennsylvania.

Kondapi, C. 1951. *Indians Overseas: 1838–1941.* London: Oxford University Press for the Indian Congress of World Affairs.

Kotkin, Joel. 1993. *Tribes: How Race, Religion and Identity Determine Success in the New Global Economy.* New York: Random House.

Kwame, Appiah, Anthony and Henry Louis Gates, Jr. (eds.). nd. *The Dictionary of Global Culture.* New York: Alfred A. Knopf, pp. 178–179.

Manget, J. S. 1969. *A History of the Asians in East Africa.* Oxford: Clarendon.

Patel, Dhiru. 2001. *South Asian Diasporas.* http://www.himalmag.com/99Dec /diaspora.htm.

Potts, Lydia. 1990. *The World Labour Market—A History of Migration.* London: Zed.

Schwartzerg, Joseph E. 1878. *A Historical Atlas of South Asia.* Chicago: The University of Chicago Press.

Singh, I. J., and Bahadur Singh (eds.). 1979. *The Other India.* New Delhi: Arnold-Heinemann.

Thaper, Romila. 1966. *A History of India, Vol. I.* Baltimore: Penguin.

Tinker, Hugh. 1974. *A New System of Slavery: The Export of Indian Labour Overseas, 1830–1920.* London: Oxford University Press.

———. 1976. *Separate and Unequal: India and the Indians in the British Commonwealth, 1920–1959.* London: C. Hurst.

———. 1977. *The Banyan Tree: Overseas Emigrants from India, Pakistan, and Bangladesh.* Oxford: Oxford University Press.

———. 1989. External Migration. In *The Cambridge Encyclopedia of Pakistan, Bangladesh, Sri Lanka, Nepal, Bhutan, and Maldives.* Francis Robinson (ed.). Cambridge: Cambridge University Press.

———. 1990. *South Asia: A Short History.* Honolulu: University of Hawaii Press.

Unsigned. 1993. *Business Week.*

———. 1996a. Passage from India: The Diaspora. *Time International, 147*: 13, March 25.

———. 1996b. *Fortune.*

Weber, Max. 1958. *The Protestant Ethic and the Spirit of Capitalism.* New York: Charles Scribner.

Chapter 2

Andrews, K. P. 1983. *Keralites in America: Community Reference Book.* Glen Oaks, NY: Literary Market Review, Inc.

Bailey, F. G. 1963. *Closed Social Stratification in India.* Archives de Europes Sociology.

———. 1965. Decisions by Consensus in Councils and Committees: With Special Reference to Village and Local Government in India. In *Political Systems and the Distribution of Power, ASA Monograph 2.* Michael Banton (ed.). London: Tavistock.

Bhachu, Parminder. 1985. *Twice Migrants: East African Sikh Settlers in Britain.* London: Tavistock.

Bhagwati, Jagdish N. 1976. The Brain Drain. *International Social Science Journal. XVIII:*691–729.

———. 1976. Taxing the Brain Drain. *Challenge. XIX:*34–38.

Caroli, Betty Boyd. 1983. Recent Immigration to the United States. In *Ethnic and Immigration Groups: The United States, Canada and England.* Patricia J. F. Rosof, William Zeisel, Jean B. Quandt, and Myriam Maayan (eds.). New York: The Institute for Research in History and The Haworth Press.

Cervantes, Mari, and Dominique Grellec. 2002. The Brain Drain: Old Myths and New Realities. *OECD Observer,* May 7.

Collins, Larry, and Dominique LaPierre. 1975. *Freedom at Midnight.* New York: Simon and Schuster.

Domrese, Robert. 2002. The Migration of Talent from India. In *The International Migration of High-Level Manpower: Its Impact on the Development Process.* New York: Praeger.

Dumont, L. 1966. *Homo Heirarchicus: The Caste System and Its Implications.* London: Weidenfeld and Nicolson.

Dumont, Louise, and D. Pocock. 1957. For a Sociology of India. Contributions to India's Sociology. o. I. April.

———. 1958a. Commented Summary of the First Part of Bougle's Essays. *Contributions to Indian Sociology, No. II.* The Hague: Mouton, April.

———. 1958b. Foreword. *Contributions to Indian Sociology No. II.* The Hague: Mouton, April.

Dutta, Manoranjan. 1982. Asian Indian Americans: Search for an Economic Profile. In *From India to America: A Brief History of Immigration Problems of Discrimination, Admission and Assimilation.* S. Chandrasekhar (ed.). LaJolla: Population Review.

Glaser, William A. 1978. *The Brain Drain: Emigration and Return.* Oxford: Pergamon.

————. 1980. International Flows of Talent. In *Sourcebook on the New Immigration: Implications for the United States and the International Community.* Roy Simon Bryce-Laporte (eds.). New Brunswick, NJ: Transaction.

Gordon, Paul, and Anne Newland. 1986. *Different Worlds: Racism and Discrimination in Britain.* London: The Runnymede Trust.

Hattori, James. 2000. Reversing India's Brain Drain. CNN.Com, August 25, 2000. http//www.cnn.com/2000/TECH /computing/08/25/brain.drain/

Helweg, Arthur. 1989. Sikh Politics in India: The Emigrant Factor. In *The Sikh Diaspora: Migration and the Experience Beyond Punjab.* N. Gerald Barrier and Verne A. Dusenbery (eds.). Columbia, MO: South Asia Books.

Helweg, Arthur, and Usha M. Helweg. 1990. *An Immigrant Success Story.* Philadelphia: University of Pennsylvania Press.

Hutton, J. H. 1946. *Caste in India.* Oxford: Oxford University Press.

Khadria, Binod. 1999. *The Migration of Knowledge Workers: Second Generation Effects of India's Brain Drain.* New Delhi: Sage.

Kubat, Daniel (ed.). 1983. *The Politics of Return: International Return Migration in Europe.* New York: Center for Migration Studies.

Lane, Hana Umlauf. 1986. *The World Almanac and Book of Facts.* New York: Newspaper Enterprise Association, Inc.

Mangat, J. S. 1969. *A History of the Asians in East Africa.* Oxford: Clarendon.

Marriott, McKim. 1955. Little Communities in an Indigenous Civilization. In *Village India: Studies in the Little Community.* McKim Marriott (ed.). Chicago: University of Chicago Press.

————. 1968. Caste Ranking and Food Transactions: A Matrix Analysis. In *Structure and Change in Indian Society.* Milton Singer and Bernard Cohen (eds.). Chicago: Aldine.

Mathew, K. M. 1986. *Manorama Year Book 1986.* Kottayam, Kerala: Manorama.

Meyer, Jean-Baptiste. 1999. Scientific Diasporas: A New Approach to the Brain Drain. Prepared for the Conference on Science, UNESCO-ICSU, Budapest, Hungary, June 26–July 1, 1999.

Nahal, Chaman. 1975. *Azadi.* New Delhi: Arnold-Heinemann.

Nayer, Deepak. 1991. *Migration Remittances and Capital Flows: The Indian Experience.* Delhi: Oxford University Press.

Newland, Kathleen. 1979. International Migration: The Search for Work. *Worldwatch Paper 33.* Washington, DC: Worldwatch Institute.

Oommen, T. K. 1989. India: "Brain Drain" or the Migration of Talent. *International Migration, XXVII.*3, September.

Pais, Arthur. 1989a. Indian Diaspora. *India Abroad. XIX.*48, September 1:10–11.

————. 1989b. U.S. Catholics Need Clergy Abroad. *India Abroad. XIX.*14, January 6:25.

Pais, Arthur, Bindu Bhaskar, and Priya Kurian. 1989. Malayalees in North America. *India Abroad. XIX.*38:12–14.

Pant, Apa. 1979. The Much Maligned Other India. In *In the Other India.* I. J. Bahadur Singh (ed.). New Delhi: Arnold-Heinemann.

Rockett, I. R. H., and S. L. Putnam. 1989. Physician-Nurse Migration to the United States: Regional and Health Status Origins in Relation to Legislation and Policy. *International Migration XXVII.*3, September.

Rogers, Rosemary. 1984. Return Migration in Comparative Perspective. In *The Politics of Return: International Return Migration in Europe.* Daniel Kubat (ed.). New York: Center for Migration Studies.

Schwartz, Barton M. 1967. *Caste in Overseas Indian Communities.* San Francisco: Chandler.

Singh, I. J. Bahadur. 1979. *The Other India.* New Delhi: Arnold-Heinemann.

Singh, Khushwant. 1956. *Train to Pakistan.* London: Greenwood.

Singh, Ram Nath. 1989. *Impact of Out Migration on Socio-Economic Conditions: A Case Study of Khutouna Block.* Delhi: Amar Prakashan.

Tinker, Hugh. 1974. *A New System of Slavery: The Export of Indian Labour Overseas, 1830–1920.* London: Oxford University Press.

———. 1976. *Separate and Unequal.* London: C. Hurst.

———. 1977. *The Banyan Tree: Overseas Emigrants from India, Pakistan and Bangladesh.* Oxford: Oxford University Press.

Unsigned. 1979. Business Brief: Migrating to Work. In *World Development Letter.* Washington, DC: Agency for International Development, September 10.

———. 1983a. The Non-resident Gods. *India Today.* September 30

———. 1983b. The Talent Trap. *India Today.* November.

———. 2002a. About Remittances. *Migration News.* June, 11. http://imigration.ucdavis.edu/Data/remit.on.www/aboutremit.html

———. 2002b. Non-Resident Indians Bread Earners. *Non-Resident Indians.* June 15. http://www.indianbest.com/nriindex_htm

———. 2002c. Money from Indians Abroad Surges Six-fold. Rediff.com. June 11, wysiwyg//18/http://www.rediff.com/money/2002/Jul/21abroad.htm

Weiner, Myron. 1980. *Indians in the Gulf: The Beginning or the End of a Diaspora?* A paper presented at the Association for Asian Studies, Washington, DC. March 23.

Wyman, Mark. 1993. *Round-trip to America: The Immigrants Return to Europe, 1880–1939.* Ithaca, NY: Cornell University Press.

Chapter 3

Buchignani, Norman, and Doreen M. Indra with Ram Srivastiva. 1985. *Continuous Journey: A Social History of South Asians in Canada.* Toronto: McClelland and Stewart, in association with the Multiculturalism Directorate.

Chandrasekhar, S. 1982. *From India to America: A Brief History of Immigration, Problems of Discrimination: Admission and Assimilation.* LaJolla: Population Review.

Daniels, Roger. 1989. *Coming to America: History and Ethnicity in American Life.* New York: HarperCollins.

Gibson, Margaret. 1988. *Accommodation without Assimilation: Sikh Immigrants in an American High School.* Ithaca, NY: Cornell University Press.

Helweg, Arthur. 1986. *Sikhs in England,* 2nd ed. Delhi: Oxford University Press.

———. 1996. The Immigration Act of 1917. In *Asian Americans and Congress: A Documentary History.* Hyung-Chan Kim (ed.). Westport, CT: Greenwood.

———. 2001. Thind, Bhagat Singh (1892–1967): Author and Community Activist, Asian Indian. In *Making It in America: A Sourcebook on Eminent Ethnic Americans.* Elliott R. Barkan (ed.). Santa Barbara, CA: ABC Cleo.

Hess, Gary R. 1982. The Asian Indian Immigrants in the United States: The Early Phase, 1900–1965. In *From India to America: A Brief History of*

Immigration; Problems of Discrimination; Admission and Assimilation. S. Chandrasekhar (ed.). LaJolla: Population Review.

Jayadev, Raj. 2002. Hi-tech Underbelly: On the Sweatshops of Silicon Valley, Immigrant Dreams Are Shattered. In *South Asian Diasporas.* Retrieved from http://www.himalmag.com/99Dec/.hitech.htm on February 12, 2001.

Jensen, Joan M. 1988. *Passage from India: Asian Indian Immigrants in North America.* New Haven, CT: Yale University Press.

Johnston, Hugh. 1979. *The Voyage of the Kamogata: The Sikh Challenge to Canada's Colour Bar.* Delhi: Oxford University Press.

Joshi, V. C. (ed.). 1965. *Lajpat Rai: Autobiographical Writings.* Delhi: Oxford University Press.

Kolsky, Elisabeth. 2002. *Less Successful Than the Next: South Asian Taxi Drivers in New York City.* Retrieved from http://www.wnyc.org/new/sixmonths/immigrationandidentity/taxiessay.html on April 22, 2002.

Kamath, M. V. 1976. *The United States and India, 1776–1976.* Washington, DC: The Embassy of India.

La Brack, Bruce. 1988. *The Sikhs of Northern California, 1904–1975.* New York: AMS.

McLeod, W. H. 1986. *Punjabis in New Zealand: A History of Punjabi*

Migration, 1890–1940. Amritsar: Guru Nanak Dev University.

Leonard, Karen Isaksen. 1992. *Making Ethnic Chilies: California's Punjabi Mexican Americans.* Philadelphia: Temple University Press.

———. 1997. *The South Asian Americans.* Westport, CT: Greenwood.

Rangaswamy, Padma. 2000. *Namasté America: Indian Immigrants in an American Metropolis.* University Park: Pennsylvania State University Press.

Saund, Dilip Singh. 1960.

Shankar, Lavina Dhingra, and Rajini Srikanth. 1998. *A Part Yet Apart: South Asians in Asian America.* Philadelphia: Temple University Press.

Singh, Khushwant. 1966. *A History of the Sikhs,* Volume II. Princeton: Princeton University Press.

Srindhar, S. A., and Nirrmal K. Mattoo. 1997. *Ananya: A Portrait of India.* Queens: The Association of Indians in America.

Tinker, Hugh. 1976. *Separate and Unequal.* London: C. Hurst.

PART II

Glazier, Jack, and Arthur Helweg. 2001. *Ethnicity in Michigan.* East Lansing: Michigan State University Press.

Chapter 4

Bains, Tara Singh, and Hugh Johnston. 1995. *The Four Quarters of the Night: The Life-Journey of an Emigrant Sikh: McGill-Queens Studies in Ethnic History, 21.* Montreal: McGill-Queens University Press.

Helweg, Arthur. 1986. *Sikhs in England.* Delhi: Oxford University Press.

———. 1996. Immigration Act of 1917: The Asian Indian Exclusion Act. In *Asian America and Congress: A Documentary History.* Hyung-Chan Kim (ed.). Westport, CT: Greenwood.

———. 2001. Bhagat Singh Thind. In *Making It in America: A Sourcebook on Eminent Ethnic Americans.* Elliott Barkan (ed.). Santa Barbara, CA: ABC Cleo.

Lal, Vinay. 1999. Establishing Roots, Engendering Awareness: A Political History of Asian Indians in the United States. In *Live like the Banyan Tree: Images of the Indian American Experience.* Philadelphia: Balch Institute for Ethics Studies.

Pettigrew, Joyce. 1978. *Robber Noblemen.* New Delhi: Ambika.

Sharma, Ursula. 1971. *Rampal and His Family: The Story of an Immigrant.* London: Collins.

Walbridge, Linda S., and Fatimah Haneef. 1999. Inter-Ethnic Relations within the Ahmadyya Muslim Community in the United States. In *The Expanding Landscape: South Asians and the Diaspora.* Carla Petievich (ed.). Delhi: Manohar.

Wyman, Mark. 1993. *Round-trip to America: The Immigrants Return to Europe, 1880–1930.* Ithaca, NY: Cornell University Press.

Chapter 5

Buchignani, Norman, and Doreen M. Indra with Ram Srivastiva. 1985. *Continuous Journey: A Social History of South Asians in Canada.* Toronto: McClelland and Stewart, in association with the Multiculturalism Directorate.

Chandrasekhar, S. 1982. *From India to America: A Brief History of Immigration, Problems of Discrimination, Admission, and Assimilation.* LaJolla, CA: Population Review.

Coelho, George. 1958. *Changing Images of America: A Study of Indian Student Perceptions.* Glencoe, IL: Free Press.

Eck, Diane L. 2000. Negotiating Hindu Identities in America. In *The South Asian Religious Diasporas in Britain,*

Canada, and the United States. Harold Coward, John R. Hinnells, and Raymond Brady Williams (eds.). Albany: State University of New York Press, p. 221.

————. 2001. *A New Religious America: How a "Christian Country" Has Become the Most Religiously Diverse Nation.* San Francisco: Harper.

Gibson, Margaret. 1988. *Accommodation without Assimilation: Sikh Immigrants in an American High School.* Ithaca, NY: Cornell University Press.

Helweg, Arthur W., and Usha M. Helweg. 1990. *An Immigrant Success Story: East Indians in North America.* Philadelphia: University of Pennsylvania Press.

Helweg, Usha, and Simran Singh. 1982. Studying in America: Then and Now. *Span XXIII.*8.

Hess, Gary. 1974. The Forgotten Asian Americans. In *Pacific Historical Review. Vol. 42,* pp. 576–596.

Jain, Ravindra K. 1993. *Indian Communities Abroad: Themes and Literature.* Delhi: Manohar.

Jensen, Joan M. 1988. *Passage from India: Asian Indian Immigrants in North America.* New Haven: Yale University Press.

Kamath, M. V. 1976. *The United States and India, 1776–1976.* Washington, DC: The Embassy of India.

Koritala, Srirajasekhar Bobby. 2000. *A Historical Perspective of Americans of Asian Indian Origins, 1990–1997.* Retrieved from http://www-useers.cs .umn.edu/-seetala/India/Articles .article001.html

Kotkin, Joel. 1993. *Tribes: How Race, Religion and Identity Determine Success in the New Global Economy.* New York: Random House.

La Brack, Bruce. 1988. *The Sikhs of Northern California, 1904–1975.* New York: AMS.

Leonard, Karen Isaksen. 1997. *The South Asian Americans.* Westport, CT: Greenwood.

Lessinger, Johanna. 1995. *From the Ganges to the Hudson: Indian Immigrants in New York City.* Boston: Allyn & Bacon.

Mann, Grander Singh. 2000. Sikhism in the United States of America. In *The South Asian Religious Diaspora in Britain,*

Canada, and the United States. Harold Coward, John R. Hinnells, and Raymond Brady Williams (eds.). Albany: State University of New York Press.

Mishra, Pramod, and Urmila Mohapatra. 2002. *South Asian Diaspora in North America: An Annotated Bibliography.* Delhi: Kalinga.

Nimbark, Ashakant. 1980. Some Observations on Asian Indians in an American Educational Setting. In *The New Ethnics: Asian Indians in the United States.* Parmatma Saran and Edwin Eames (eds.). New York: Praeger.

Pais, Arthur. 1989. Student Associations. *India Abroad. XIX.*20:12–4.

Pais, Arthur, Andy McCord, and Ela Dutt. 1989. Indians in U.S. Universities. *India Abroad.* XIX.15:12–4.

Patel, Dhiru. 2001. South Asia Diasporas. Retrieved from http://www.himalmag .com/99DEc/diaspora.htm December 12, 2001.

Pradhan, Kachin N. 1996. *India in the United States: Contributions of India and Indians in the United States of America.* Bethesda: SP Press International, Inc.

Rajghatta, Chidanand. 1998. More Indian Students Go to US Now. Most of Them Stay On. Report. Retrieved from http://expressindia.com/ie/daily /199812114/34850444.html

Rangaswamy, Padma. 2000. *Namasté America: Indian Immigrants in an American Metropolis.* University Park: Pennsylvania State University Press.

Saberwall, Satish. 1968. The Problem. In *To See Ourselves: Anthropology and Modern Social Issues.* Thomas Weaver (ed.). Glenview: Scott Foresman.

Shukla, Sandhdya. 2001. Nations for South Asian Diasporas. In *Annual Review of Anthropology, Vol. 30.* Palo Alto: Annual Reviews.

Tandon, Prakash. 1980. *Return to Punjab, 1961–1975.* New Delhi: Vikas.

Tinker, Hugh. 1977. *The Banyan Tree: Overseas Emigrants from India, Pakistan, and Bangladesh.* Oxford: Oxford University Press.

Unsigned. 1986. Britons Fete Fulbright and His Legacy. *New York Times.* CXXXV1.46, 974. November 30:Y13.

Chapter 6

Anderson, Benedict. 1993. *Imagined Communities: Reflections on the Origins and Spread of Nationalism.* London: Verso.

Bellah, Robert N., Richard Madsen, William M. Sullivan, Ann Swidler, and Steven M. Tipton. 1985. *Habits of the Heart: Individualism and Commitment in American Life.* New York: Perennial Library, Harper & Row.

Conzens, Kathleen. 1991. Presidential address to the American Immigration Society.

de Tocqueville, Alexis. 1840. *Democracy in America.* George Lawrence (trans.), J. P. Mayer (ed.). New York: Doubleday, Anchor.

Dumont, Louise. 1958a. Commented Summary of the First Part of Bougle's Essays. *Contributions to Indian Sociology, No. II.*

————. 1958b. Foreword. *Contributions to Indian Sociology, No. II.*

————. 1966. *Homo Heirarchicus: The Caste System and Its Implications.* London: Weidenfeld and Nicolson.

Dumont, Louise, and D. Pocock. 1957. For a Sociology of India. *Contributions to Indian Sociology* No. I. 1957, April.

Glazier, Jack. 2001. Issues in Ethnicity. In *Ethnicity in Michigan: Issues and People.* Jack Glazier and Arthur Helweg (ed.). East Lansing: Michigan State University Press.

Helweg, Arthur. 1986. *Sikhs in England,* Second Edition. Delhi: Oxford University Press.

Kroeber, A. L., and T. Parsons. 1958. The Concept of Cultural and Social Systems. *American Sociological Review,* pp. 583–584.

Lynch, Owen. 1969. *The Politics of Untouchability.* New York: Columbia University Press.

Mandelbaum, David G. 1972a. *Society in India: Continuity and Change.* Berkeley: University of California Press.

————. 1972b. *Society in India: Change and Continuity.* Berkeley: University of California Press.

Murray, Henry. 1986. *Conversation with Viktor Frankl.* Videotape. Pennsylvania State University.

Naisbitt, John. 1982. *Megatrends: Ten New Directions Transforming Our Lives.* New York: Warner.

Shankar, Lavina Dhingra, and Rajini Srikanth (eds.). 1988. *A Part Yet Apart: South Asians in Asian America.* Philadelphia: Temple University Press.

Singh, Khazan. 1914a. *History of the Sikh Religion.* Channdigarh: Department of Languages. Government of Punjab.

————. 1914b. *Philosophy of the Sikh Religion.* Channdigarh: Department of Languages. Government of Punjab.

Srinivas, M. N. 1969. *Social Change in Modern India.* Berkeley: University of California Press.

Stewart, Edward C. 1985. *American Cultural Patterns: A Cross-Cultural Perspective.* Yarmouth, ME: Intercultural Press.

Terkel, Studs. 1980. *American Dreams: Lost & Found.* New York: Pantheon.

Tyler, Stephan A. 1974. *India: An Anthropological Perspective.* Prospect Heights, IL: Waveland.

Chapter 7

Bharati, Aghenanda. 1990. Religious Revival in Modern Times. In *The Cambridge Encyclopedia of India, Pakistan, Bangladesh, Sri Lanka.* Francis Robinson (ed.). Cambridge: Cambridge University Press.

Chahal, Devinder Singh. nd. The Text and Meaning of the *Adi Granth.* Photocopy.

Cole, W. Owen, and Piara Singh Sambhi. 1990. *A Popular Dictionary of Sikhism.* London: Curzon.

Grewal, J. S. 1991. *The New Cambridge History of India: The Sikhs of Punjab.* Cambridge: Cambridge University Press.

Helweg, Arthur. 1986. *Sikhs in England.* Delhi: Oxford University Press.

Hunter, James Davidson. 1991. *Culture Wars: The Struggle to Define America.* New York: Basic.

Inden, Ronald B. 1990. *Imagining India.* Bloomington: Indiana University Press.

Kohli, Surinder Singh. nd. *Research Coverage of Blasphemy*. Photocopy.

———. 1972a. *The Sikh Philosophy*. Amritsar: Singh Brothers.

———. 1972b. *A Conceptual Encyclopedia of Guru Granth Sahab*. New Delhi: Manohar.

———. 1973. *Outlines of Sikh Thought*. New Delhi: Munshiram Manohar.

Kroeber, A. L., and T. Parsons. 1958. The Concepts of Cultural and Social Systems. *American Sociological Review*. pp. 582–583.

Mann, Jasbir Singh, and Harbans Singh Saraon. 1988. *Advanced Studies in Sikhism*. Irvine: Sikh Community of North America.

Mann, Jasbir Singh, Sukhmander Singh Sandhu, Gurmail Singh Sidhus, Surjit Singh, S. S. Sodhi. nd. *The Future of Sikh Studies*. Photocopy.

McLeod, W. H. 1980. *Early Sikh Tradition*. Oxford: Clarendon.

———. 1988. *Who Is a Sikh? The Problem of Sikh Identity*. Oxford: Clarendon.

Oberoi, Harjot. 1994. *The Construction of Religious Boundaries: Culture, Identity and Diversity in the Sikh Tradition*. Delhi: Oxford University Press.

Ruse, Michael (ed.). nd. *Interview on God, Darwin and Dinosaurs*. A PBS Presentation.

Schneider, David M. 1968. *American Kinship: A Cultural Account*. Englewood Cliffs, NJ: Prentice-Hall.

Singh, Harbans Saraon. 1983. *The Heritage of the Sikhs*. Delhi: Manohar.

———. 1992. *The Encyclopedia of Sikhism, Vol. I, A–D*. Patiala: Punjab University Press.

Tinker, Hugh. 1990. *South Asia: A Short History*. Honolulu: University of Hawaii Press.

Whiting, Robert. 1989. *You Gotta Have Wa*. New York: Vintage.

PART III

Helweg, Arthur W. 1986. *Sikhs in England*. New Delhi: Oxford University Press.

Helweg, Arthur W., and Usha M. Helweg. 1990. *An Immigrant Success Story: East Indians in North America*. Philadelphia: University of Pennsylvania Press.

Chapter 8

Bailey, F. G. 1965. Decisions by Consensus in Councils and Committees: With Special Reference to Village and Local Government in India. In *Political Systems and the Distribution of Power, ASA Monograph* 2, Michael Banton (ed.). London: Tavistock.

Bellah, Robert N., Richard Madsen, William M. Sullivan, Ann Swidler, and Steven M. Tipton. 1985. *Habits of the Heart: Individualism and Commitment in American Life*. New York: Perennial Library, Harper & Row.

Bhardwaj, Surinder M. 1989. Transference and Development of Sacred Space: The South Indian Example in North America, unpublished paper.

Charbonnier, G. 1961. *Conversations with Claude Levi-Strauss*. London: Jonathan Cape.

Elkhanialy, Hekmat, and Ralph W. Nicholas. 1976. Racial and Ethnic Designation, Experiences of Discrimination, and Desire for Legal Minority Status Among Indian Immigrants in the U.S.A. In *Immigrants from the Indian Subcontinent in the U.S.A.: Problems and Prospects,* Hekmat Elkhanialy and Ralph W. Nicholas (eds.). Chicago: India League of America.

Fenton, John Y. 1988. *Transplanting Religious Traditions: Asian Indians in America*. New York: Praeger.

Fisher, Maxine P. 1980. *The Indians of New York City*. Columbia, MO: South Asia.

Helweg, Arthur. 1986. The Indian Diaspora: Influence on International Relations. In *Modern Diasporas in International Relations*. Gabriel Sheffer (ed.). London: Croom Helm.

Leach, Edmund. 1976. *Culture and Communication*. Cambridge: Cambridge University Press.

Machanda, Rita. 1989. Indian-Americans: The Lobbying Game. *India Today* *XIV*.18. September.

Mauss, Marel. 1967. *The Gift*. New York: W. W. Norton.

Sahlins, Marshall. 1965. On the Sociology of Primitive Exchange. In *The Relevance of Models for Social Anthropology. ASA Monograph 1*.

Michael Banton (ed.). London: Tavistock.

Schwartz, Barton M. 1967. *Caste in Overseas Indian Communities*. San Francisco: Chandler.

Sundaram, Vijay. 1989. Indo-Crisis Hotline Fields Calls From Battered Women. *India West. XIV*.14:30–31.

Chapter 9

Assisi, Francis. 1988. Rights Commission Report Addresses Economic Status of Indo-Americans. Chandrasekhar, S. (ed.). *India West, XII*.49, October 14:4, 32.

Chandrasekhar, S. 1982. *From India to America: A Brief History of Immigration: Problems of Discrimination, Admission, and Assimilation*. LaJolla: Population Review.

Coelho, George. 1958. *Changing Images of America: A Study of Indian Student Perceptions*. Glencoe, IL: Free Press.

Dutta, Monoranjan. 1982. Asian Indian Americans: Search for an Economic Profile. In *From India to America: A Brief History of Immigration; Problems of Discrimination, Admission, and Assimilation*. S. Chandrasekhar (ed.). LaJolla: Population Review.

Elkhanialy, Hekmat, and Ralph W. Nicholas. 1976. Racial and Ethnic Designation, Experiences of Discrimination, and Desire for Legal Minority Status among Indian Immigrants in the U.S.A. In *Immigrants from the Indian Subcontinent in the U.S.A.: Problems and Prospects*. Hekmat Elkhanialy and Ralph W. Nicholas (eds.). Chicago: India League of America.

George, Geo. 2001. South Asians Invisible to American Media. Jivan Online. Retrieved from http://www.jivanonline.com/world/invisible.html, January 18.

Gibson, Margaret. 1988. *Accommodation without Assimilation: Sikh Immigrants in an American High School*. Ithaca, NY: Cornell University Press.

Gune, Ramesh. 1987. Enemy Within: Rivalry Splits Rights Group. *India Abroad. XVIII*.13:13.

Helweg, Arthur. 2001. Ethnicity in Michigan. In *Ethnicity in Michigan: Issues and People*. Jack Glazier and

Arthur Helweg (eds.). East Lansing: Michigan State University Press.

———. 1993. An Immigrant Success Story. *Ethnic and Racial Studies*. 1:570–572.

Helweg, Arthur W. and Usha M. Helweg. 1990. An Immigrant Success Story: East Indians in North America. Philadelphia: University of Pennsylvania.

Helweg, Usha, and Simran Singh. 1982. Studying in America: Then and Now. *Span XXIII*.8.

Howe, Marvin. 1986. Status of India Immigrants Is Debated. *New York Times CXXXV*. 46, 750. Sunday, April 20:19.

Hu, Arthur. 1989. Asian Americans: Model Minority or Double Minority? *Amerasia Journal XV*, 8:245–57.

Hudson, Lynn. 1985. Survey Describes Average Reader of India Abroad. *India Abroad. XXXXVIII*. August 30.

———. 1986. From Farms to Floppies: The Achievers: Some Stories of Success from the Indian Immigrant Community in This Land of Opportunities. *India Abroad. XVI*. 40, July 4:I.

———. 1986. In the Land of Liberty. *India Abroad. XVI*. 40, Friday, July 4:I.

———. 1987a. Invoking the Law to Fight Discrimination. *India Abroad. XVIII*.13, December 25:12, 13.

———. 1987b. 25,539 Indian Businesses Listed. *India Abroad. XVII*. 14, January 2:14.

Jafrey, Irfan M. 2002. Thought Fountains Essays in Business. Retrieved from http://students.washington.edu/cannut/bizessays.html on March 25.

Kamath, M. V. 1976. *The United States and India, 1776–1976*. Washington, DC: The Embassy of India.

Krishna, Bala Murali. 2001. South Asians Main Targets of Sept. 11 Backlash. Retrieved from http://news.nconline .com/news/view_article.html?article_id =163 on November 25.

Mishra, Pramod, and Urmila Mohapatra. 2002. *South Asian Diaspora in North America: An Annotated Bibliography.* Delhi: Kalinga.

Mohapatra, Manindra Kumar. 1977. *Orientation of Overseas Indians toward Discrimination in American Society: Preliminary Findings from a Survey Research.* Norfolk: Dominion University.

———. 1979. *Studies on Overseas Indian Ethnic Minorities: A Select Bibliography.* Monticello, IL: Vance Bibliographies.

Namias, June. 1978. *First Generation: In the Words of Twentieth-Century American Immigrants.* Boston: Beacon.

Nimbark, Ashakant. 1980. Some Observations on Asian Indians in an American Educational Setting. In *The New Ethnics: Asian Indians in the United States.* Parmatma Saran and Edwin Eames (eds.). New York: Praeger.

Pais, Arthur. 1989. Student Associations. *India Abroad,* XIX.20:12–14.

Pais, Arthur, and Andy McCord. 1989. The "Myth" of Model Minority. *India Abroad.* XX.2, October 6:14–17.

Pais, Arthur, Andy McCord, and Ela Dutt. 1989. India in U.S. Universities. *India Abroad.* XIX.15:12–14.

Rajghatta, Chidanand. 1998. More Indian Students Go to US Now. Most of Them Stay On. Report. Retrieved from http://expressindia.com/ie/daily /199812114/34850444.html

Saberwall, Satish. 1968. The Problem. In *To See Ourselves: Anthropology and Modern Social Issues,* Thomas Weaver (ed.). Glenview: Scott Foresman.

Saran, Parmatma. 1977. Cosmopolitans from India. *Society* 6.

———. 1980. New Ethnics: The Case of the East Indians in New York City. In *Sourcebook on the New Immigration.* Roy Simon Bryce-Laporte (ed.). New Brunswick, NJ: Transaction.

———. 1985. The Asian Indian Experience in the United States. Cambridge, MA: Schenkman.

Sikri, Aprajita. 1987. Illegal Is Reverse Discrimination by Minorities. *India Abroad.* XVIII. 13, December 25:12.

———. 1987. Latent Prejudice, Envy Now Surface to Confront Indians. *India Abroad.* XVIII. 13, December 25:12–13.

———. 1989. Student Wins Minority Status Suit. *India Abroad. XX.3,* October 20:32.

Singer, Milton. 1980 [1972]. *When a Great Tradition Modernizes: An Anthropological Approach to Indian Civilization.* New York: Praeger.

Tandon, Prakash. 1980. *Return to Punjab, 1961–1975.* New Delhi: Vikas.

Thandi, Jaya. 1971. Indians in Washington. *Illustrated Weekly of India, XCIV,* 9, August:547–549.

Index

Abraham, Thomas, 13
academic scholarship, 96–104
Adam, William, 51
Advani, Saroj, 110
African Indian immigrants, 43
Akal Takht in Amritsar, 97
Alcott, Amos Bronson, 52
Alexander the Great, 17, 34
Alfred, King of Wessex, 17
American experience, 2
American Federation of Labor War Relief
    Committee, 59
American letters syndrome, 112, 113
American Oriental Society, 52
American Vedanta Society of New York
    City, 53
Anand, Geeta, 83
Andhra Pradesh, 43
Antonine, 17
Aryan
    defined, 16
    invasions by, 17
ashram, 26
ASIA games, 118
Asian Indians, 2, 5
    accents of, 115
    accomplishments and contributions of, 80
    backlash against after September 11th,
        112
    communities of, 10, 76, 80
    concerns about children, 119
    cuisine of, 75
    dances of, 75
    dress of, 75
    economy of, 77
    employment of, 77
    as ethnic group, 86
    family dynamics of, 76
    feelings against, 55
    globalization of, 78
    governmental responsibility for, 118
    health issues of, 76
    incomes of, 64
    language of, 76
    lifestyles in America, 105
    mental health issues of, 76
    music of, 75
    politics of, 79

pride of, 121
prominent, 115, 116, 117
relations with India, 79
religions of, 77
religious holidays and celebrations of, 76
student experience of, 80
as students, profiles of, 83
traditions, customs, and beliefs of, 74
in U.S., 9, 74
weddings of, 77
youth culture of, 120
Asian Pacific Islanders, 60
Asiatic Barred Zone, 56
Asiatic Exclusion League, 55
Asoka, Emperor, 16
assimilation theory, 6
Association of Indian Associations (AIA),
    109
ayah, 114

Babar, 34
Bahrain, 24
Balaam, 17
Bangalore, 46
Bangladeshi Americans, 87
Banias, 93
Barth, Fredrik, 26
Bhachcu, Parminder, 9
Bhagavad Gita, 52
Bhajan, Yogi, 53
Bhandari, Manju, 82
Bhangra Dance Troupe, 121
Bhuddhism, 17
Bhuyan, Bijoy, 65, 71
bindi, 62
Bollywood, 120
Boxer Rebellion, 54
Brahmins, 16, 93
brain drain, 42
brain gain, 46
British colonial mentality, 103
British Guiana, 19
British Indian Army, 19
British Public Health Service, 53, 54
British raj, 34
    encroachment on India, 18
    exploitation by, 50
    influence on education, 4

Mother India, 32–49
Mughals, 16
muhabbat, 92, 93

Nair, Jivan, 63
nam, 100, 103
Nanak, Guru, 20, 34
Narayan, Jayaprakash, 58
nationalism, 48
Nehru, Jawaharlal, 33, 41
Network of Professional and Self-
    Employed Women, 110
New Commonwealth, 21
new immigration, 3, 5, 21
non-resident Indians (NRIs), 9, 38
    contributions to India, 43
    investments of, 39
    perspective on, 13
    privileges of, 39
    visible influence of in India, 40

Odule, Friar, 17
Organization of Economic Cooperation and
    Development (OECD), 42
overseas Indians, 9

Pakistani Americans, 87
pan-Asian movement, 87
Parliament of Religions, 52
parochial associations, 109
parochialization, 48
Parsees, 50, 77
part-societies, 10, 107
passenger Indians, 17
Patel, Kaushak, 28
Patel, Vijay, 108
Patels, 20, 22
people of Indian origin (PIOs), 9, 32
    loyalties of, 41
    perspective on, 13
    responsibility for, 41
PIO card, 47
pirhi, 93
plantation economies, 19
plantation system, 19
Portuguese, encroachment on India, 18
Prahaled, C. K., 14
preadapted, 10, 29
privacy, concepts of, 95
promised land concept, 5
Protestant ethic, 90
Punjab, 2, 22, 29, 93
    current population in U.S., 59, 60
    history of, 34
    immigrants from, 34

influence of NRIs in, 40
    language of, 88
Punjabi-Mexican communities, 57
Puritan culture, 91

Queen Victoria's Diamond Jubilee, 20, 54
quota system, 56

railroads, 18
Ramayana, 17
refugee mentality, 117
regionalism, 107
religion
    comparative, 51
    conflicts with science, 99
    methods of, 100
remittances, 43
returnees, 40
    contributions of, 43
    perceptions of, 113
robh, 92, 93
Roy, M. N., 58
Roy, Raja Ram Mohan, 51

Saegal, Raju, 11
Saigal, Nandani, 114
sanskritization, 94, 111
sant, 100
Saund, Dilip Singh, 57
Schumpeter, Joseph, 26
science, conflicts with religion, 99
scientific diaspora, 47
Self-Realization Fellowship, 53
September 11, 2001 backlash, 112
servants, 3
Sethi, Rajin, 84
seva, 92
Shah, Neil, 30
Shah, Pram, 30
Sharma, Jagdish, 84, 113
Sharon, Kaushal, 62
Shepherd, Matthew, 118
Shiah, 20
Sikh Golden Temple in Amritsar, 89, 97
Sikhism
    history of, 34
    validation of, 101, 102, 103
Sikh Jats, 22
Sikh Reformer, 97
Sikhs, 20
    and academic scholarship, 96–104
    beliefs of, 97
    in Canada, 54
    community involvement of, 81
    conflict with Judeo-Christian beliefs, 99